GW01396171

ROBE
AFGHANISTAN

OSAMA BIN LADEN: 9/11 TO DEATH IN PAKISTAN

The ☻INDEPENDENT

Mango Media
Miami
in collaboration with
The Independent

Independent Print Limited

Published by Mango Media, Inc.
www.mangomedia.us

This is a work of non-fiction adapted from articles and content by journalists of The Independent and published with permission.

Front Cover Image: Fat Jackey/Shutterstock.com
Back Cover Image: Oleg Zabielin/Shutterstock.com

ROBERT FISK ON AFGHANISTAN *Osama bin Laden: 9/11 to Death in Pakistan*

ISBN: 978-1-63353-363-9

"Bin Laden doesn't matter anymore, alive or dead. Because, like nuclear scientists, he has invented the bomb."

– Robert Fisk, The Independent

Table of Contents

PREFACE

It began on a surge of international consensus, following the terrorist atrocities of 11 September 2001. Thirteen years later, the US-led coalition's war in Afghanistan came to a quiet close. Britain and America are still counting the cost. Some 3,224 international troops lost their lives in the conflict, including 453 Britons, while Afghan civilian casualties exceeded 21,000. More than 140,000 British servicemen and women served in the conflict, at a total operational cost of £21.5bn. It was the longest war in modern British or American history, and by the end of it more than 10 per cent of the Afghan population were classified as refugees.

Throughout that time, one journalist above all others has reported on the conflict with unfailing insight, perspective and courage. Robert Fisk has used the accumulated wisdom and contacts of a lifetime to capture the trauma and heroism of a military engagement that was never going to be as simple as Western politicians liked to imagine.

Spanning the full 13 years of the conflict, this collection shows Fisk at his best. Reporting with dedication, compassion and in-depth knowledge, he tells a heart-breaking story of a country ravaged by war and a destitute people desperate for peace. Whether he is warning Western statesmen of pitfalls ahead or recounting his own hair-raising experiences, Fisk tells the truth unflinchingly, but also with compassion.

This is journalism at its best, informing and dissecting. If you wish to understand what the war in Afghanistan was about, this is as good a first draft of history as you will find.

PROLOGUE

9/11

World Trade Center ruins

12 September 2001

PROVOKING AMERICA INTO A COSTLY MILITARY ADVENTURE

I can imagine how Osama bin Laden received the news of the atrocities in the United States. In all, I must have spent five hours listening to him in Sudan and then in the vastness of the Afghan mountains, as he described the inevitable collapse of the United States, just as he and his comrades in the Afghan war helped to destroy the power of the Red Army.

He will have watched satellite television, he will have sat in the corner of his room, brushing his teeth as he always did, with a miswak stick, thinking for up to a minute before speaking; he is one of the few Arabs who doesn't feel embarrassed to think before he speaks. He once told me with pride how his own men had attacked the Americans in Somalia. He acknowledged that he knew personally two of the Saudis executed for bombing an American military base in Riyadh. Could he have been behind yesterday's mass slaughter in America?

Of course, we need a health warning here. If Mr bin Laden was really guilty of all the things he has been blamed for, he would need an army of 10,000. And there is something deeply disturbing about the world's habit of turning to the latest hate figure whenever blood is shed. But when events of this momentous scale take place, there is a new legitimacy in casting one's eyes at those who have constantly threatened America.

Mr bin Laden had a kind of religious experience during the Afghan war. A Russian shell had fallen at his feet and, in the seconds as he waited for it to explode, he said he had a sudden, religious feeling of calmness. The shell - and Americans may come to wish the opposite happened - never exploded. The United States must leave the Gulf, he would say every 10 minutes. America must stop all sanctions against the Iraqi people. America must stop using Israel to oppress Palestinians. It was his constant theme, untouched by doubt or the real complexities of the Middle East. He was not fighting an anti-colonial war, but a religious one. In the Arabia that he would govern, there would be more, not less, head chopping, more severe punishments, no Western-style democracy.

His supporters - Algerians, Kuwaitis, Egyptians and Gulf Arabs - would gather round him in his tent with the awe of men listening to a messiah. I watched them one night in Afghanistan in a mountain camp so cold that I woke to find ice in my hair. They were obedient to him, not the kind of obedience of schoolchildren but the sort of adherence you find among people whose minds are made up. And the words they listened to were fearful in their implications. American civilians would no more be spared than military targets. This was not a man who would hesitate to carry out his promises if he could. He was a man who would have appreciated the appalling irony of creating a missile defence shield against "rogue states" but unable to prevent men crashing domestic airliners into the centre of America's financial and military power.

Yet I also remember one night when Mr bin Laden saw a pile of newspapers in my bag and seized upon them. By a sputtering oil lamp, he read them page by page in the corner of his tent, clearly unaware of the world around him, reading aloud of an Iranian Foreign Minister's visit to Saudi Arabia. Was this really a man who could damage America, who would have laughed when he heard that the United States had placed a $5m (£3.3m) reward on his head? Was it not America, I wondered then, which was turning Mr bin Laden into the face of "world terror?" Was he really so powerful and so deadly?

If - and we must keep repeating this word if - the shadow of the Middle East falls over yesterday's destruction, then who else in the region could produce such meticulously timed assaults on the world's only superpower? The rag-tag and corrupt Palestinian nationalist groups that used to favour hijacking are unlikely to be able to produce a single suicide bomber. Hamas and Islamic Jihad have neither the capability nor the money that this assault needed. Perhaps the old satellite groups that moved close to the Lebanese Hezbollah in the 1980s, before the organisation became a solely resistance movement, could plan something like this. The bombing of the US Marines in 1983 needed precision, timing and infinite planning. But Iran, which supported these groups, has changed out of recognition since then, now more involved in its internal struggles than in the long-dead aspiration to "export" a religious revolution. Iraq lies broken, its agents more intent on torturing their own people than striking at the country that defeated it so suddenly in 1991.

So the mountains of Afghanistan will be photographed from satellite and high-altitude aircraft in the coming days, Mr bin Laden's old training camps - and perhaps a few new ones - highlighted on the overhead projectors in the Pentagon. But to what end? When America last tried to strike at Mr bin Laden, it destroyed an innocent pharmaceuticals plant in Sudan and a few of Mr bin Laden's Muslim followers in Afghanistan. For if this is a war between the Saudi millionaire and President Bush's America, it cannot be fought like other wars. Indeed, can it be fought at all without some costly military adventure overseas.

Or is that what Mr bin Laden seeks above all else?

14 September 2001

AFGHANISTAN ALWAYS BEATS ITS INVADERS

On the heights of the Kabul Gorge, they still find ancient belt buckles and corroded sword hilts. You can no longer read the insignia of the British regiments of the old East India Company but their bones - those of all 16,000 of them - still lie somewhere amid the dark earth and scree of the most forbidding mountains in Afghanistan. Like the British who came later, like the Russians who were to arrive more than a century afterwards, General William Elphinstone's campaign was surrounded with rhetoric and high principles and ended in disaster. George Bush Junior and Nato, please note.

Indeed, if there is one country - calling it a nation would be a misnomer - that the West should avoid militarily, it is the tribal land in which Osama Bin Laden maintains his obscure sanctuary. Just over two decades ago, I found out what it was like to be on an invasion army in that breathlessly beautiful, wild, proud plateau. Arrested by the Russian Parachute Regiment near the Salang Tunnel, I was sent with a Soviet convoy back to Kabul. We were ambushed, and out of the snowdrifts came the Afghans, carrying knives. An air strike and the arrival of Soviet Tadjik troops saved us. But the mighty Red Army had been humbled before men who could not write their own names and whose politics were so remote that a mujahid fighter would later insist to me that London was occupied by Russian troops.

Back in 1839 we British were also worried about the Russians. General Elphinstone lead an East India Company army of 16,500 - along with 38,000 followers - into Afghanistan, anxious to put an end to Dost Mohamed's flirtation with the Tsar, took Kandahar and entered Kabul on 30 June with the first foreign force to occupy the city in modern times. Dost Mohamed - the British Superpower of the time knew how to deal with recalcitrant natives - was dispatched to exile in India, but the Afghans were not prepared to be placed under British tutelage. To garrison a foreign army in Kabul was folly, as Elphinstone must have realised when, on 1 November, 1840, a British official, Alexander Burns, was hacked to pieces by a mob in the souk and his head impaled on a stake. A 300-strong British unit in the field fled for its life back to Kabul. And when Dost Mohamed's son turned up, leading an Afghan army of 30,000, Elphinstone was doomed.

He bartered his freedom in return for a safe passage back to the British fort in Jalalabad, close to the Indian frontier. It was one of the coldest winters on record and with few supplies, virtually no food and false promises of safety, he led his army - their columns 10 miles in length - out into the frozen desolation of the Kabul Gorge. The camp followers were left by the wayside; contemporary records describe Indian women attached to the British army's colonial force, stripped naked, starving, raped and knifed by Afghan tribesmen, their corpses left in the snow. Elphinstone had long since given up trying to protect them. Yet each new foray down the chasm of the Kabul Gorge - I was to see the remains of a Russian convoy littered across the same track almost 140 years later - led to further ambushes and massacres.

Elphinstone secured the safety of himself, a few officers and a party of English ladies. The last British guardsmen were cut down on the heights, surrounded by thousands of Afghans, firing to the last round, the company commander dying with the Union flag wrapped around his waist. Days later, the last survivor of the massacres, galloping his exhausted horse Jalalabad was attacked by two Afghan cavalry. Hacking them away from him, he broke his sword, Hollywood-style, on one of the men. But with his horse dying beneath him, he reached the British fort. It was to date the greatest defeat of British arms in history.

The British clung to Afghanistan as if it was a jewel in the crown. Under the Treaty of Gandamak, the Amir Yakub Khan could rule Kabul and a British embassy would be opened in the city. But within months, in 1879, the residency was under siege, its few occupants fighting - once more - to the last man. With the embassy on fire, the handful of Britons inside made repeated forays into the ranks of the Afghans. "When charged," a later British account would claim, "the Afghan soldiers ran like sheep before a wolf". But within hours, the British were fighting from the burning roof of the residency, slashed to bits with swords, stripped and their bodies burned. The Consul, born to a French father and an Irish mother, was Major Sir Pierre Louis Napoleon Cavagnari, KCB, CSI. A British journalist with the Kabul Field Force found a few scorched bones in the residency yard; they included, no doubt, Sir Pierre's remains.

Ironically, one of Elphinstone's successors was visiting the site of the 1842 massacre in 1880 when he heard that his army - this was the Second Afghan War - had been attacked in a remote semi-desert called

Maiwand where the 30th Bombay Infantry was fighting off thousands of ghazi warriors who were charging suicidally at British cannon and Egyptian colonial troops. Savage in their assaults, waving green Islamic banners and utterly heedless of their own lives - and the word "suicidal" is not used loosely here - they threw themselves among the British.

We were to conduct a military inquiry into the disaster that followed and now, in the fragile, yellowing pages of the Indian British Army's Intelligence Branch report we can find chilling evidence of what this meant. Captain Wainwaring was to recall how "the whole of the ground to the left of the 30th Native Infantry, and between it and the Grenadiers, was covered with swarms of ghazis and banner-men. The ghazis were actually in the ranks of the Grenadiers, pulling the men out and hacking them down with their swords ...". A young Afghan woman - all we know is that her name was Malaleh - feared that the tribesmen might withdraw and so tore off her veil, holding it above her head as a flag and charging at the Grenadiers herself. She was shot down by British rifle fire. But the British fled. In all, they lost 1,320 men including 21 officers, along with 1,000 rifles and at least 600 swords.

The Great Game was supposed to be about frontiers - about keeping a British-controlled Afghanistan between the Indian Empire and the Russian border - but it was a history of betrayals. Those we thought were on our side turned out to be against us. Until 1878, we had thought the Amir Sher Ali Khan of Kabul was our friend, ready to fight for the British Empire - just as a man called Osama bin Laden would later fight the Russians on "our" behalf - but he forbade passage to British troops and encouraged the robbery of British merchants.

He had "openly and assiduously endeavoured ... to stir up religious hatred against the English," our declaration of war had announced on 21 November, 1878. The Amir's aiding and abetting of the murder of the British Embassy staff was "a treacherous and cowardly crime, which has brought indelible disgrace upon the Afghan people," Sir Frederick Roberts announced in 1879 when, yet again, the British had occupied Kabul. The Amir's followers "should not escape ... penalty and ... the punishment inflicted should be such as will be felt and remembered ... All persons convicted of bearing a part (in the murders) will be dealt with according to their deserts." It was an ancient, Victorian warning, a ghostly preamble to the words we have been hearing from President Bush - and, indeed, Mr Blair - in the last 48 hours.

The Russians were to endure their 10 years of Calvary exactly a century later, though in truth it was the Afghans who suffered a virtual genocide under the Soviets. Osama bin Laden, who had himself escaped several murder attempts by Russian agents, survived. Perhaps Vladimir Putin who is being asked to subscribe to the West's new battle for "democracy and liberty" against the forces of darkness might remind Mr Bush just how painful Russia's military adventure in Afghanistan proved to be. Perhaps we could all go back to the history books before suggesting - and the idea of such an adventure is clearly being dreamed of in Washington - that the Great Game should be taken up once more

15 September 2001

THE WEEK THAT SHOOK THE WORLD

The first time I met Osama bin Laden inside Afghanistan it was a hot, humid night in the summer of 1996. Huge insects flew through the night air, settling like burrs on his Saudi robes and on the clothes of his armed followers. They would land on my notebook until I swatted them, their blood smearing the pages. Bin Laden was always studiously polite: each time we met, he would offer the usual Arab courtesy of food for a stranger: a tray of cheese, olives, bread and jam. I had already met him in Sudan and would spend a night, almost a year later, in one of his mountain guerrilla camps, so cold that I awoke in the morning with ice in my hair.

I had been given a rough blanket and my shoes were left outside the tent. Whenever we met, he would interrupt our interviews to say his prayers, his armed followers - from Algeria, Egypt, the Gulf Arab states, Syria - kneeling beside him, hanging on his every word as he spoke to me as if he was a messiah.

On 20 March, 1997, I would meet him again. Although only 41 at the time, his ruggedly groomed beard had white hairs, and he had bags under his eyes; I sensed some infirmity, a stiffness of one leg that gave him the slightest of limps. I still have my notes, scribbled in the frozen semi-darkness as an oil lamp sputtered between us. "I am not against the American people," he said. "Only their government." I had heard this so often in the Middle East. I told him I thought the American people regarded their government as their representatives. Bin Laden listened to this in silence. "We are still at the beginning of our military action against the American forces,' he said.

I remembered those words this week as I watched those airliners scything into the World Trade Centre towers. And I remembered, too, how in that last meeting he had seized on the Arabic-language newspapers I was carrying in my satchel (a schoolbag I use in rough countries) and scurried to a corner of the tent to read them for 20 minutes, ignoring both his fighters and myself. Although a Saudi, he did not even know that the Iranian foreign minister had just visited the Saudi capital of Riyadh. Didn't he even have a radio, I asked myself? Was this really the "godfather of world terror?" The US administration and Time magazine had both blessed him with this sobriquet. I rather thought he would have liked that. And the $5 million reward that the American administration offered for him. As a multimillionaire himself, bin Laden would have been insulted at such a low price on the "wanted" poster.

The bin Ladens are a construction family, respected in their native Saudi Arabia although their roots lie on the Yemeni border, a family who honoured the young man who, after the Soviet invasion of Afghanistan in 1979, took his followers and his road construction machinery to a volcanic landscape of tribal leaders to fight "the West". For the Russians - to a Saudi - were Westerners and their incursion into Islamic Afghanistan was a heretical, corrupting act. He paid from his own packet to fly thousands of young Arab Muslims to fight alongside him.

They came - from Algeria, from Egypt and the Arabian Gulf and from Syria - and many of them died as martyrs in the ferocious battles, torn to pieces by mines, shredded by the machine-gun fire of the Soviet Hind helicopter gunships that raided the villages of Panchir.

The first time we met, in Sudan, I persuaded bin Laden - much against his will - to talk about those days. And he recalled how, during an attack on a Russian firebase not far from Jalalabad, a mortar shell had fallen at his feet. He had waited for it to explode. And in those milliseconds of rationality, he had - so he said - felt a great sense of tranquillity, a sense of calm acceptance which he ascribed to God. The shell - and many an American may now wish the opposite had happened - failed to explode.

Even the Russians came to know of the esteem in which bin Laden was held among the Afghan resistance. In Moscow in 1993, I met a Soviet adviser who was supposed to arrange his liquidation. "A dangerous man," the Russian said of bin Laden. At the time, of course, the Americans loved him, provided him with weapons, never dreaming that within two decades they, too, would be dreaming of his murder. Bin Laden told me once that he never met an American agent during the anti-Russian war, never accepted a single bullet from the West.

But his bulldozers and earth-removers carved highways through the mountains for the Mujahedin to carry their British-made Blowpipe anti-aircraft missiles high enough to strike the Soviet Migs; years later, one of his armed followers would take me up the "bin Laden trail", a terrifying two-hour odyssey along fearful ravines in rain and sleet, the windscreen misting as we climbed the cold mountain. "When you believe in jihad (holy war), it is easy," the gunman informed me, fighting with the steering wheel as stones scuttered from the tyres, bouncing down the valleys into the clouds below. From time to time - this was in 1997 - lights winked at us from far away in the darkness. "Our brothers are letting us know they see us," the gunman said. It was two hours more before we reached bin Laden's old wartime camp, the jeep skidding backwards towards sheer cliffs, the headlights illuminating frozen waterfalls above. "Toyota is good for Jihad," bin Laden's man smiled. I could only agree. I never heard bin Laden make a joke.

If the United States regarded him as the foremost "terrorist" in the world - as I told him they did - then "if liberating my land is called terrorism, this is a great honour for me." There was no difference, he said, between the American and Israeli governments, between the American and Israeli armies. But Europe - especially France - was beginning to distance itself from the Americans. He did condemn French policy towards north Africa; although he did not mention Algeria, the name hovered over us for several minutes like a ghost.

Bin Laden gave me a Pakistani wall poster in Urdu which proclaimed the support of Pakistani scholars for his "holy war" against the Americans; he even handed to me colour photographs of graffiti on the walls of Karachi that demanded the ousting of US troops from "the place of the two Holy shrines (Mecca and Medina)". He had, he claimed, received some months ago an emissary from the Saudi royal family who said that his Saudi citizenship - taken away after pressure from Washington - would be restored along with a new Saudi passport and 2 billion Saudi riyals (£339 million) for his family if he abandoned his jihad and went back to Saudi Arabia. He and his family, he said, had rejected the offer.

At the time, bin Laden had three wives, the elder of them the mother of his bright, 16-year-old Bon Omar, the youngest herself a teenager. Another son, Saad, was brought to meet me; they spoke some English and were clearly excited - in an innocent way - to be surrounded by so many armed men. All lived with him - along with other Mujahedin wives and children -- and stayed in a compound outside Jalalabad. Bin Laden even invited me to visit these hot, dank, miserable homes in the company of one of his Egyptian fighters. Of course, his wives - the youngest was later to return to her family in the Gulf - were not there. "These are ladies who are used to living in comfort," the Egyptian said. The encampment was protected by sheets of canvas and a few strands of barbed wire; a drainage ditch and three separate latrines had been dug in the earth, in one of which floated a dead frog. The Egyptian's teenage son, sitting beside us with a rifle in his lap, insisted that Egyptian Intelligence men had viewed the camp. "There are people in the towns who work for the Americans," he said. "We see these people and we have to be careful."

Another of the Arabs in that camp was more forthcoming. There was, he said, "no other country left for Mr bin Laden" outside of Afghanistan. "When he was in Sudan, the Saudis wanted to capture him with the help of the Yemenis. We know that the French government tried to persuade the Sudanese to hand him over to them because the Sudanese had given them a south American. The Americans were pressing the French to get hold of bin Laden in Sudan. An Arab group paid by the Saudis tried to kill him, but bin Laden's guards fired back and two were wounded."

In all, bin Laden lost 500 of his men in the war against the Russians. Their graves lie near the Pakistani border at Torkum. After the Russian withdrawal, bin Laden left for Sudan, disgusted by the Afghans' internecine fighting. His closest followers went with him to build highways and invest in Sudanese industry.

Bin Laden is a tall, slim man and towers over his companions.

He has narrow, dark eyes which stared hard at me when he spoke of his hatred of Saudi corruption. Indeed, in my long conversation with bin Laden in 1996 - on that hot night of mosquitoes - the Saudi kingdom and its apparatchiks probably consumed more time than his views of America. He picked his teeth with a piece of miswak wood, a habit that accompanied all his conversations with me. History - or his version of it - was the basis of almost all his remarks. And the pivotal date was 1990, the year Saddam Hussein invaded Kuwait. "When the American troops entered Saudi Arabia, the land of the two Holy places, there was as strong protest from the ulema (religious authorities) and from students of the Sharia law all over the country against the interference of American troops.

"This big mistake by the Saudi regime of inviting the American troops revealed their deception. They had given their support to nations that were fighting against Muslims. They helped the Yemen communists against the southern Yemeni Muslims and are helping (Yasser) Arafat's regime fight Hamas. After it insulted and jailed the ulema ... the Saudi regime lost its legitimacy."

Bin Laden paused to see if I had listened to his careful if frighteningly exclusive history lesson. "We as Muslims have a strong feeling that binds us together... We feel for our brothers in Palestine and Lebanon. The explosion at Khobar did not come as a direct result of American occupation but as a result of American behaviour against Muslims...

"When 60 Jews are killed inside Palestine (in suicide bombings in 1996), all the world gathers within seven days to criticise this action, while the deaths of 600,000 Iraqi children (under UN sanctions) did not receive the same reaction. Killing those Iraqi children is a crusade against Islam. We, as Muslims, do not like the Iraqi regime but we think that the Iraqi people and their children are our brothers and we care about their future."

But it was America that captured bin Laden's final attention. "I believe that sooner or later the Americans will leave Saudi Arabia, and that the war declared by America against the Saudi people means war against Muslims everywhere. Resistance against America will spread in many, many places in Muslim countries. Our trusted leaders, the ulema, have given us a fatwa that we must drive out the Americans. The solution to this crisis is the withdrawal of American troops... their military presence is an insult to the Saudi people."

I've been thinking a lot about that last statement this week. American forces are still in Saudi Arabia. And about his earlier remark in

July, 1996 - after a truck bomb had killed 19 Americans - that this incident marked "the beginning of the war between Muslims and the United States". Of the later bombing and the killing of 24 US servicemen, he was to tell me that it was "a great act in which I missed the honour of participating". He spoke then in a chilling, lower voice of his hatred of the American "occupiers".

Intelligent - and eloquent in Arabic - bin Laden undoubtedly is. But his understanding of foreign affairs is decidedly eccentric. At one point, he even suggested to me that individual US states might secede from the Union because of Washington's support for Israel. But the historical perspective was deeply disturbing. "We believe that God used our holy war in Afghanistan to destroy the Russian army and the Soviet Union," he said. "We did this from the top of this very mountain on which you are sitting - and now we ask God to use us one more time to do the same to America, to make it a shadow of itself. We also believe that our battle against America is much simpler than the war against the Soviet Union because some of our Mujahedin who fought here in Afghanistan also participated in operations against the Americans in Somalia (during the doomed UN mission) - and they were surprised at the collapse of American morale. This convinced us that the Americans are a paper tiger.

He was also to tell me that "swift and light forces working in complete secrecy" would be needed to oust America from Saudi Arabia. In the following two years, bin Laden was to form his al-Qaeda movement and declare war on the American people - not just the government and army of the United States. There would follow the near-sinking of the USS Cole in Aden harbour - by suicide bombers - and the Cruise missile attacks on the old CIA base that bin Laden uses in southern Afghanistan. He walks now with a stick - a development of the foot problem I noticed four years ago - and speaks more slowly.

But could he really command an army of suicide bombers from the desolation of the Afghan mountains? He did admit to me once that he knew two of the three men executed - beheaded - in Saudi Arabia for bombing the second American military base. He wanted a "real" Islamic sharia law government in Arabia - there would, I suspected, be even more head-chopping in a bin Laden regime - and he wanted an end to those dictators installed by the Americans, those men who supported US policies while repressing their own people.

And it occurred to me that this was, for many millions of Arabs in the Middle East, a very powerful message. You didn't need instructions from bin Laden to form your own small group of followers, to decide on your own individual actions. Bin Laden wouldn't have to plan bombings or the overthrow of regimes. You had only to listen to the thousands of cassette tapes of his voice circulated clandestinely around the Middle East. Which is why I wonder - always supposing bin Laden is connected to the crime against humanity committed in the United States this week - if it would even be necessary to command a para-military organisation for such acts to happen. Arabs are angry enough with the injustices that they blame on America without needing orders from Afghanistan. Inspiration might be just enough.

And I wondered, after those images from New York last week, whether bin Laden was not as astonished as myself to see them. Always supposing he watched television. Or listened to the radio. Or read a newspaper

THE GRAVEYARD OF EMPIRES

SEPTEMBER 2001: INVASION OF AFGHANISTAN

War on Terrorism

18 September 2001

COULD BECOME MORE COSTLY THAN VIETNAM

President Bush is talking about a "crusade" - it would be difficult to find a word more likely to enrage Muslims - but if he plans to wage it in Afghanistan, the United States faces a military campaign more fraught and potentially even more costly than Vietnam.

Ground troops may be necessary to seize Osama bin Laden but they will be entering a country containing one tenth of the world's land mines, left by Soviet occupation forces across 80 per cent of the land.

Besides, anyone who wants to invade Afghanistan needs friends. The Russians had the communist government of Babrak Karmal. But, with the murder of Shah Masood, the only serious opponent of the Taliban, by Arab suicide bombers nine days ago, the United States hasn't a single friend in that cemetery of foreign armies.

So, are the Americans planning a mere attack by cruise missiles? They fired 70 missiles at Osama bin Laden's camps after the bombing of the US embassies in Nairobi and Dar es Salaam - they knew where they were, of course, because the camps were built by the CIA during the Afghan-Russian war - but they did not touch Mr bin Laden. Do they plan to use special parachute units to descend on the areas around Kandahar where Mr bin Laden has been known to live in the past?

And what about those mines? If the Americans are even contemplating a ground force, it can enter only from Pakistan - the most dangerous main supply route it would be possible to find - and up the Kabul Gorge from Jalalabad. But the Russians seeded the perimeters of Jalalabad, Kandahar, Khost and Herat with anti-armour mines. There are, in Afghanistan today, more than 10 million mines. They lie in fields, on mountainsides, beside roads, around the big cities, along irrigation ditches. On average, between 20 and 25 Afghan men, women and children are blown up by mines every day - even if we take the lower figure, this indicates 73,000 civilian casualties from these mines in the past 10 years alone.

A military incursion would, therefore, need an army of mine clearance specialists as well as soldiers, men who would have to inch their way over the roughest terrain in the world - while under attack - to make the roads and countryside safe for the Americans and their allies. Of Afghanistan's 29 provinces, 27 are littered with mines.

During their savage 10-year occupation, the Russians also planted thousands of mines in "security zones" around Afghanistan's airports, power stations and government installations. Western non-governmental organisations working in the country two years ago estimated that it would cost £80 per mine to clear Afghanistan's 10 million mines - and 45 days to clear merely a square mile of land. There are now two million disabled men, women and children in Afghanistan. No infantry can march across this territory.

And then there is that main supply route. Pakistan has already made clear that it will not involve its own military in a campaign, although there are suspicions that enough money might persuade General Musharraf - now respectfully referred to as President by the Americans even though he took the presidency illegally - to change his mind. However, the "Jihadi" culture has already impregnated the Pakistan army and there is a real possibility of unrest turning to civil war if the Americans arrived to invade Muslim Afghanistan.

The very border areas through which a Western army would have to pass are held by men loyal to the Taliban. On the Pakistani side of the frontier, there are now 2,000 Taliban madrassas (schools) where religious teaching is given not only to potential mujahedin but to Chechen and Tadjik fighters as well. The policemen who guard these madrassas constitute a mere facade of governmental control.

Even if the Americans penetrated Afghanistan, their shells would only plough over the ruins. The Russians tried to destroy the Taliban's predecessors with 10 years of bombing, destroying whole villages, with their people, farm animals, fields, trees and mud huts. And still they could not get rid of the mujahedin, still they could not - to use Mr Bush's inappropriately folksy phrase - "smoke them out of their holes".

With Pakistan as its only, broken ally among Afghanistan's neighbours, with no friends inside the country and 10 million hidden land mines lying across its mountains and fields and cities, Mr Bush's "crusade" looks more than dangerous. We are now being told that the United States is no longer afraid to take casualties. America, the President says, will have to accept losses. He'd better be right if he sends his men into Afghanistan.

18 September 2001

TALIBAN FIND THEY HAVE FEW MUSLIM FRIENDS

They have been lining up in their condemnation. Mullahs, sheikhs and sayeds, from Beirut to Tehran, are criticising last week's assault on the United States, sending condolences and sympathy and - by their actions - distancing themselves from the atrocity that millions of Arab Muslims watched live on television.

There is genuine outrage, true, but it would be as well to place it in context. Because the Taliban, the shield of Osama bin Laden, has almost as many enemies in the Middle East as it has in America.

For two consecutive days, Sayed Mohamed Hussein Fadlallah, the spiritual guide to the Hizbollah guerrilla movement - the group that reinvented the art of suicide bombing against the Israeli occupation army in Lebanon and which Washington still blames for the kidnapping of Americans in Beirut in the 1980s - has been excoriating those responsible.

"No religion justifies such an action," the Shia Muslim cleric announced in Beirut. "It is not permissible to use innocent and peaceful civilians as a card to change a specific policy." Muslims and Islamists opposed American policy in the region - "which is totally biased in favour of the Zionist enemy" - but they wanted to be friends with the American people, the cleric said.

Sheikh Abdul-Amir Qabalan, the vice-president of the Higher Shia Muslim Council in Lebanon, insisted Islam was "a religion of justice and equality and it condemns any attack on civilians and the innocent".

Now this makes interesting reading. No such condemnations followed the Palestinian suicide bombings that killed 15 civilians, including six children, in a Jerusalem pizzeria in August or the suicide bombing that slaughtered 21 Israeli teenagers in Tel Aviv. Hizbollah's satellite groups were held responsible for the 1983 bombing of the US embassy in Beirut in which more than 50 Lebanese civilians were killed.

In Iran, whose boy soldiers perfected suicide attacks on the Iraqi army in the 1980-88 war and whose government has always supported Palestinian suicide bombers, President Mohammad Khatami and his conservative opponents condemned totally the New York and Washington bombings. This is not surprising.

For in Tehran the rulers of Afghanistan have been called the "black Taliban" for years, long before the US identified them as Mr bin Laden's protectors. The Iranians, and by extension their Hizbollah proteges, have long regarded the Taliban's "Wahabi" Sunni Muslim leaders as obscurantists and potential "terrorists".

At least two million Afghan refugees are living in great poverty in eastern Iran, many of whom would have stayed at home were it not for the Taliban's rule and the mass starvation that the Taliban has done little to alleviate. Iran has now closed its border with Afghanistan to prevent a further exodus of refugees and America has said that it would "consider" inviting Iran to join a coalition against "world terrorism". Iran will most certainly decline.

The Saudis, of course, can scarcely do anything but join in the chorus of condemnation. They helped to create the Taliban, to legitimise its presence in Afghanistan and to fund and arm the so-called "students" who destroyed most of the rival "mujahedin" groups who had been pillaging Kabul and other great Afghan cities in the years that followed the Soviet military withdrawal. Mr bin Laden is himself a Saudi - though one officially deprived of his citizenship - and, as is becoming clearer, some of the hijackers were Saudi citizens.

In Egypt, Sunni Muslim clerics added their own condemnation although President Mubarak has been one of the few Middle Eastern leaders to warn of the consequences of indiscriminate American retaliation. He it was who warned two short weeks ago that, unless a peace was restored, he feared "an explosion outside the region".

Back in Lebanon, the Hizbollah itself issued a crafty statement yesterday, regretting the loss of innocent lives in America but warning Washington not to take advantage of the atrocities "to practise all sorts of aggression and terrorism under the pretext of fighting aggression and terrorism".

23 September 2001

HOW CAN THE US BOMB THIS TRAGIC PEOPLE?

We are witnessing this weekend one of the most epic events since the Second World War, certainly since Vietnam. I am not talking about the ruins of the World Trade Centre in New York and the grotesque physical scenes which we watched on 11 September, an atrocity which I described last week as a crime against humanity (of which more later). No, I am referring to the extraordinary, almost unbelievable preparations now under way for the most powerful nation ever to have existed on God's Earth to bomb the most devastated, ravaged, starvation-haunted and tragic country in the world. Afghanistan, raped and eviscerated by the Russian army for 10 years, abandoned by its friends - us, of course - once the Russians had fled, is about to be attacked by the surviving superpower.

I watch these events with incredulity, not least because I was a witness to the Russian invasion and occupation. How they fought for us, those Afghans, how they believed our word. How they trusted President Carter when he promised the West's support. I even met the

CIA spook in Peshawar, brandishing the identity papers of a Soviet pilot, shot down with one of our missiles - which had been scooped from the wreckage of his Mig. "Poor guy," the CIA man said, before showing us a movie about GIs zapping the Vietcong in his private cinema. And yes, I remember what the Soviet officers told me after arresting me at Salang. They were performing their international duty in Afghanistan, they told me. They were "punishing the terrorists" who wished to overthrow the (communist) Afghan government and destroy its people. Sound familiar?

I was working for The Times in 1980, and just south of Kabul I picked up a very disturbing story. A group of religious mujahedin fighters had attacked a school because the communist regime had forced girls to be educated alongside boys. So they had bombed the school, murdered the head teacher's wife and cut off her husband's head. It was all true. But when The Times ran the story, the Foreign Office complained to the foreign desk that my report gave support to the Russians. Of course. Because the Afghan fighters were the good guys. Because Osama bin Laden was a good guy. Charles Douglas-Home, then editor of The Times would always insist that Afghan guerrillas were called "freedom fighters" in the headline. There was nothing you couldn't do with words.

And so it is today. President Bush now threatens the obscurantist, ignorant, super-conservative Taliban with the same punishment as he intends to mete out to bin Laden. Bush originally talked about "justice and punishment" and about "bringing to justice" the perpetrators of the atrocities. But he's not sending policemen to the Middle East; he's sending B-52s. And F-16s and AWACS planes and Apache helicopters. We are not going to arrest bin Laden. We are going to destroy him. And that's fine if he's the guilty man. But B-52s don't discriminate between men wearing turbans, or between men and women or women and children.

I wrote last week about the culture of censorship which is now to smother us, and of the personal attacks which any journalist questioning the roots of this crisis endures. Last week, in a national European newspaper, I got a new and revealing example of what this means. I was accused of being anti-American and then informed that anti-Americanism was akin to anti-Semitism. You get the point, of course. I'm not really sure what anti-Americanism is. But criticising the United States is now to be the moral equivalent of Jew-hating. It's OK to write headlines about "Islamic terror" or my favourite French example "God's madmen", but it's definitely out of bounds to ask why the United States is loathed by so many Arab Muslims in the Middle East. We can give the murderers a Muslim identity: we can finger the Middle East for the crime - but we may not suggest any reasons for the crime.

But let's go back to that word justice. Re-watching that pornography of mass-murder in New York, there must be many people who share my view that this was a crime against humanity. More than 6,000 dead; that's a Srebrenica of a slaughter. Even the Serbs spared most of the women and children when they killed their menfolk. The dead of Srebrenica deserve - and are getting - international justice at the Hague. So surely what we need is an International Criminal Court to deal with the sorts of killer who devastated New York on 11 September. Yet "crime against humanity" is not a phrase we are hearing from the Americans. They prefer "terrorist atrocity", which is slightly less powerful. Why, I wonder? Because to speak of a terrorist crime against humanity would be a tautology. Or because the US is against international justice. Or because it specifically opposed the creation of an international court on the grounds that its own citizens may one day be arraigned in front of it.

The problem is that America wants its own version of justice, a concept rooted, it seems, in the Wild West and Hollywood's version of the Second World War. President Bush speaks of smoking them out, of the old posters that once graced Dodge City: "Wanted, Dead or Alive". Tony Blair now tells us that we must stand by America as America stood by us in the Second World War. Yes, it's true that America helped us liberate Western Europe. But in both world wars, the US chose to intervene after only a long and - in the case of the Second World War - very profitable period of neutrality.

Don't the dead of Manhattan deserve better than this? It's less than three years since we launched a 200-Cruise missile attack on Iraq for throwing out the UN arms inspectors. Needless to say, nothing was achieved. More Iraqis were killed, and the UN inspectors never got back, and sanctions continued, and Iraqi children continued to die. No policy, no perspective. Action, not words.

And that's where we are today. Instead of helping Afghanistan, instead of pouring our aid into that country 10 years ago, rebuilding its cities and culture and creating a new political centre that would go beyond tribalism, we left it to rot. Sarajevo would be rebuilt. Not Kabul. Democracy, of a kind, could be set up in Bosnia. Not in Afghanistan. Schools could be reopened in Tuzla and Travnik. Not in Jaladabad. When the Taliban arrived, stringing up every opponent, chopping off the arms of thieves, stoning women for adultery, the United States regarded this dreadful outfit as a force for stability after the years of anarchy.

Bush's threats have effectively forced the evacuation of every Western aid worker. Already, Afghans are dying because of their absence. Drought and starvation go on killing millions - I mean millions - and between 20 and 25 Afghans are blown up every day by the 10 million mines the Russians left behind. Of course, the Russians never went back to clear the mines. I suppose those B-52 bombs will explode a few of them. But that'll be the only humanitarian work we're likely to see in the near future.

Look at the most startling image of all this past week. Pakistan has closed its border with Afghanistan. So has Iran. The Afghans are to stay in their prison. Unless they make it through Pakistan and wash up on the beaches of France or the waters of Australia or climb through the Channel Tunnel or hijack a plane to Britain to face the wrath of our Home Secretary. In which case, they must be sent back, returned, refused entry. It's a truly terrible irony that the only man we would be interested in receiving from Afghanistan is the man we are told is the evil genius behind the greatest mass-murder in American history: bin Laden. The others can stay at home and die.

24 September 2001

NOT FROM SAUDI AIRFIELDS

Supposedly allied in close friendship with the United States, Saudi Arabia declined to allow America to use its airfields for President George Bush's "war on terrorism" yesterday. It specifically forbade US bombers to take off for retaliatory strikes from the massive Prince Sultan airbase near the capital, Riyadh. The decision comes only a week after Lt-Gen Charles Wald, the head of air operations for US Central Command, moved his headquarters to the airbase from South Carolina.

With truly ambiguous courtesy, a Saudi official announced that "Saudi Arabia will not accept any infringement on its national sovereignty, but it fully backs action aimed at eradicating terrorism and its causes." Many thousands of Saudis - not least the "prime suspect" himself, Osama bin Laden - will ask how Saudi Arabia suddenly intends to protect its sovereignty when 4,500 US military personnel are still stationed in the kingdom and when American planes still use its airfields - including the Prince Sultan base - for bombing raids over southern Iraq. In any event, eradicating the "causes" of the atrocities in New York and Washington are not President Bush's priority.

Off the record, the Saudis are saying they are worried about possible strikes on other Muslim states - presumably including Afghanistan - and that they want some power of decision over air operations, an idea that is not going to commend itself to Messrs Bush and Powell. In reality, however, Saudi authorities know that many thousands of Muslims in the kingdom - including, it is said, prominent ulema (religious teachers) and a number of Saudi princes - have voiced quiet support for Mr bin Laden's demand that the Americans pack up and leave Saudi Arabia.

The Americans will not be amused. More than half of the 19 hijackers who took over the four American airliners on 11 September appear to have been Saudi nationals - even those who used the identities of other Saudis - and Mr bin Laden is himself a Saudi, though long since deprived of citizenship. The Taliban, whom Washington now holds responsible for Mr bin Laden, were the theological creation of the Saudi "wahabi" Sunni sect, and - until sanctions were imposed on Afghanistan - a regular flight linked Riyadh and the south-western Afghan city of Jalalabad.

The kingdom's alliance with the US began more than half a century ago when President Franklin D Roosevelt invited King ibn Saud on board the USS Quincy in 1945. The king set up his desert tent on the deck of the American destroyer with seven sheep tied to the fantail to provide daily fresh meat. He was promised that the US would never do anything which might prove hostile to the Arabs. Three days later, Winston Churchill forfeited Britain's hitherto leading influence with the Saudis by declaring to the king that "if it was the religion of His Majesty to deprive himself of smoking and alcohol, I must point out that my rule of life prescribes as an almost sacred rite smoking cigars and also the drinking of alcohol before, after, and - if need be - during all meals and in the intervals between them."

These days, the Saudis might prefer a less forceful British prime minister to a US president whose nation so swiftly betrayed Roosevelt's promise. But it was King Fahd who invited half a million US forces into the kingdom after Saddam Hussein's invasion of Kuwait in 1990 - a "historical decision" according to the king, a historical betrayal according to Mr bin Laden - and it is Crown Prince Abdullah's burden to support a continued US presence to deter further aggression from Iraq.

No such doubts assail President Saddam's victim, Kuwait. Although the Emir, Sheikh Jaber al-Ahmed al-Sabah, only recently suffered a brain hemorrhage, the Kuwaiti government has been more than happy to invite the Americans - the liberators of 1991 - to send more armour and fighter-bombers to the emirate. Bahrain, cleansed of its sinister secret policemen and their British mentors, has also offered its facilities to the US; its Gulf fleet has for years been based in the Bahraini capital of Manama. The United Arab Emirates cut diplomatic relations with the Taliban at the weekend, a decision which may be followed by Saudi Arabia.

Yet it is not difficult to see the predicament of the Saudis and their neighbours. The real problem for Gulf Arabs is the vagueness of America's proposed military response to the mass murders in New York and Washington. President Bush's talk of a "crusade" caused near heart attacks among the Saudi rulers while the idea of a "long war on terror" has an unhappy ring for the emirs and sultans of the Gulf. They would much prefer their own dictatorial stability than the necessity of explaining to their own people why it is necessary to host another American bombing campaign against Muslim nations.

The Saudis are genuinely mystified about American plans. Do they intend to fire Cruise missiles into Afghanistan, as President Bill Clinton did after the US embassy bombings in Africa? Is Iraq to be included in the list of nations to be punished for the World Trade Centre atrocities? Or the Hizbollah in Lebanon, who clearly have no connection with the crime but who are eagerly being fingered by the Israelis? The FBI were infuriated when they were refused permission by the Saudis to interrogate the men accused of bombing the Al-Khobar military barracks in which 24 US soldiers were killed. The Americans were still pleading for the right to talk to the three accused on the day they had their heads chopped off.

Last night, Saudi and US diplomats were dancing a very odd tango. The Saudis would make no official statement about their refusal to deny their bases to the Americans while the US embassy in Riyadh referred all questions to the Pentagon. In turn, the Pentagon told journalists to call the State Department - which declined to make any comment at all. In retrospect, the Saudis may look back with some nostalgia to the tough-talking, cigar-chomping, whisky-drinking British prime minister who made a last vain attempt to maintain his country's supremacy in the kingdom by sending King ibn Saud a veteran Rolls Royce - complete with a throne behind the driving wheel.

25 September 2001

A FIGHT AGAINST AMERICA'S ENEMIES

While covering the Russian occupation of Afghanistan, I would, from time to time, drive down through Jalalabad and cross the Pakistan border to Peshawar to rest. In the cavernous, stained interior of the old Intercontinental Hotel, I would punch out my stories on a groaning telex machine beside an office bearing the legend "Chief Accountant" on the door. On the wall next to that office - I don't know if it was the Chief Accountant who put it there - was a framed piece of paper bearing four lines of Kipling that I still remember:

A scrimmage at a border station

A canter down a dark defile

Five thousand pounds of education

Felled by a five-rupee jezail

Or, I suppose today, a Kalashnikov AK-47, home-produced in Quetta, or one of those slick little Blowpipe missiles that we handed over to the mujahedin with such abandon in the early Eighties so that they could kill their - and our - Russian enemies.

But I've been thinking more about the defiles, the gorges and overhanging mountains, the sheer rock walls 4,000 feet in height, the caves and the massive tunnels which Osama bin Laden cut through the mountains. Here, presumably, are the "holes" from which the Wes is going to "smoke out" Mr bin Laden, always supposing that he's been obliging enough to run away and hide in them. For there is already a growing belief - founded on our own rhetoric - that Mr bin Laden and his men are on the run, seeking their hiding places.

I'm not so certain. I'm very doubtful about what Mr bin Laden is doing right now. In fact, I'm not at all sure what we - the West - are doing. True, our destroyers and aircraft carriers and fighter aircraft and heavy bombers and troops are massing in the general region of the Gulf. Our SAS boys - so they say in the Middle East - are already climbing around northern Afghanistan, in the region still controlled by the late Shah Masoud's forces. But what exactly are we planning to do? Kidnap Mr bin Laden? Storm his camps and kill the lot of them, Mr bin Laden and all his Algerian, Egyptian, Jordanian, Syrian and Gulf Arabs?

Or is Mr bin Laden merely chapter one of our new Middle Eastern adventure, to be broadened later to include Iraq, the overthrow of Saddam Hussein, the destruction of the Lebanese Hezbollah, the humbling of Syria, the humiliation of Iran, the reimposition of yet another fraudulent "peace process" between Israel and the Palestinians?

If this seems fanciful, you should listen to what's coming out of Washington and Tel Aviv. While The New York Times Pentagon sources are suggesting that Saddam may be chapter two, the Israelis are trying to set up Lebanon - the "centre of international terror" according to Israeli prime minister Ariel Sharon - for a bombing run or two, along with Yasser Arafat's little garbage tip down in Gaza where the Israelis have discovered, mirabile dictu, a "bin Laden cell".

The Arabs, of course, would also like an end to world terror. But they would like to include a few other names on the list. Palestinians would like to see Mr Sharon picked up for the Sabra and Chatila massacre, a terrorist slaughter carried out by Israel's Lebanese allies - who were trained by the Israeli army - in 1982. At 1,800 dead, that's only a quarter of the number killed on 11 September. Syrians in Hama would like to put Rifaat Al-Assad, the brother of the late president, on their list of terrorists for the mass killings perpetrated by his Defence Brigades in the city of Hama in the same year. At 20,000, that's more than double the 11 September death toll.

The Lebanese would like trials for the Israeli officers who planned the Israeli invasion of Lebanon in 1982, which killed 17,500 people, most of them civilians - again, well over twice the 11 September statistic. Christian Sudanese would like President Omar al-Bashir arraigned for mass murder.

But, as the Americans have made clear, it's their own terrorist enemies they are after, not their terrorist friends or those terrorists who have been slaughtering populations outside American "spheres of interest". Even those terrorists who live comfortably in the US but have not harmed America are safe: take, for example, the pro-Israeli militiaman who murdered two Irish UN soldiers in southern Lebanon in 1980 and who now live in Detroit after flying safely out of Tel Aviv. The Irish have the name and address, if the FBI are interested - but of course they're not.

So we are not really being asked to fight "world terror". We are being asked to fight America's enemies. If that means bagging the murderers behind the atrocities in New York and Washington, few would object. But it does raise the question of why those thousands of innocents are more important - more worthy of our effort and perhaps blood - than all the other thousands of innocents. And it also raises a much more disturbing question: whether or not the crime against humanity committed in the US on 11 September is to be met with justice - or a brutal military assault intended to extend American political power in the Middle East.

Either way, we are being asked to support a war whose aims appear to be as misleading as they are secretive. We are told by the Americans that this war will be different to all others. But one of the differences appears to be that we don't know who we are going to fight and how long we are going to fight for. Certainly, no new political initiative, no real political engagement in the Middle East, no neutral justice is likely to attend this open-ended conflict. The despair and humiliation and suffering of the Middle East peoples do not figure in our war aims - only American and European despair and humiliation and suffering.

As for Mr bin Laden, no one believes the Taliban are genuinely ignorant of his whereabouts. He is in Afghanistan. But has he really gone to ground? During the Russian war, he would emerge, again and again, to fight Afghanistan's Russian occupiers, to attack the world's second superpower. Wounded six times, he was a master of the tactical ambush, as the Russians found out to their cost. Evil and wicked do not come close to describing the mass slaughter in the US. But - if it was Mr bin Laden's work - that does not mean he would not fight again. And he would be fighting on home ground. There are plenty of dark defiles into which we may advance. And plenty of cheap rifles to shoot at us. And that wouldn't be a "new kind of war" at all.

26 September 2001

REJECTING THE MONSTER THEY HELPED CREATE

The Saudis, who helped to create the Taliban regime in Afghanistan, thereby spawning a baby that turned into a monster, severed all diplomatic ties with the Kabul government yesterday.

Their decision, which ended seven years of shameless Saudi support for the most obscurantist and cruel regime in the region, came scarcely a month after the Saudi Royal Family fired the man who did more than any individual to cement the Taliban's power in Afghanistan: Prince Turki bin Feisel al-Saud, the head of the Saudi secret service.

Saudi Arabia's break with the Taliban ends a relationship that embarrassed the Saudis as much as it infuriated the United States - even though it was studiously ignored by US administrations and the American media.

The links began in 1994 when Saudi and other Arab princes flew to Afghanistan's second city of Kandahar for a hunting expedition, bringing with them jeeps, money and an entire mobile phone system for their Afghan hosts. Among them was Prince Turki, who was not only a close acquaintance of Osama bin Laden but had enthusiastically embraced Mr bin Laden's original call for Arab fighters to join the war against the Russians in 1980.

Prince Turki had first promoted the Wahhabi Sunni Muslim Taliban - reared in the ignorance of the Afghan refugee camps in Pakistan - as adherents to the al-Saud family sect and a counter-balance to the Shia Muslim Hazara tribe of Afghanistan, which was supported by Iran. Wahhabism, a form of "pure" Islam first preached in the 18th century by Abdul Wahab - whose daughter's marriage to an al-Saud sealed the alliance between the theological zealot and the future rulers of Saudi Arabia - enforced strict sharia religious law, which was applied with obsessional relish by the Pashtun-speaking Taliban.

The Saudis had few doubts about supporting them. Mr bin Laden's flight from Sudan to Afghanistan in 1995 placed him under Taliban, and therefore Saudi, control.

There are many accounts of the Arab hunt for game birds - bustards in this case - around Kandahar and of the Arab princes' generosity to the Taliban. According to the Pakistani journalist Ahmad Rashid, whose 20-year study of Afghanistan, Taliban, is probably the most authoritative source on the subject, the head of the Pakistani Jema'a Ulema Islami (Group of Islamic Religious Scholars), Maulana Faz-lur Rehman, organised the Arabs' trip.

Within 18 months, Prince Turki had returned to Kandahar, this time to provide millions of dollars, vehicles and petrol for the Taliban assault on Kabul - the battle that finally drove the feuding and largely secular mujahedin guerrillas out of the city and led to the imposition of the ruthless religious laws that within months destroyed culture, entertainment, science and women's rights in most of Afghanistan. The involvement of two Saudi companies in a gas pipeline project across the country provided further reason for the Saudis to pursue their friendship.

The Saudi religious leaders, the ulema, had insisted that the Royal Family should support the Taliban after they themselves had been forced to approve the presence of half a million US troops in the land of Mecca and Medina five years earlier. The ulema, including Sheikh Abdul Aziz bin Baz, the Grand Mufti and chairman of the Council of Senior Preachers, demanded Saudi support for the Taliban and preached in favour of its rule in Afghanistan in the madrassahs (religious schools) and mosques across Saudi Arabia.

In April 1997, Mullah Rabbani, the Taliban leader, arrived in Riyadh to announce that "Saudi Arabia is the centre of the Muslim world (and) we would like to have Saudi assistance. King Fahd expressed happiness at the good measures (sic) taken by the Taliban and over the imposition of Sharia (law) in our country." According to Mr Rashid, the Saudis were now extremely reluctant to demand the return of Mr bin Laden.

Ironically, the Iranians, who have always opposed the Taliban and their regime, had by 1996 found themselves in a position remarkably similar to that in which the US finds itself today. The Taliban had given sanctuary to Ahl-e-Sunnah Wal Jamaar, head of an opposition "terrorist" group that had been recruiting among Iranians around Khorasan, many of them from Iran's Baluchi, Turkmen and Afghan minorities. The Taliban gave the Iranians the same reply as they have done in response to demands for Mr bin Laden's expulsion: he is a Muslim "guest" and cannot be asked to leave.

The state visit by Mohammad Khatami, the Iranian President, to Saudi Arabia in May 1999 doomed the Saudi-Taliban relationship. The Saudis had grown to distrust the Taliban's other prop, Pakistan, and were appalled at the massacre of Iranian diplomats by the Taliban in Mazar-I-Sharif in 1998. When Prince Turki paid one more visit to Kabul last year to demand the expulsion of Mr bin Laden, he was brusquely told to leave.

But the ghost of Wahhabism continued to haunt Afghanistan. In Saudi Arabia, there had long been rumours that members of the Royal Family were in the habit of "marrying" a new wife each year and discarding an older wife to make room for her. In Kabul, the Taliban are now reported to have adopted similar mores. Several families have said that squads of armed Taliban men have turned up at their door to take a daughter for an arranged marriage - to a husband who will then divorce another of his wives. Whether the habit was picked up from the Saudis, the kingdom has already done its best to make a final break with the Taliban. By cutting diplomatic ties with Afghanistan, Saudi Arabia is hoping the world will forget how culpable it was in the whole Taliban catastrophe.

27 September 2001

AFGHANISTAN NURTURES WHAT SAUDI ARABIA PRODUCES

Our fleets and aircraft may be heading for the land and sea close to Afghanistan but, in the days to come, the attention of diplomats and intelligence agents is likely to be focused on an ally whose citizens - perhaps as many as 12 of them - were among the 19 hijackers who slaughtered more than 7,000 people: Saudi Arabia.

The Saudis are not handing out visas to journalists right now - and why should they when their enquiries would reveal a kingdom that is ever more dangerously balanced between religious extremists and the royal family which first invited American troops to Saudi Arabia more than 11 years ago? At least six of the hijackers aboard the four jets come from Saudi Arabia, most from middle-class, even wealthy families. Some of them are followers of Safar Hawali, a dissident cleric who has repeatedly demanded - like Osama bin Laden - that US forces be withdrawn from the Gulf.

Saudi Arabia's internal tensions are becoming more transparent as the full story of the attacks is pieced together. If the Taliban government in Afghanistan - itself a Saudi creation funded with millions of dollars by the now-fired head of the Saudi secret police, Prince Turki bin Faisal al-Saud - is hiding Mr bin Laden, what of the Saudis whose intelligence service was so poor it had no idea six of its citizens were planning an attack on the US? In private, most Saudis acknowledge the growing strains - if not open hostility - between the Saudi ulema (religious authorities) and the royal family.

"This has always been a problem and we know the sensitivities that exist now," an old Saudi friend remarked yesterday. "Hawali is a fanatic and I had an argument with him once. He has no idea of compromise. His mind is made up about everything. But every country has its fanatics and mad guys. You had them in Lebanon. They exist in Chechnya and Pakistan." None of those countries, however, can boast six - perhaps 12 - of its citizens among the suicide crews who killed so many thousands in America this month.

Hamza Alghamdi was from Baljurchi, in the Saudi province of Baha, the same town from which Ahmed Alghamdi and Ahmed Alhaznawi - both named as hijackers - came. The Saudi newspaper Al-Watan published a report this week that a man named Hamza Saleh Alghamdi had left home for Chechnya and then telephoned his parents to ask them to forgive him and pray for him. His father insists that the photograph of Alghamdi published by the FBI is not that of his son.

So is this a case of yet another stolen passport being used to create a false identity for the hijackers? Hani Hanjour, the hijacker who piloted the plane that crashed into the Pentagon, came from the Saudi hill resort of Ta'if. Like the Lebanese family of Ziad Jarrahi, who apparently piloted the airliner that crashed in Pennsylvania after a revolt by passengers, Hanjour's parents insist that he must have been an innocent passenger on the plane.

The brothers Wail and Waleed M Alshehri came from Khamis Mushayt near Abha, the city where Safar Hawali preaches. Ahmed Alnami was also from Asir province - Abha is its capital and he appears to have been a prayer leader in its mosque.

Despite this clear evidence that Saudi Arabia has been a cradle of determined killers, no debate has been opened in the kingdom as to how - or why - these young men, all of whom were in their twenties, would form a suicide squad. To ask this question would open the schism within Saudi society and demonstrate the power of the ulema, the same religious leaders whom Mr bin Laden has always claimed were on his side. The most recent rift between the ulema and the Saudi government came over, of all things, insurance - with the religious leaders claiming it is un-Islamic. Instead of opposing the powerful religious elite, the government allowed policies to be issued by "offshore" companies with representatives living in the kingdom.

Fearful that the US will discover the deep-seated friction within Saudi society, the Saudis have effectively neutered American efforts to interview men arrested for suspected bombings. Prince Turki al-Saud has made no comment since his dismissal last month. As usual, the Saudis want to keep a very thick Arab robe tied tightly around their own dissidents - lest the world discovers that Afghanistan only nurtures what Saudi Arabia produces.

OCTOBER 2001: AMERICA'S NEW WAR

Northern Alliance fighters, Afghanistan

1 October 2001

TALIBAN WARNS US MUSLIMS AGAINST 'TREASON'

A prominent Taliban cleric has been flooding mosques and Islamic centres in the United States with faxes, telling Muslims that an American assault on the Taliban government in Kabul would be "treason against God" and claiming the Israeli secret service "orchestrated" the atrocities in New York and Washington.

Israr Ahmed's Koranic teaching is highly influential among the 2,000 Taliban schools along the Pakistani-Afghan frontier and his message to Muslim Americans - while it belongs to the outer reaches of conspiracy theorists - is unprecedented.

A copy of his message, sent from the Tanzeem-e-Islami (the Islamic Association), has been obtained by The Independent and it reveals that Dr Ahmed, a Pakistani, was among the "ulema" (religious authorities) who met the Pakistani leader, General Pervez Musharraf, to warn him that Pakistan would descend into civil war if it co-operated with the United States.

The purpose of Dr Ahmed's appeal is to undermine General Musharraf's promise to help the US forces in any attacks on Afghanistan, and to question the evidence which the United States says it has against the Saudi dissident Osama bin Laden.

"The way that America is naming Usama (sic) bin Laden as a criminal, without any clear evidence, is against all laws of justice," he writes in his letter to American Muslims. "In this situation, an attack on Afghanistan will be absolutely inhuman and an example of extreme state terrorism ..."

Ignoring the growing evidence of connections between groups in Afghanistan and the bombing of the US embassies in Africa and the suicide attacks on the World Trade Centre, Dr Ahmed claims that "it is becoming clear that the secret Israeli service Musad (sic) orchestrated these terrorist attacks to change the world opinion against Islam and Muslims ... These terrorist attacks are a vital link in the chain of events that the Jews are undertaking to fulfil their dream of world domination ... in this Zionist plan, Pakistan and its atomic capability are the topmost in their hit list."

Taliban supporters have insisted several times that an Israeli "plot" lies behind the crimes against humanity of 11 September and Dr Ahmed's letter suggests he has little idea how dismissive most American Muslims would be of such an idea.

But his attempt to enlist the support of Arab Americans - indeed all American Muslims - in his campaign to end Pakistan's support for the United States shows the lengths to which Taliban clerics will now go to sabotage President Bush's plans.

Dr Ahmed says: Pakistan should stand firm against the American "Pharaoh".

"Afghanistan," he says, "is our brother Muslim country and its Taliban government is based on upholding the supremacy of Islamic Sharia (law); Pakistan's co-operation in the unjust American attack against the Islamic Taliban government will not only be a treason against Allah and his messenger (the Prophet Mohamed) but a betrayal of Pakistan's ideology."

3 October 2001

IT'S REALLY AN OLD WAR

"America's new war," is what they call it on CNN. And of course, as usual, they've got it wrong. Because in our desire to "bring to justice" - let's remember those words in the coming days - the vicious men who planned the crimes against humanity in New York and Washington last month, we're hiring some well-known rapists and murderers to work for us.

Yes, it's an old war, a dreary routine that we've seen employed around the world for the past three decades. In Vietnam, the Americans wanted to avoid further casualties; so they re-armed and re-trained the South Vietnamese army to be their foot-soldiers. In southern Lebanon, the Israelis used their Lebanese militia thugs to combat the Palestinians and the Hizbollah. The Phalange and the so-called "South Lebanon Army" were supposed to be Israel's foot-soldiers. They failed, but that is in the nature of wars - by-proxy. In Kosovo, we kept our well-armed Nato troops safely out of harm's way while the KLA acted as our foot-soldiers.

And now, without a blush or a swallow of embarrassment, we're about to sign up the so-called "Northern Alliance" in Afghanistan. America's newspapers are saying - without a hint of irony - that they, too, will be our "foot-soldiers" in our war to hunt down/bring to justice/smoke out/eradicate/liquidate Osama bin Laden and the Taliban. US officials - who know full well the whole bloody, rapacious track record of the killers in the "Alliance" - are suggesting in good faith that these are the men who will help us bring democracy to Afghanistan and drive the Taliban and the terrorists out of the country. In fact, we're ready to hire one gang of terrorists - our terrorists - to rid ourselves of another gang of terrorists. What, I wonder, would the dead of New York and Washington think of this?

But first, let's keep the record straight. The atrocities of 11 September were a crime against humanity. The evil men who planned this mass-murder should (repeat: should) be brought to justice. And if that means the end of the Taliban - with their limb-chopping and execution of women and their repressive, obscurantist Saudi-style "justice" - fair enough. The Northern Alliance, the confederacy of warlords, patriots, rapists and torturers who control a northern sliver of Afghanistan, have very definitely not (repeat: not) massacred more than 7,000 innocent civilians in the United States. No, the murderers among them have done their massacres on home turf, in Afghanistan. Just like the Taliban.

Even as the World Trade Centre collapsed in blood and dust, the world mourned the assassination of Ahmed Shah Masood, the courageous and patriotic Lion of Panjshir whose leadership of the Northern Alliance remained the one obstacle to overall Taliban power. Perhaps he was murdered in advance of the slaughter in America, to emasculate America's potential allies in advance of US retaliation. Either way, his proconsulship allowed us to forget the gangs he led.

It permitted us, for example, to ignore Abdul Rashid Dustum, one of the most powerful Alliance gangsters, whose men looted and raped their way through the suburbs of Kabul in the Nineties. They chose girls for forced marriages, murdered their families, all under the eyes of Masood. Dustum had a habit of changing sides, joining the Taliban for bribes and indulging in massacres alongside the Wahhabi gangsters who formed the government of Afghanistan, then returning to the Alliance weeks later.

Then there's Rasoul Sayaf, a Pashtun who originally ran the "Islamic Union for the Freedom of Afghanistan", but whose gunmen tortured Shia families and used their women as sex slaves in a series of human rights abuses between 1992 and 1996. Sure, he's just one of 15 leaders in the Alliance, but the terrified people of Kabul are chilled to the bone at the thought that these criminals are to be among America's new foot-soldiers.

Urged on by the Americans, the Alliance boys have been meeting with the elderly and sick ex-King Mohamed Zahir Shah, whose claim to have no interest in the monarchy is almost certainly honourable - but whose ambitious grandson may have other plans for Afghanistan. A "loya jerga", we are told, will bring together all tribal groups to elect a transitional government after the formation of a "Supreme Council for the National Unity of Afghanistan". And the old king will be freighted in as a symbol of national unity, a reminder of the good old days before democracy collapsed and communism destroyed the country. And we'll have to forget that King Zahir Shah - though personally likeable, and a saint compared to the Taliban - was no great democrat.

What Afghanistan needs is an international force - not a bunch of ethnic gangs steeped in blood - to re-establish some kind of order. It doesn't have to be a UN force, but it could have Western troops and should be supported by surrounding Muslim nations - though, please God, not the Saudis - and able to restore roads, food supplies and telecommunications. There are still well-educated academics and civil servants in Afghanistan who could help to re-establish the infrastructure of government. In this context, the old king might just be a temporary symbol of unity before a genuinely inter-ethnic government could be created.

But that's not what we're planning. More than 7,000 innocents have been murdered in the USA, and the two million Afghans who have been killed since 1980 don't amount to a hill of beans beside that. Whether or not we send in humanitarian aid, we're pouring more weapons into this starving land, to arm a bunch of gangsters in the hope they'll destroy the Taliban and let us grab bin Laden cost-free.

I have a dark premonition about all this. The "Northern Alliance" will work for us. They'll die for us. And, while they're doing that, we'll try to split the Taliban and cut a deal with their less murderous cronies, offering them a seat in a future government alongside their Alliance enemies. The other Taliban - the guys who won't take the Queen's shilling or Mr Bush's dollar - will snipe at our men from the mountainside and shoot at our jets and threaten more attacks on the West, with or without bin Laden.

And at some point - always supposing we've installed a puppet government to our liking in Kabul - the Alliance will fall apart and turn against its ethnic enemies or, if we should still be around, against us. Because the Alliance knows that we're not giving them money and guns because we love Afghanistan, or because we want to bring peace to the land, or because we are particularly interested in establishing democracy in south-west Asia. The West is demonstrating its largesse because it wants to destroy America's enemies.

Just remember what happened in 1980 when we backed the brave, ruthless, cruel mujahedin against the Soviet Union. We gave them money and weapons and promised them political support once the Russians left. There was much talk, I recall, of "loya jergas", and even a proposal that the then less elderly king might be trucked back to Afghanistan. And now this is exactly what we are offering once again.

And, dare I ask, how many bin Ladens are serving now among our new and willing foot-soldiers?

America's "new war", indeed.

7 October 2001

THE HANDS WE SHAKE ARE COVERED IN BLOOD

Almost four weeks after the crimes against humanity in New York and Washington, we are playing politics on the hoof and allying ourselves to some of the nastiest butchers around.

Mr Blair may believe that "the values we believe in should shine through what we do in Afghanistan" but few of our "friends" in the region have many values, and some of them have a lot of blood on their hands. For as we search for facilities and jumping-off points and air space and access - and we are now creating policies by the day - we are being asked to forget a lot of recent history.

First out of the memory goes Chechnya. The savage repression of this Muslim republic - complete with mass executions, mass rape and mass graves - was the brainchild of Vladimir Putin, the former serving KGB officer into whose soul Mr Bush believes he peered in Slovenia.

Mr Putin's assault on Grozny was timed to bring him the Russian presidency, and within weeks his undisciplined troops had turned the rubble of Chechnya into something approaching Afghanistan. Mr Putin now seems our strongest ally in the "war against terror". And why not, when he is himself such a master of terror?

Second out of the memory goes the nasty little dictatorship run by the Saudi royal family whose religious "mouttawa" police taught the Taliban how to run their Ministry for the Prevention of Vice and Promotion of Virtue.

We should forget that women are not even allowed to drive a car in Saudi Arabia, we must ignore the weekly head-choppings outside mosques, the country's disgraceful and unfair judicial system - everything, in fact, which might remind us of Saudi Arabia's carbon copy, the Taliban, whose destruction we are now seeking.

Then we must turn our attention away from the not terribly democratic regime of General Pervez Musharraf. Only a little while ago, the general was the Pakistani army commander who overthrew the democratically elected - though corrupt - government of Nawaz Sharif. Indeed, General Musharraf was rather keen to hang Mr Sharif until

President Clinton dropped by Islamabad early last year to condemn Osama bin Laden and appeal for Sharif's life.

Only a few weeks ago, the general appointed himself president. And while the world tut-tutted then, it now respectfully accords General Musharraf the title of "president" too.

Fourth down the memory hole goes our new friend Uzbekistan whose President Islam Karimov currently holds 7,000 political prisoners in his jails. There is no free press, no political opposition.

Mikhail Ardzinov, one of the few human rights activists in Uzbekistan - who was brutally beaten by Karimov's secret police two years ago - now says that although America had promised not to sell out human rights to get Karimov's friendship, "We know that the tone will change now". Too true. Karimov has promised that his air space can be "used in the fight against terrorism for humanitarian and security aims".

And this is not the moment to remind anyone that Uzbekistan has its own reasons to destroy the Taliban - not just because the Taliban has been exporting its revolution over the Afghan-Uzbek border, but because President Karimov wants to run an oil pipeline through Afghanistan to a Pakistani port, a project that will help to fund his bankrupt police state (as well as a few American oil companies).

One of Karimov's allies is the anti-Taliban war criminal Abdul Rashid Dustum whose men went on a rampage of rape in Kabul in the early Nineties and who, for several months, went to fight for the Taliban after receiving a massive bribe for his change of allegiance. So it's amnesia too for the anarchy and mass human rights abuses perpetrated when the Northern Alliance - our friends in northern Afghanistan - ruled Kabul. We must remember with sorrow its former leader, Ahmed Shah Massoud, a genuine patriot murdered by Arab suicide bombers on 9 September, but we must forget his colleague Rasoul Sayaf whose men used Shia women as sex slaves in the early Nineties.

Now it's true that Churchill, when told in 1941 that Germany had invaded the Soviet Union and that Stalin was now his ally, announced that if Hitler invaded Hell, he would at least make "a favourable reference" to the Devil in the House of Commons. But we're not making any references at all to our "friends" in the region. We have drawn the shining bright sword and have no time to worry if the hands we shake are covered in blood.

This is a war of democracy versus evil, according to President Bush. It's just that there's not an awful lot of democracy around.

8 October 2001

WORLD'S MOST DANGEROUS POLITICAL TECTONIC PLATE

The most powerful military force on earth has now begun its bombardment of the world's poorest, most ravaged Muslim nation. And no matter how many loaves of bread are dropped with our bombs, will there be a Muslim who will approve?

Is it possible, is it conceivable - even with our most sophisticated missiles - that we are not killing the innocent as well as the guilty in Afghanistan? We may say we are punishing Osama bin Laden. We may believe it. But will the Muslim world believe it?

There has been much talk of a coalition these past four weeks but it's not a coalition that includes any Muslim nation, albeit that Pakistan and Saudi Arabia and the little dictatorship up in Uzbekistan are being dragged along behind it.

There are no Saudi Arabian or Kuwaiti pilots in the night skies over Afghanistan. This is not a Western-Muslim coalition. This is the West on its own, bombing a Muslim country that has a standard of living close to the Middle Ages.

The bombing, I suppose, came in time for prime-time television. But do we seriously think that Mr bin Laden and his cronies are going to be caught out by this?

President George Bush talks about "sustained, comprehensive and relentless" operations. But where does it go from here?

Those of us who remember the start of the Kosovo war - or, indeed, the beginning of the air bombardment of Iraq - remember how we were assured that our opponents would sue for peace in a few days. But that did not happen and the Taliban, a monster created by our two "Alliance" friends Pakistan and Saudi Arabia, are unlikely to throw down their arms.

Of course, we will be firing missiles and dropping bombs on at least 12 of Mr bin Laden's training camps. That won't be difficult. After all we - or rather the CIA - built them for Mr bin Laden and his comrades just under 20 years ago.

With more time and more work, perhaps we could have cobbled together a bigger alliance but what we are doing now is plunging into the very centre of jihadi culture.

The issue is not how many bombs we dropped last night or dropped today but where the cracks begin to appear in the next 24 hours. Because Saudi Arabia, Pakistan and Afghanistan lay on the most dangerous political tectonic plate in the world.

On Wednesday, if not before, we may find out the answer when the Islamic conference opens in Qatar. It will be intriguing - perhaps even frightening - to listen to what Muslim leaders say when they meet.

True, Mr Bush has done his best to find a sop, pushing humanitarian aid into the package of bombs and manhunts.

As usual, we've been told that the Afghans are not our enemies. That's what we said before we bombed Iraq in 1991. And it's what we said before we bombed Libya in 1985. And it's what the Americans said before they shelled Lebanon in 1982. And, as a matter of fact, it's what we told the Egyptians before we bombed them on the Suez canal in 1956. But will the Muslim world believe it?

And just as a footnote to this bleak moment of 21st-century history, are we setting up any judicial process, any courts, any legislation to ensure that bad men are punished with the law? That is one answer we are unlikely to get from our leaders in the next few days.

9 October 2001

LOST IN THE RHETORICAL FOG OF WAR

A few months ago, my old friend Tom Friedman set off for the small Gulf emirate of Qatar, from where, in one of his messianic columns for The New York Times, he informed us that the tiny state's Al-Jazeera satellite channel was a welcome sign that democracy might be coming to the Middle East. Al-Jazeera had been upsetting some of the local Arab dictators - President Mubarak of Egypt for one - and Tom thought this a good idea. So do I. But hold everything. The story is being rewritten. Last week, US Secretary of State Colin Powell rapped the Emir of Qatar over the knuckles because - so he claimed - Al-Jazeera was "inciting anti-Americanism".

So, goodbye democracy. The Americans want the emir to close down the channel's office in Kabul, which is scooping the world with tape of the US bombardments and - more to the point - with televised statements by Osama bin Laden. The most wanted man in the whole world has been suggesting that he's angry about the deaths of Iraqi children under sanctions, about the corruption of pro-western Arab regimes, about Israel's attacks on the Palestinian territory, about the need for US forces to leave the Middle East. And after insisting that bin Laden is a "mindless terrorist" - that there is no connection between US policy in the Middle East and the crimes against humanity in New York and Washington - the Americans need to close down Al-Jazeera's coverage.

Needless to say, this tomfoolery by Colin Powell has not been given much coverage in the Western media, who know that they do not have a single correspondent in the Taliban area of Afghanistan. Al-Jazeera does.

But why are we journalists falling back on the same sheep-like conformity that we adopted in the 1991 Gulf War and the 1999 Kosovo war? For here we go again. The BBC was yesterday broadcasting an American officer talking about the dangers of "collateral damage" - without the slightest hint of the immorality of this phrase. Tony Blair boasts of Britain's involvement in the US bombardment by talking about our "assets", and by yesterday morning the BBC were using the same soldier -speak. Is there some kind of rhetorical fog that envelops us every time we bomb someone?

As usual, the first reports of the US missile attacks were covered without the slightest suggestion that innocents were about to die in the country we plan to "save". Whether the Taliban are lying or telling the truth about 30 dead in Kabul, do we reporters really think that all our bombs fall on the guilty and not the innocent? Do we think that all the food we are reported to be dropping is going to fall around the innocent and not the Taliban? I am beginning to wonder whether we have not convinced ourselves that wars - our wars - are movies. The only Hollywood film ever made about Afghanistan was a Rambo epic in which Sylvester Stallone taught the Afghan mujahedin how to fight the Russian occupation, help to defeat Soviet troops and won the admiration of an Afghan boy. Are the Americans, I wonder, somehow trying to actualise the movie?

But look at the questions we're not asking. Back in 1991 we dumped the cost of the Gulf War - billions of dollars of it - on Saudi Arabia and Kuwait. But the Saudis and Kuwaitis are not going to fund our bombing this time round. So who's going to pay? When? How much will it cost us - and I mean us? The first night of bombing cost, so we are told, at least $2m, I suspect much more. Let us not ask how many Afghans that would have fed - but do let's ask how much of our money is going towards the war and how much towards humanitarian aid.

Bin Laden's propaganda is pretty basic. He films his own statements and sends one of his henchmen off to the Al-Jazeera office in Kabul. No vigorous questioning of course, just a sermon. So far we've not seen any video clips of destroyed Taliban equipment, the ancient Migs and even older Warsaw Pact tanks that have been rusting across Afghanistan for years. Only a sequence of pictures - apparently real - of bomb damage in a civilian area of Kabul. The Taliban have kept reporters out. But does that mean we have to balance this distorted picture with our own half-truths?

So hard did a colleague of mine try, in a radio interview the other day, to unlink the bin Laden phenomenon from the West's baleful history in the Middle East that he seriously suggested that the attacks were timed to fall on the anniversary of the defeat of Muslim forces at the gates of Vienna in 1683. Unfortunately, the Poles won their battle against the Turks on 12, not 11, September. But when the terrifying details of the hijacker Mohamed Atta's will were published last week, dated April 1996, no one could think of any event that month that might have propelled Atta to his murderous behaviour.

Not the Israeli bombardment of southern Lebanon, nor the Qana massacre by Israeli artillery of 106 Lebanese civilians in a UN base, more than half of them children. For that's what happened in April, 1996. No, of course that slaughter is not excuse for the crimes against humanity in the United States last month. But isn't it worth just a little mention, just a tiny observation, that an Egyptian mass-murderer-to-be wrote a will of chilling suicidal finality in the month when the massacre in Lebanon enraged Arabs across the Middle East?

Instead of that, we're getting Second World War commentaries about western military morale. On the BBC we had to listen to how it was "a perfect moonless night for the air armada" to bomb Afghanistan. Pardon me? Are the Germans back at Cap Gris Nez? Are our fighter squadrons back in the skies of Kent, fighting off the Dorniers and Heinkels? Yesterday, we were told on one satellite channel of the "air combat" over Afghanistan. A lie, of course. The Taliban had none of their ageing Migs aloft. There was no combat.

Of course, I know the moral question. After the atrocities in New York, we can't "play fair" between the ruthless bin Laden and the West; we can't make an equivalence between the mass-murderer's innocence and the American and British forces who are trying to destroy the Taliban.

But that's not the point. It's our viewers and readers we've got to "play fair" with. Must we, because of our rage at the massacre of the innocents in America, because of our desire to kowtow to the elderly "terrorism experts", must we lose all our critical faculties? Why at least not tell us how these "terrorism experts" came to be so expert? And what are their connections with dubious intelligence services?

In some cases, in America, the men giving us their advice on screen are the very same operatives who steered the CIA and the FBI into the greatest intelligence failure in modern history: the inability to uncover the plot, four years in the making, to destroy the lives of almost 6,000 people. President Bush says this is a war between good and evil. You are either with us or against us. But that's exactly what bin Laden says. Isn't it worth pointing this out and asking where it leads?

10 October 2001

BUSH AND BLAIR HAVE ALREADY LOST THE TALKING WAR

Messrs Bush and Blair may tell the world they are going to win the "war against terrorism" but in the Middle East, where Osama bin Laden is acquiring almost mythic status among Arabs, they have already lost.

Whether it be a Lebanese minister, a Saudi journalist, a Jordanian bank clerk or an Egyptian resident, the response is always the same: Mr bin Laden's voice, repeatedly beamed into millions of homes, articulates the demands and grievances - and fury - of Middle East Muslims who have seen their pro-Western presidents and kings and princes wriggling out of any serious criticism of the Anglo-American bombardment of Afghanistan.

Viewing Mr bin Laden's latest video tape, Western nations concentrated (if they listened at all) on his remarks about the atrocities in the United States. If he expressed his approval, though denied any personal responsibility, didn't this mean that he was really behind the mass slaughter of 11 September?

Arabs listened with different ears. They heard a voice which accused the West of double standards and "arrogance" towards the Middle East, a voice which addressed the central issue in the lives of so many Arabs: the Palestinian-Israeli conflict and the continuation of Israeli occupation.

Now, as a long-time resident of Cairo put it yesterday, Arabs believe America "is trying to kill the one man ready to tell the truth".

Arab civilians, usually uneasy about identifying themselves when their views conflict with their government, are now speaking more freely about their anger. "They say their target is bin Laden," Samar al-Naji said in Jordan. "Then they strike at innocent people in Afghanistan who have nothing to do with terrorism. They strike Muslims while ignoring the acts of Israel, the terrorist state which is demolishing Palestinian homes and killing women and children." Mr al-Naji is only a bank clerk, at 29 hardly a seasoned politician.

At the Ain Shams University in Cairo, prayers were performed for the dead of Afghanistan and in the Nile delta town of Zagazig, students went to the heart of the problem in all pro-Western Arab regimes. "Our rulers, why are you silent?" they chanted. "Have you got orders from America?" This is rubbish, of course. Rulers of what we like to call "moderate" Arab states don't need orders to give their discreet support to the West. And Mr bin Laden is, after all, calling for their own overthrow.

Only in the freer Arab countries could ministers speak their minds. The Lebanese information minister, Ghazi Aridi, regards Mr bin Laden's video tape as "a stroke of intelligence". There was, he said, "an international incitement against one person. If he is killed, he will become a symbol and if he survives he will become a stronger symbol."

In the Gulf, feelings are very fragile. "Look, I know old women who are staying up late at night to say prayers for Mr bin Laden," a Saudi journalist says. "His appearance on television was very good public relations for him, especially when he talked about Palestine. In public, people don't praise him; there has been no comment in the mosques. But in private, they are all talking about him."

A Saudi editor, Jamal Kashoggi, insisted that many Saudis were far more critical of Mr bin Laden - believing that he is defaming Islam

- and ready to see a less pessimistic outcome in Afghanistan. "Kandahar contains supporters of the monarchy as well as the Taliban," he said. "Afghans who were disappointed by the anti-Russian mujahedin and turned to the Taliban are now disappointed with the Taliban and may accept a royalist comeback." But this, a view that would most certainly coincide with Saudi Arabia's own royal family, may be a minority one.

In countries which have been afflicted by a "terrorism" far greater in suffering and death than the crimes against humanity in New York and Washington, the very language used by President Bush has been a cause for great anger.

"I'm sick of hearing about terrorism, terrorism, terrorism," a prominent Lebanese construction manager shouted at me. "When you have enemies, they are 'terrorists' or 'madmen' or 'evildoers'. When we have enemies, we are asked to compromise with them. You have bin Laden. We have Sharon - who is your friend and whose hand Mr Bush shakes".

Many Lebanese believe that Israel's Prime Minister, Ariel Sharon, should be indicted as a war criminal for his role in the Sabra and Chatila Palestinian camps massacre of 1982, in which up to 1,800 civilians - almost half the number of victims slaughtered in America on 11 September - were killed in three days by Israel's Christian militia allies while Israel's army watched from the camp perimeters.

11 October 2001

WAR OF WORDS

Was Sulemain Abu Gheit's statement a code? No wonder the Americans asked the Arabic Al-Jazeera channel last night to censor the group's statements off the air. Or was it just a strident appeal? Or a declaration of war? Surely, you might say, Osama bin Laden's al-Qa'ida group - the "foundation" might be a better translation than the "base" - had said it all before. Weren't the suicide aircraft attacks of 11 September the declaration of war?

Or last Sunday's American attacks - plus British missiles - our declaration of war on Mr bin Laden? But Mr bin Laden's spokesman appeared to want the last word. "America has opened a door that, God willing, will not be closed," he said.

It's not difficult to see what Mr bin Laden was intending to do. After his, "tour de force" last week - the round-up of Middle East grievances, the Koranic quotations, the historical resonance, Muslim versus infidel - it might have been necessary to ensure that Arabs as well as all Muslims had understood the message: there is no turning back now. "The Americans must know that the storm of aircraft will not stop, God willing," the turbaned Mr Abu Gheit said. "And there are thousands of young people who are as keen about death as Americans are about life."

As usual, it wasn't difficult to find the parallels. President Bush also promised - in his way - that the "storm of aircraft" would not stop. In the past 24 hours, he has told us that his war "against terror" may last for a week, a year or "a decade" - this was not to be censored off the air. And this was bin Laden-speak, just as the "with-us-or-against-us" Bush rhetoric was straight out of the bin Laden lexicon.

Or is Mr bin Laden taking his language from the US President? "I direct this message to the entire Islamic nation," Mr Abu Gheit said. "I say to them that all sides today have come together against the nation of Islam and the Muslims." But isn't this very like Mr Bush's "us against them" approach, that democracy is being attacked by the forces of "evil", that this is war unto the end?

Even Mr Abu Gheit's assertion that "we will fight them with the material and spiritual strength that we have, and our faith in God - we will be victorious" was a carbon copy of the Bush speech-writer's promise of success. Arabs, who could understand Mr bin Laden's spokesman in his original Arabic, might have been forgiven for thinking that the White House and the cave in which Mr bin Laden is supposedly hiding have had a linguistic hot-line.

Given the demonstrations and burning and curses against America, however, it is more likely that the al-Qa'ida statement was a backup to the 12-minute monologue delivered by Mr bin Laden when the American bombing of Afghanistan began, a kind of "he-really-meant-what-he-said-about-holy-war" reminder to encourage further demonstrations in Pakistan, Gaza and elsewhere and - more chillingly - to activate long dormant cells into action.

"The Americans must know that by invading the land of Afghanistan they have opened a new page of enmity and struggle between us and the forces of the unbelievers," Mr Abu Gheit said.

Oddly, for such a Wahabi sect, the statement urged Muslim women as well as men to fight the Americans; deprived of education they may be, but Afghan women are expected to die for their faith.

In earlier wars, however, Christians were content to urge women to fight without the right to education or the vote. It is tempting indeed to see a kind of ghastly mirror-image of our own conceit in the arrogance of this message. Did they learn from us or did we learn from them?

Mr bin Laden and Mr Abu Gheit appeared together in the earlier videotape in which the al-Qa'ida leader, speaking below a wall of sullen rock, explained that the day of holy war had arrived, that all Muslims should line up against the infidel, that the death of tens of thousands of Iraqi children, the corrupt Arab regimes and Israeli occupation were the West's responsibility. In a land without television, Mr bin Laden knew how to use it.

11 October 2001

BIN LADEN'S BROADCASTS MAY CONTAIN SECRET ORDERS

The White House urged the major American television networks yesterday to cut back on the screening of statements by Osama bin Laden and his spokesmen, warning they could contain secret orders to his followers in the US.

The Secretary of State, Colin Powell, said intelligence analysts were scrutinising the videotaped appearances of Mr bin Laden on Sunday, shortly after the air strikes against Afghanistan began, and of the Al-Qa'ida spokesman, Sulemain Abu Gheit, who on Tuesday (9 October) praised the 11 September attacks and warned that others would follow. The tapes could contain "some kind of message", General Powell said.

The White House made its appeal after Qatar's Al Jazeera channel aired the pre-recorded statements by Mr bin Laden and Mr Abu Gheit, which in turn were picked up by the US networks. The request was issued to senior executives of the four main broadcast networks and CNN. Afterwards, the five said they would examine incoming feeds of such statements from Al-Jazeera and not air them live.

"At best, Osama bin Laden's message is propaganda, calling on people to kill Americans. At worst, he could be issuing orders to his followers to initiate such attacks," Ari Fleischer, the White House spokesman, said

The US embassy in Doha has already filed a formal diplomatic complaint about Al-Jazeera with the tiny Qatari state which funds it.

It is no wonder the US wants to censor Al-Jazeera. It is a phenomenon in the Arab world, a comparatively free, bold initiative in journalism that was supported by the Americans - until it became rather too free.

With more than 35 offices around the world - including Kabul - the channel's 350-strong staff have had reporters in the Pentagon, northern Afghanistan (with the so-called Northern Alliance) and Gaza. It was the first channel to show Palestinians firing mortars at Israeli settlements and scooped Iraqi television with a speech by Saddam Hussein inviting Arabs to overthrow their pro-Western leaders.

The channel has its critics inside and outside the station. One member of staff used to fear that Al-Jazeera was "run by the CIA" - an idea quickly dismissed now that the Americans want to muzzle it. Others thought it lacked respect for authority.

Alas for the Americans, Israel and local Arab despots, Al-Jazeera is now the best-selling, highest-rated channel in the Middle East. And when it comes to footage of the American bombing of Kabul, whose material does CNN show? Al Jazeera's, of course.

11 October 2001

ARAB SUMMIT – NO GUILT, NO RESPONSIBILITY

Listening to the speeches of the Muslim leaders at the Organisation of the Islamic Conference emergency summit yesterday, it was possible to believe that Osama bin Laden represented Arabs more faithfully than their tin-pot dictators and kings.

Please give us more evidence about 11 September, asked the Emir of Qatar. Please don't forget the Palestinians, pleaded Yasser Arafat. Islam is innocent, insisted the Moroccan Foreign Minister.

Everyone - but everyone - wished to condemn the 11 September atrocities in the United States. No one - absolutely no one - wanted to explain how 19 Arabs decided to fly planeloads of innocent people into buildings full of civilians.

The very name of "bin Laden" did not sully the Qatar conference hall. Not once. Not even the name "Taliban". Had a Martian landed in the Gulf - which looks not unlike Mars - he might have concluded that the World Trade Centre in New York was destroyed by an earthquake or a typhoon.

Was it not President Hosni Mubarak of Egypt who said, back in 1990, that the Iraqi invasion of Kuwait would blow over "like a summer's breeze"? Thus delegates condemned to a man the slaughter in America without for a moment suggesting why this slaughter might have taken place.

Like the Americans, the Arabs didn't want to look for causes. Indeed, the conference hall was a strangely perverse place, in which introspection included neither guilt nor responsibility. Mr Arafat demanded an international force - a good idea for a new Afghanistan - but it quickly turned out that he was talking about an international force to protect Palestinians in the West Bank and Gaza which, according to the map, is about 1,800 miles from Kabul.

Of course, he condemned the World Trade Centre massacre. So did Sheikh Hamad al-Thani, the Emir of Qatar, and Mohamed bin Issa, the Moroccan Foreign Minister, and Abdul-Aziz Bilqazeez, the Islamic Conference's secretary-general. But that was about it. Indeed, the collected speeches amounted to a collected theme: please don't kill innocent Afghans, but - whatever happens - don't bomb Arab countries. Indeed, for much of the day, Afghanistan appeared a faraway country of which they knew little - a mendacious thought, given that Saudi Arabia and Pakistan were midwives to the Taliban - and wanted to know even less.

Only Farouq al-Sharaa, the Syrian Foreign Minister, stated frankly that attacking Muslim states was "forbidden". This meant, he said, "that all Arabs and Muslims will stand with the country that is attacked". Which must have made them shiver in their boots on board the US carriers in the Gulf.

There was the usual rhetoric bath from other conference delegates. The communique from the 56 conference members claimed that they rejected "the linking of terrorism to the Arab and Muslim people's rights, including the Palestinian and Lebanese people's right to self-determination, self-defence and resisting Israeli and foreign occupation and aggression". Translation: please, America, don't take the Israeli side and bomb Hamas, Islamic Jihad, the Lebanese Hizbollah, Damascus, Tehran et al. "Resistance is not terrorism" has become as familiar a slogan in the Arab world as "war against terrorism" has in the Western world.

There was little that George Bush or Tony Blair would have disagreed with. Retaliation "should not extend to any but those who carried out those attacks (which) requires conclusive evidence against the culprits," Sheikh Hamad pronounced. "The Islamic world was the first to call for the dialogue of civilisation." This might have been scripted for Mr Blair.

But the Qatari Emir got off one quick biff at the Americans. The world should not, he said, fall "into conflicting sects, camps and clashing dichotomies based on the principle of 'If you are not on my side, then you are against me'." Mr Bilqazeez made the point that Afghans had suffered two decades of war and should suffer no more - and that they should decide the future of their country for themselves. He neglected to mention that the West seems set on doing the "deciding" bit for the Afghans and that the Americans had funnelled almost as many weapons into Afghanistan as the Russians had done.

The Islamic American organisations, represented by Jamal Bazranji, wanted it known that they represented 2.5 per cent of the American population, that their role was to "bridge civilisations" and that they were Americans "with no other homeland" - an argument which Mr bin Laden would no doubt disagree with.

Wasn't Israel the real problem, the delegates tried to ask? Principle among them, of course, was our old friend Mr Arafat. Of course he condemned the attacks in America. Of course he felt "solidarity" with the American people - the old socialist "solidarity" being put to an original new use. But Israel was using these attacks as an excuse for its increased aggression against Palestinians and there must be an international observer force in Palestine to oversee the Mitchell report and there must be condemnation of Israel.

Money was to be had in a good cause. Qatar opened a fund for the Afghans and the Saudis put in $10m (£6.8m), the United Arab Emirates $3m, Oman $1m. But what the delegates wanted was evidence - "conclusive evidence", according to Sheikh Hamad - that Washington had identified the culprits of 11 September.

This at least allowed him to avoid the fatal words "bin Laden". Indeed, it allowed everyone to duck this annoying, dangerous, frightening man who is calling for the overthrow of almost every single one of the Islamic delegates.

An interesting day, then, for the Islamic conference. We're sorry about 11 September, they said. Please don't bomb Afghanistan more than you have to. Please don't kill the innocent. And please don't bomb us. You couldn't put it simpler than that.

14 October 2001

PUNCHING HOLES IN THE RUNWAY OF KANDAHAR AIRPORT

How kind of the Americans to suspend bombing on Fridays. Will it, I wonder, be halted on all Muslim sabbaths? For the festival that marks the ascent of the Prophet Mohamed to Heaven? For Ramadan?

Do not think these comments cynical. I just began to wonder - once General Richard Myers obliged the Muslims of Afghanistan by suspending war on Fridays - whether this war was serious or not. What did we think we were doing by emphasising our affection for Islam in the middle of bombing Afghanistan?

This is not the only way we are fooling ourselves. When we opened our air bombardment of Afghanistan, we went straight into Kosovo mode. We were, so we were told, going to attack ground to air defences, command and control centres and achieve total "air superiority". Forget the fact that the Taliban have already taken Afghanistan back to the Middle Ages, that scarcely any of their 20 clapped-out Mig-21s can fly, that they probably wouldn't know the difference between a command and control centre and a dustbin. In just a few short hours last week, we turned the Taliban into the Serbs.

True, we bombed Osama bin Laden's camps. I bet we did. There would have been no difficulty in spotting their location because, of course, most of them were built by the CIA when Mr bin Laden and his men were the good guys - although this salient fact oddly eluded the generals when they came to tell us what they had bombed.

But do we really believe that punching holes into the runway of Kandahar airport is going to have any military effect on men who smash televisions and hang videotapes from trees? Do we think that blowing up fuel dumps is going to stop bearded men from shooting at us in the mountains? If the equally bloody men of the Northern Alliance are to be our foot soldiers, do we intend - once they reach the ruins of Kabul - to allow them to return to their good old days of rape and looting? Or are we going to send in the Americans and the British to capture the cities - which is exactly what the Russians did in 1980 - and leave the mountains to the bad guys?

We've been making much of the Mountain Division recently, supposedly poised in Uzbekistan. But poised to do what? The only conceivable military tactic that might work for us - that is, if we still remember we're after Mr bin Laden, not the destruction of the ruins of Afghanistan - would be to slice off bits of the country, one at a time, for search missions. But anyone who has visited Afghanistan knows how awesome that task would be. A journey down the Kabul Gorge with its towering, sheer peaks and freezing rivers, suggests that the Mountain Division would have to spend years picking its way through the rocks.

And all the while, a humanitarian catastrophe is growing closer. Can our soldiers fight their way across a country teeming with starving, emaciated people, distributing ration packs along with cheerful requests for information on the whereabouts of Mr bin Laden. How are we to concentrate on retribution for 11 September when armies of Afghan civilians are appealing for us to save their lives?

Even if we find Mr bin Laden and his men, are we then just going to allow Afghanistan to rot back into the muck, its people dying of hunger and landmines? It's only a matter of time before the clerks of Pakistan accuse the West of responsibility for the humanitarian tragedy about to occur - and the worst thing is that they may be partly right.

I'm struck by what President Bush said last week; that this could last weeks, months, even a decade. I wonder how many Afghans will be left alive in 10 years' time to appreciate the respect we showed them by not bombing on Fridays.

15 October 2001

ARAB SUSPICION - THIS IS A WAR AGAINST ISLAM

In Baghdad we had the bunker where our missile fried more than 300 people to death. In Kosovo we had a refugee column torn to pieces by our bombs. Now in Afghanistan, a village called Karam is our latest massacre.

Of course it's time for that tame old word "regret". We regretted the Baghdad bunker. We were really very sorry for the refugee slaughter in Kosovo. Now we are regretting the bomb that went astray in

Kabul on Friday night; the missile that killed the four UN mine clearers last Monday; and whatever hit Karam.

It's always the same story. We start shooting with "smart" weapons after our journalists and generals have told us of their sophistication. Their press conferences produce monochrome snapshots of bloodless airbase runways with little holes sprinkled across the apron. "A successful night," they used to say, after bombing Serbia.

They said that again last week and no one - until of course we splatter civilians - suggests going to war involves killing innocent people. It does. That is why the military invented that repulsive and morally shameful phrase "collateral damage". And they are always ready to smear the reporters on the ground

At first, Nato claimed its aircraft had not butchered the refugee convoy in April 1999. Once we found the bomb parts, with US markings, they changed their tune.

The new tune went like this: "If we killed the innocent we regret it, but why don't the reporters 'break free' of their Serb minders and see what else is going on in Kosovo?' We might be asked the same again, now we are involved in what, historically, is for us in Britain the Fourth Afghan War. What are we journalists doing giving succour to Mr bin Laden and his thugs?

There is one big difference this time round. In 1991, we had a real Muslim coalition on our side. In 1999, we so bestialised the Serbs that the death of their innocent civilians could be laid at the hands of Slobodan Milosevic, and anyway - in theory at least - we were trying to save the Albanian Muslims.

No doubt some idiot general will tell us this time round that Karam is Mr bin Laden's fault - idiot, because this is not going to wash with the hundreds of thousands of Muslims who are outraged at our air strikes on Afghanistan.

And here's the rub. In every Middle Eastern country, even tolerant Lebanon, suspicion is growing that this is a war against Islam.

That is why the Arab leaders are mostly silent and why the Saudis don't want to help us. That is why crowds tried yesterday to storm a Pakistani airbase used by the American forces.

It reveals a dislocation of thought among Arabs about the crimes against humanity in New York and Washington, a disturbing disconnection that allows them to condemn the atrocities in America without reference to America's response - and condemn the response without reflecting on the carnage on the other side of the Atlantic.

The Muslim world now sees innocent Muslims who have died in Western air strikes on Afghanistan. If Karam turns out to be as terrible as the Taliban claims, all of Mr Blair's lectures and denials that this is a religious war will be in vain.

The Prime Minister can now only reflect upon the irony that an obscurantist sect that smashes television sets and hangs videotapes from trees is now using television and videotape for its own propaganda.

17 October 2001

PROMISES, PROMISES

Colin Powell tells Pakistan's General Musharraf that he will help solve the problem of Kashmir. Tony Blair offers Yasser Arafat the vision of a Palestinian state. But should we take them at their word? History shows that assurances made in wartime aren't always everything they seem.

Tea on the lawn. Perhaps only in the old British Empire do they make black tea and milk in the same scalding pot, poured with lashings of sugar into fragile cups. The bougainvillea blasted crimson and purple down the brick wall beside me while big, aggressive black birds pursued each other over the cut grass of my tiny Peshawar hotel. At the end of my little road lies the tiny British cemetery wherein gravestones mark the assassination of the 19th century Raj's good men from Surrey and Yorkshire, murdered by what were called ghazis, the Afghan fundamentalists of their age who were often accompanied into battle - and I quote Captain Mannering of the Second Afghan war - "by religious men called talibs".

In those days, we made promises. We promised Afghan governments our support if they kept out the Russians. We promised our Indian Empire wealth, communications and education in return for its loyalty. Little has changed. Yesterday - all day long into the sweaty evening - fighter-bombers pulsed through the yellow sky above my little lawn, grey supersonic streaks that rose like hawks from Peshawar's mighty runway and headed west towards the mountains of Afghanistan. Their jet engines must have vibrated among the English bones in the cemetery at the end of the road, as Hardy's Channel firing once disturbed Parson Thirdly's last mortal remains. And, on the great black television in my bedroom, the broken, veined screen proved that Imperial history does indeed repeat itself.

General Colin Powell stood on the right hand of General Pervez Musharraf after promising a serious look at the problems of Kashmir and Pashtu representation in a future Afghan government. The US Secretary of State and the general whom we must now call the President of Pakistan spent much of their time chatting above the overnight artillery bombardment by that other old Empire relic, the Indian army. General Musharraf wanted a "short" campaign against Afghanistan, General Powell a promise of continued Pakistani support in the US's "war against terror". Musharraf wanted a solution to the problem of Kashmir. Powell, promising that the United States was now a close friend of Pakistan, headed off to India to oblige.

Vain promises have ever been a part of our conflict. In the 1914-18 war - another struggle against "evil", we should remember - it was the British who made the promises. To the Jews of the world, especially to Russian Jews, we promised our support for a Jewish homeland in Palestine. To the Arabs, Lawrence of Arabia promised independence. There's a wonderful moment in the film of the same name when Peter O'Toole, clad in an Arab gown and looking not unlike Osama bin Laden, asks General Allenby (Jack Hawkins) if he can promise Sherif Husseyn independence in return for Arab support in destroying the Turkish army. For just a brief, devastating moment, Hawkins hesitates; then his face becomes all smiling benevolence: "Of course!" he says. Did I not see that very same smile on Tony Blair's face as he clutched Arafat's hand in both of his before leading him through the door of 10 Downing Street this week?

In the end, we imposed an Anglo-French military occupation on the Arabs who had helped us and, three decades later gave the Jews only half of Palestine. "Promises", as the Palestinian academic Walid Khalidi once pointed out, "are meant to be kept." But not the kind you make in wartime.

By the Second World War, we were promising the Lebanese independence from the French if they turned against their Vichy masters. Then the French broke their promise and tried to stay on until driven out in ignominy in 1946. Two years earlier, President Roosevelt - anxious to secure Saudi oil rights from the British as the war came to an end - promised the Saudi monarchy that he would not allow the Palestinians to be dispossessed.

By 1990, after the invasion of Kuwait, we wanted the Arab and Muslim world on our side against Iraq. President Bush Senior promised a "New World Order" in which a nuclear-free - indeed arms-free - Middle East would live in an oasis of peace. Once the Iraqis were driven out, however, we called a short-lived "Middle-East" summit in Madrid and then sold more missiles, tanks and jet fighters to the Arabs and Israelis than in the preceding 30 years. Israel's nuclear power was never mentioned.

And here we go again. Scarcely three days before Mr Powell acquired his sudden interest in the problems of Kashmir, Yasser Arafat, the discredited old man of Gaza - "our bin Laden", as ex-General Ariel Sharon indecently called him - was invited to Downing Street where Tony Blair, hitherto a cautious supporter of Palestinian independence, declared the need for a "viable Palestinian state", including Jerusalem - "viable" being a gloss for a less chopped-up version of the Bantustan originally proposed for Mr Arafat. Mr Blair, of course, had no need to fear American wrath since President Bush Jnr had already discovered that even before 11 September - or so he told us - he had a "vision" of a Palestinian state that accepted the existence of Israel. Mr Arafat - speaking English at length for the first time in years - instantly supported the air bombardment of Afghanistan. Poor old Afghans. They were not on hand to remind the world that the same Mr Arafat had once enthusiastically supported the Soviet invasion of Afghanistan.

Why do we always play politics on the hoof, making quick-fix promises to vulnerable allies of convenience after years of accepting, even creating, the injustices of the Middle East and South-west Asia? How soon before we decide - and not before time - to lift sanctions against Iraq, and allow tens of thousands of Iraqi children to live instead of die? Or promise (in return for the overthrow of Sadam) to withdraw our forces from the Arabian peninsula? After all - say this not too loudly - if we promised and fulfilled all that, every one of Osama bin Laden's demands will have been met.

It's intriguing to read the full text of what bin Laden demanded in his post-World Trade Centre attack video tape. He said in Arabic, in a section largely excised in English translations, that "our (Muslim) nation has undergone more than 80 years of this humiliation..." and referred to "when the sword reached America after 80 years". Bin

Laden may be cruel, wicked, ruthless or evil personified, but he is very intelligent. I think he was referring specifically to the 1920 Treaty of Sevres, written by the victorious allied powers, which broke the Ottoman Empire and did away - after 600 years of sultanates and caliphates - with the last dream of Arab unity. As the American Professor James Robbins has shrewdly spotted, bin Laden's lieutenant, Ayman Zawahri - shouting into the video recorder from his Afghan cave 11 days ago - stated that the al-Quaida movement "will not tolerate a recurrence of the Andalusia tragedy in Palestine". Andalusia? Yes, the debacle of Andalusia marked the end of Muslim rule in Spain in 1492.

We may sprinkle quick-fix promises around. The people of the Middle East have longer memories. Back in the mid-1990s, I used to visit the bookshops of Algiers. Out in the triangle of death around Bentalha, hundreds of innocents were having their throats slit by an Islamist group - possibly also by government forces - many of whose members had fought in Afghanistan against the Russians. In the shops I would look for books on Islam. Muslim culture, Islamic history, Koranic thought. They were all there. And on the very next shelves - the same applied, I found, in Cairo bookshops - would invariably be text books on nuclear science, chemical engineering, aeronautics and biological research.

The aeronautical texts have, of course, a fearful new resonance today. So have the books on biological research. But the reason for their concurrence, I suspected, lay in the history of Arab humiliation. The Arabs were among the first scientists at the start of the second millennium, while the Crusaders - another of bin Laden's fixations - were riding in technological ignorance into the Muslim world. So while in the past few decades, our popular conception of the Arabs vaguely embraced an oil-rich, venal and largely backward people, awaiting our annual handouts and their virgins in heaven, many of them were asking pertinent questions about their past and future, about religion and science, about - so I suspect - how God and technology might be part of the same universe.

No such long-term thought or historical questions for us. We just went on supporting our Muslim dictators around the world - especially in the Middle East - in return for their friendship and our vain promises to rectify historical injustice.

We allowed our dictators to snuff out their socialist and communist parties; we left their population little place to exercise their political opposition except through religion. We went in for bestialisation - Messrs Khomeini, Abu Nidal, Gaddafi, Arafat, Saddam and bin Laden - rather than historical questioning. And we made more promises. Presidents Carter and Reagan, I recall, made promises to the Afghan mujahedin. Fight the Russians and we will help you. There would then be assistance in Afghanistan's economic recovery. A rebuilding of the country, even (this from the innocent Mr Carter) "democracy" - not a concept to be sure that we would now be promising to the Pakistanis, Palestinians, Uzbeks or Saudis. Of course, once the Russians were gone in 1989, there was no economic assistance. But last year, there was President Clinton, loud once more in America's promises of economic help for Pakistan, asking for a rejection of bin Laden; yet his only sense of perspective was to tell the Pakistani people that their history was - wait for it - "as long as the river Indus".

The problem, I fear, is that without any sense of history, we do not understand injustice. We only compound that injustice, after years of indolence, when we want to bribe our would-be allies with promises of immense historical importance - a resolution to Palestine, Kashmir, an arms-free Middle East, Arab independence, an economic Nirvana - because we are at war - tell them what they want to hear, promise them what they want - anything, so long as we can get our armadas into the air in our latest "war against evil".

So there was General Powell yesterday promising to deal with Kashmir while General Musharraf pleaded for a short war and while the jets went sweeping off towards Afghanistan from the Peshawar airbase.

18 October 2001

WATCHING THE WAR FROM KABUL'S ROOFTOPS

Mohamed saw the "Arabs" of Kabul leaving at dawn the day after the suicide attacks in New York and Washington, with their families and their guns.

"They were taking their possessions out of their homes with their wives and children and they were in a hurry," the 63-year-old driver says. "I had just heard about the attacks on Iranian radio and I was

driving around Kabul very early on 12 September and they were everywhere leaving: Taliban and their families, Arabs and their people.

"The Arabs had Kalashnikov rifles and rocket-propelled grenades. One of their trucks had a tarpaulin over the top so no one could
see what was inside."

Shirahmed - whose surname, like Mohamed's, has been withheld
so he cannot be identified - was in Kabul to sell the 10-roomed family
home he built 19 years ago with his own hands. He saw the exodus of
the "Arabs" and went to call a friend from the central telephone office.
"There was an Arab there trying to get through on the phone to Sudan
and four other Arabs in a car outside," he says. "They were shouting
and angry. The man couldn't get through to Khartoum. They left at
speed in their car. All the big Taliban families went the same day."

Mohamed noticed that the Arab fighters were wearing Taliban
clothes, complete with black turbans, but their children wore white
caps with a rectangle cut into the front. "That is the way the children
dress in Kandahar," he says.

The Arabs fleeing their suburban apartments in Shahrenov,
Kalfatullah, Parwaneseh and Merken knew what was coming. Everyone in Kabul knew. "I listened to the Persian service of the BBC and
Voice of America and to Iranian radio and the moment I heard about
New York and that it might involve Osama (bin Laden), I thought there
would be a war in Afghanistan," says Shirahmed, who is in his sixties.
"That morning, everyone rushed to the shops to buy food and live-
stock and prices went very high. Later, when the American attacks
started, they went very low. No one thought about Osama. They had
their own problems."

Listening to the two men - Shirahmed now a permanent refugee
in Pakistan, Mohamed waiting for Pakistani permission to return
home to Kabul - it is clear that a kind of frightening normality settled
over the Afghan capital in the month after the attacks in America.

Pro-Taliban Pakistani fighters were seen all over Kabul. Mohamed remembers that the Taliban carried out one of their bloody
punishments on 22 September: the amputation of the left hand of
three men for theft and rape.

"It was the last of the punishments," he says. "Once the American
attack started on 7 October, the Taliban wanted to be very friendly
with us. They would say: 'OK, we are all brother Muslims, we have to
be united. We will rebuild the country. Allah will help us.' But people

didn't believe them - they knew the Taliban very well. They knew the Taliban's links with Pakistan were cut. They were all alone now."

Neither Shirahmed nor Mohamed are Pashtuns, so you would not expect them to like the largely Pashtun Taliban. Even so, their memories of the American bombardment seem extraordinarily clear and precise. Both remember how, for the first three days, US aircraft would start their attacks at 9pm. Shirahmed watched the flash of explosions of the first raid from the roof of his brother's home in Khaikhana.

"The first we heard was the roar of an aircraft and anti-aircraft fire from the Taliban side about two miles from the airport," he says. "Everyone was frightened, but they were also happy because they thought this would change the Taliban government.

"But I think the Americans have made their biggest mistake: if they want to get the Taliban or Osama, that's fine. But they don't have to kill innocent people. The Pashtuns were very angry, although many had left Kabul before the attacks."

The American aircraft would bomb their targets every 10 minutes for three hours, one after another, "one aircraft at a time in the sky", according to Mohamed. Shirahmed noticed how, after four days, the Americans appeared to open a "second stage" - attacking at 9pm, breaking off after a few hours, then resuming at 3am.

"So many people went to the roof of their homes to see the bombing, it was like a cinema show," he says. "On the third night, the Americans bombed the medium wave transmitter tower at Yekatut and Radio Shariat (the Taliban station) went off the air. Nobody listened to it anyway."

But Mohamed did. "The Taliban radio told us to stay in our homes and not to leave Kabul. They said 'everything is normal and Taliban morale is very high and we are preparing to resist the Americans.' (They) started to act very kindly towards us. Most of the checkpoints disappeared. The prices came down. Ninety-eight kilograms of flour before the attacks cost 1,600,000 Afghanis; afterwards, it went down to 750,000.

"People were happy to think the Taliban might collapse because most of them had no jobs. When the Americans bombed, officials were told not to go to work, which meant they were not paid - and that made the Taliban even more unpopular."

Four days into the bombings, Shirahmed heard the television transmitter tower at Kohe Asmai was under attack. "I heard that women and children were killed near the airport but saw no bodies or ambulances."

Mohamed, living in the centre of Kabul, left his wife and family late last week on routine work for the charity in Peshawar for which he works. At the border at Torkham, the Taliban - suddenly friendly towards non- Pashtuns - pleaded successfully with the frontier guards to let Mohamed cross. He is now trapped in Pakistan: he has not been able to return across the border.

Shirahmed, having sold his family home left in near misery over the mountains south of Torkham. "I built that house myself and four of my five children were born there," he says. "It had a basement and two storeys and a little garden and we were happy, and now we are sad. Now seven members of my family live in one room in Peshawar and we pay $40 a month in rent."

As for Mohamed, he is thinking of the winter. "If the American attacks continue, the people will be in a terrible situation," he says. "The roads will be closed, the snow is coming, there will be no food, no warmth. It will be a catastrophe for us."

20 October 2001

THIS IS NOT CNN COUNTRY

Ghaziabad lay under a grey, smouldering sky. Its brick-stacks pumping black smog over the equally angry Mosque. "Now Afghanistan is like a bloody river," a voice shouted over three tin loudspeakers fitted to a tiny minaret. In Ghaziabad, they make bricks, not money. A wide, pale green river of sewage floated gently between the road and the mosque. "Blood ... blood ... why?" the voice appealed.

I stopped the car and walked over the bridge and approached the Afghan imam - white-turbaned, with intelligent eyes, a well-combed black beard, and a deep black scar above his left eye. But an old man shouted at him: "Why do you let the kaffir (unbeliever) into our mosque?" he shouted at the imam. Fisk the Kaffir. I hadn't come across him before.

This was definitely not CNN country. Indeed, there are times when I would like all those Westerners who preach to Muslims about their respect for Islam - all those Bushes and Blairs and Powells and

Straws with their sermons about Osama bin Laden's perversion of religion - to cross the dirty concrete bridge above the sewer to brown-
brick mosques like the one at Ghaziabad. The names of all the Pakistani villages around here have a meaning. Bad, of course, means
town. Ghazi is a warrior, one who is honoured to kill unbelievers. So
this was the town of the infidel killer. And after a few minutes listening
to the imam, you can see why.

Maulawi Tajmohmed had been about to lead me into the mosque.
When the old man complained, he waited patiently on the steps.
"Bring some chairs," he said, bowing to the old man who hated kaffirs.
But no one brought any chairs. So the Maulawi and I stood together,
surrounded by an ever-growing number of Afghan youths and elderly
men, their eyes avoiding the cleric but searching the face of the "unbeliever".

What, I asked Maulawi Tajmohmed, had he been praying for today. There was a muttering and a perceptible movement of anger, that
ever-so-slight closing in of the crowd. A young man on the Maulawi's
left drew in his breath.

But I got my sermon. Looking at his congregation, only occasionally at me, the Maulawi answered my question: "I will tell you what
we pray. We pray to God like this - O God, in all your great majesty,
hear our prayer. Please show to our human world the correct way. If
some do not walk this road, they are not from Islam. We believe they
will go to hell. O God, if these people cannot hear you and will not obey
your word, please keep true Muslims safe. And kill those people, as
Moussa (Moses) killed the Pharoah, Rhamses."

The crowd were silent now, though they had been joined by a
score of children, boys in grubby brown robes and small girls with sil-
ver braid in their hair. I rather guessed what was coming next.
Maulawi Tajmohmed was in his stride. The chairs had been forgotten.
Indeed, I rather thought - and hoped - that I had been forgotten.

"And what more do we pray?" the Maulawi asked. "We pray - O
God, you are all powerful and you can destroy all American equipment
(sic) which the Americans use in our country against Muslims. O God,
please help the Afghans and give them victory over the people who
are non-believers."

Across the drainage ditch, a bus groaned past, its cloth curtains
sewn with black eyes to ward off evil. Two horses clopped down the

stony road, hauling trailers of logs and undergrowth, the leaves brushing the highway, the drivers hunched over the reins. Yes, winter will be here soon; winter up in those high mountains that you could see, far away in Afghanistan, over the fields of rubble and shacks.

Maulawi Tajmohmed's eyes moved around the crowd, at the old man, at the youth by his side. "O God," he said, his voice rising, "You know our situation better than all others. We trust your promises. When you tell us in the Koran that Muslims will be victorious over the unbelievers. Mullah Mohammed Omar, the Emir of the Faithful, and Osama are the great mujahedin of Allah and we believe they will be victorious." The Maulawi turned to me: "That is what we said in our prayers today."

The youth by his side piped up: "Why did I want to know what they prayed? Who was I to ask such things? What had it got to do with me?" Good questions. But the Maulawi interrupted. "The people of this town tell me that if American soldiers come to our land, our blood will race and boil and we are ready to fight them." He paused, his hand motioning towards me. "I pray that God shows you how to write the truth."

So let us tell a few truths. All through the Afghan refugee villages outside Peshawar they were saying this yesterday. All along the drainage ditches, past the brick stacks and across the old railway line outside the Peshawar ring road, they were talking about the Americans in the mosques. They were not bad people. They meant what they said. They felt it. The Maulawi shook hands with me when we said goodbye. Even the old man who hated kaffirs shook hands. "God says in the Koran," Maulawi Tajmohmed added, "that He gives to all people a heart, eyes, hair, hands - so why do they not understand him? Those who do not will perish in hell."

I wonder what Messrs Bush and Blair will say about that. They would prefer, no doubt, the even smaller, even poorer village of Bahader - "bahader" means "brave heart" - three miles from Ghaziabad, where the Afghans live alongside Pakistanis and remember that this was the birth place of the great Pashtu Sufi poet Rahman Baaba. The villagers say that he died 400 years ago, but most claim they could quote his verse by heart.

A smiling, middle-aged man urged me to sit on a cane sofa by a little sewer. "Rahman," he said, "wrote this: 'Can you see the first step on the journey to paradise? - Yes, of course I can see this, when the

Sufi walks to paradise.' I'll tell you another: 'If you don't love to see Rahman, why do you sew those big eyes on to cloth?'"

Yes, this was definitely CNN country. Bush and Blair would feel more comfortable in this mystical town whose imam kept strictly to the Koran text for his Friday sermon. Just don't mention the name of Osama bin Laden. Because when I did, the faces of the villagers lit up as if they had heard the name of the Messiah.

22 October 2001

OBSESSED WITH BIN LADEN

After Osama, "Godfather of Terror" - our very own cliché - comes Osama, "Saviour of the Muslim World", Osama, the "New Saladin", Osama "V Mahdi". Amid the blue moped fumes of the Peshawar bazaar, his face beams out of a hundred bookshops, turbaned, wise, half-smiling, disembodied.

On the front cover of Khaled Choudhury's Osama bin Laden: Freedom Fighter or Terrorist? - readers may guess which conclusion the author draws - Mr bin Laden gazes down at us from the sky above the snows of the Afghan mountains. Printed by Shaheed Publishers (shaheed means martyr) Choudhury's slim, hard-cover volume is dedicated "to all Islamic Fighters".

But let's be fair. Only a month ago, the photo-editors of Time magazine asked to buy for a possible front cover one of my snapshots of Mr bin Laden - which I took in one of his desert camps in Afghanistan in 1996 - and then announced that they intended to "age" the photo digitally to make the world's bete noir look older. I told Time to go jump in the lake. No photo. But few lakes are deep enough for the white T-shirt currently hanging in the bazaars here. "Jihad is our mission," says one, beneath Mr bin Laden's face, followed by the quotation, "As a Muslim, it is my aim to spread Islam throughout the world by love or power". Another exhorts the wearer to remember that Osama "is a Muslim brother - Osama is one of us".

Western journalists will no doubt be sending this little keepsake to their editors; in the days of the Iranian revolution, most of us bought watches illustrated with Ayatollah Khomeini's face in which the minute hand was composed of a splodge of martyr's blood. But we should not mock the purpose, or possible result, of this hero worship in the souks of Pakistan. Reading Choudhury's work, you can see why men and women here regard Mr bin Laden as a just and good man, persecuted by the United States not because he blows up buildings but because he defies the greatest power on Earth. The Americans may have the most sophisticated military equipment, the author says, but Mr bin Laden proves they don't have faith in God.

Tareq Ismael Sagar's Osama bin Laden: One Man, One Movement, begins in fairy-tale style. "On a cold evening in December, 1997," Sagar writes, "a handsome young Arab sits in his room, thinking about what he can do for the world ... his father advised him to go to Afghanistan." Forget that Mr bin Laden was already in Afghanistan by 1997 and that it was a senior member of the Saudi intelligence service who originally asked him to go there - not Mr bin Laden senior. Sagar's hero worship knows no bounds. He wishes "love to Osama" and praises his military and economic assistance to Bosnia, Chechnya, Sudan ...

But who can blame Muslims for being obsessed with Mr bin Laden when the West has been equally obsessed with him for years? Choudhury proudly tells us that his book has entered its second edition "by public demand", and I can believe it. Sagar's work informs readers that its English distributors are Green Dome International Limited, operating from 148-164 Gregory Boulevard, Nottingham, NG7 5JC. "Every Muslim," Sagar says, "must get to know their new leader, especially young people ... Saddam Hussein never had our support, but Osama does."

If Choudhury lays on the jam - Mr bin Laden is "majestic" and "legendary" - he deals in a now-familiar style with the World Trade Centre attacks. Assaults on America had hitherto only happened outside the United States: in Dar es Salaam, Nairobi, Aden and Al-Khobar (in Saudi Arabia). So the World Trade Centre destruction, of which there is a powerful graphic in the volume, was obviously the work of the CIA and Mossad. And there follow the now familiar questions about the supposedly "missing" 4,000 Israelis who did not go to work in the buildings on 11 September. There is no reference to the Jewish Americans slaughtered.

Sagar includes an intriguing account of one of Mr bin Laden's "hiding places", a system of caves in Logar province, which the author says he visited. "I saw three places there ... three rooms; one was a library, the second contained sophisticated communications technology. But the third contained just a single Kalashnikov rifle, which bin

Laden had taken from a Russian officer whom he had killed in the war against the Soviets."

Some of the texts are a little confusing. One goes to great lengths to deny the (hitherto unheard) argument that Mr bin Laden killed a close Palestinian friend, Abdullah Azzam - blown up by a car bomb in Peshawar - while others carry quotations Mr bin Laden has allegedly given in interviews with Arab journalists. The destruction of America, he reportedly says, "is in my hands". After the Clinton flurry of cruise missiles at his camps after the bombings of American embassies in Africa, Mr bin Laden is quoted as promising that "my war has not started yet - I believe in action, not words", which might have come straight from a speech by George Bush or, indeed, by Ariel Sharon.

There is an element of fantasy. Choudhury insists that Mr bin Laden thinks in "threes". Thus we are told the most important elements in his life are trust in God, fighting for God and fighting for a Muslim's rights. Thus his three favourite places are the mosques of Mecca, Medina and Jerusalem. His three most hated countries - in decreasing order of importance, of course - are the United States, Israel and Russia.

But all is not lost. The American journalist John Cooley's Unholy Wars has pride of place in several bookshops.

And lunatics who demand the withdrawal of any book that dares to praise Mr bin Laden can rest assured that another personality is well represented among the book stacks of Peshawar. I don't know why, but Pakistanis seem obsessed with a man some regard as responsible for more deaths than Mr bin Laden. A certain Henry Kissinger.

23 October 2001

REFUGEES CROWD THE BORDERS

Mullah Mohammed Omar's 10-year-old son is dead. He was, according to Afghan refugees fleeing Kandahar, taken to one of the city's broken hospitals by his father, the Taliban leader and "Emir of the Faithful", but the boy - apparently travelling in Omar's car when it was attacked by US aircraft - died of his wounds.

No regrets, of course. Back in 1985, when American aircraft bombed Libya, they also destroyed the life of Colonel Muammar Gaddafi's six-year-old adopted daughter. No regrets, of course. In 1992, when an Israeli pilot flying an American-made Apache helicopter fired an American-made missile into the car of Said Abbas Moussawi, head of the Hizbollah guerrilla army in Lebanon, the Israeli pilot also killed Moussawi's 10-year-old. No regrets, of course.

Whether these children deserved their deaths, be sure that their fathers - in our eyes - were to blame. Live by the sword, die by the sword - and that goes for the kids too. Back in 1991, The Independent revealed that American Gulf War military targets included "secure" bunkers in which members of Saddam Hussein's family - or the families of his henchmen - were believed to be hiding. That's how the Americans managed to slaughter well over 300 people in an air raid shelter at Amariya in Baghdad. No Saddam kids, just civilians. Too bad. I wonder - now that President George Bush has given permission to the CIA to murder Osama bin Laden - if the same policy applies today?

And so the casualties begin to mount. From Kandahar come ever more frightful stories of civilians buried under ruins, of children torn to pieces by American bombs. The Taliban - and here the Americans must breathe a collective sigh of relief - refuse to allow Western journalists to enter the country to verify these reports. So when a few television crews were able to find 18 fresh graves in the devastated village of Khorum outside Jalalabad just over a week ago, the US Defence Secretary Donald Rumsfeld could ridicule the deaths as "ridiculous". But not, I suspect, for much longer.

For if each of our wars for infinite justice and eternal freedom have a familiar trade mark - the military claptrap about air superiority, suppression of "command and control centres", radar capabilities - each has an awkward, highly exclusive little twist to it. In 1999, Nato claimed it was waging war to put Kosovo Albanian refugees back in their homes - even though most of the refugees were still in their homes when the war began. Our bombing of Serbia led directly to their dispossession. We bear a heavy burden of responsibility for their suffering - since the Serbs had told us what they would do if Nato opened hostilities - although the ultimate blame for their "ethnic cleansing" clearly belonged to Slobodan Milosevic.

But Nato's escape clause won't work this time round. For as the Afghan refugees turn up in their thousands at the border, it is palpably evident that they are fleeing not the Taliban but our bombs and missiles. The Taliban is not ethnically cleansing its own Pashtun population. The refugees speak vividly of their fear and terror as our bombs fall on their cities. These people are terrified of our "war on terror", victims as innocent as those who were slaughtered in the World Trade Centre on 11 September. So where do we stop?

It's an important question because, once the winter storms breeze down the mountain gorges of Afghanistan, a tragedy is likely to commence, one which no spin doctor or propaganda expert will be able to divert. We'll say that the thousands about to die or who are dying of starvation and cold are victims of the Taliban's intransigence or the Taliban's support for "terrorism" or the Taliban's propensity to steal humanitarian supplies.

I have to admit - having been weaned on Israel's promiscuous use of the word "terror" every time a Palestinian throws a stone at his occupiers - that I find the very word "terrorism" increasingly mendacious as well as racist. Of course - despite the slavish use of the phrase "war on terrorism" on the BBC and CNN - it is nothing of the kind. We are not planning to attack Tamil Tiger suicide bombers or Eta killers or Real IRA murderers or Kurdish KDP guerrillas. Indeed, the US has spent a lot of time supporting terrorists in Latin America - the Contras spring to mind - not to mention the rabble we are now bombing in Afghanistan. This is, as I've said before, a war on America's enemies. Increasingly, as the date of 11 September acquires iconic status, we are retaliating for the crimes against humanity in New York and Washington. But we're not setting up any tribunals to try those responsible.

The figure of 6,000 remains as awesome as it did in the days that followed. But what happens when the deaths for which we are responsible begin to approach the same figure? Refugees have been telling me on the Pakistan border that the death toll from our bombings in Afghanistan is in the dozens, perhaps the hundreds. Once the UN agencies give us details of the starving and the destitute who are dying in their flight from our bombs, it won't take long to reach 6,000. Will that be enough? Will 12,000 dead Afghans appease us, albeit that they have nothing to do with the Taliban or Osama bin Laden? Or 24,000? If we think we know what our aims are in this fraudulent "war against terror", have we any idea of proportion?

Sure, we'll blame the Taliban for future tragedies. Just as we've been blaming them for drug exports from Afghanistan. Tony Blair was at the forefront of the Taliban-drug linkage. And all we have to do to believe this is to forget the UN Drug Control Programme's announcement last week that opium production in Afghanistan has fallen by 94 per cent, chiefly due to Mullah Omar's prohibition in Taliban-controlled areas. Most of Afghanistan's current opium production comes - you've guessed it - from our friends in the Northern Alliance.

This particular war is, as Mr Bush said, going to be "unlike any other" - but not in quite the way he thinks. It's not going to lead to justice. Or freedom. It's likely to culminate in deaths that will diminish in magnitude even the crime against humanity on 11 September. Do we have any plans for this? Can we turn the falsity of a "war against terror" into a war against famine and starvation and death, even at the cost of postponing our day of reckoning with Osama bin Laden?

27 October 2001

THE AFGHANS CAN TRUST ONLY THEMSELVES

The doctor thinks before he speaks, long moments for reflection and concern. His is not the usual story from Kabul and he is too well known to speak freely. He asks me three times not to publish his name. When I ask him what he'd like to be called, he says he hates falsity. So he will be the Doctor, a children's doctor as it happens, who tells his story wearing a little round white hat and a big, sad smile. He doesn't like the Taliban. But he doesn't like the Americans. He speaks with great precision. When I ask him what the Americans have destroyed at Kabul airport, he replies at once. "Three military aircraft and a Russian-made Tupolev TU-152 airliner of Ariana airlines." I trust him.

In a city without newspapers, Kabul whispers radios. "We follow all the stations because they begin at different times - the Voice of America in Pashtu at 7pm, then we turn to the Pashtu service of the BBC at 8pm," the doctor says. "The best programme is on the BBC Dari (Persian) service - it's Majalaya Osyayeh Miona (Central Asia Magazine) which knows what is happening in Afghanistan - and the worst is Iranian Radio which is very wrong. Before the American attack, it concentrated on anti-Taliban propaganda. But after the attack, it said nothing about the Taliban - it was just against the American attacks and there was a lot of anti-Pakistan propaganda."

And despite all the Taliban prohibitions, some Kabul families still watch television. "They watch it underground, in basements, with wires leading up to little dishes. And when they saw Powell and Musharraf together, holding hands and being friends, well the majority of people when they saw this - when they realised there was to be US-Pakistani co-operation - they felt it was a new aggression against them." The US Secretary of State Colin Powell and Pakistan's self-proclaimed president Pervez Musharraf met in Islamabad on 16 October.

It's not difficult to comprehend the suspicions in those Kabul basements as the radios and television sets mutter ever so softly. The Iranians hate the Taliban, but they hate the Americans even more. The Pakistanis helped to create the Taliban. Now the Americans are friends with the Pakistanis. The Doctor pauses while I work out the underground equations.

"You must understand something," he says suddenly. "Most people, neutral people who're not connected with political groups, they hate the American policy - and if the Taliban would change just 20 per cent of their policy against the people, then the people would stand shoulder-to-shoulder with them. We are waiting for an end to the Taliban policy against women and against education. You see, people will never forget what Pakistan has done to undermine Afghanistan - they see Pakistan as the eternal enemy."

The Doctor wonders if I see what he is trying to say. That Afghans can trust only themselves, I ask? He nods vigorously. "Among educated people, 11 September created a new situation. We knew that America helped to create the Taliban and Osama," - no one in Afghanistan bothers to add "bin Laden" - "and we call them the 'kids' of America and Pakistan. When the first night of attacks came, we didn't know what to expect. It was very sudden but the bombs were on target. There were no injured civilians. Later, the Americans started hitting civilians. Some were very badly wounded and were taken to the Jumhuriyet hospital in the centre of the city. But we were blocked by the Taliban from going to the hospital. We had no contact."

The Doctor complains bitterly that Afghan hospitals have neither medicine nor equipment - "better to have treatment at home," he says at one point - but he is more resentful of the subsequent bombing of Kabul. "On the second night, our neighbour's house was hit. People were buried when a wall collapsed on them but they were not killed. They came out smiling. When military targets were attacked, the Taliban blocked us from going there, just like they did the hospitals. Then the Taliban announced that people were not to come out of their houses. We had to remain close to home. Then they told us to stay inside our houses." When mountain homes were destroyed above Kabul, the Doctor asked if he could help the wounded. The Taliban blocked the roads again.

"At the beginning, 90 per cent of the bombing was on target, but then the Americans started using 1,000 lb bombs and areas were badly damaged. When they hit the television transmitter towers, our houses shook and the earth moved and we smelled a lot of smoke. Then Radio Shariat (Taliban Radio) went off the air but the next day I saw them re-assembling a new antenna. The Taliban always did this. Every time something was destroyed, they replaced it at once. They would go round and collect up all the wrecked equipment. The Taliban were very relaxed about this." Here the Doctor pauses again. "I'm trying to describe the Taliban reaction to the American bombing. You know? They weren't interested in the attacks. It was very intriguing - and strange - for me to see this.

"The Taliban told many people that they were going to have the victory. Every night, the Americans bombed around Kabul. But each night, the circle of bombing got closer and closer to the centre - it got narrower and narrower." The Doctor says that the four Afghan de-mining officials killed in the American attacks died because their offices had been rented from Radio Afghanistan - they were killed, he says, when the transmitters were destroyed.

"At night, we heard very heavy sounds, propellers, like low planes and we were told these were 'discovery' aircraft. What are 'discovery' aircraft?" I told the Doctor I thought these were pilotless reconnaissance aircraft to photograph the bomb sites, "drones" in military parlance, the only kind of plane the Taliban can shoot down - so far, at least.

The Doctor's tale is chronological. On the first Friday, the Americans resumed their attacks after Muslim evening prayers, hitting a petrol storage depot. "It was like an earthquake - the ground moved again." Then the Americans turned to a transport depot, old trucks and buses left behind by the Soviets in 1990 then the empty barracks of the so-called Babajan battalion. Babajan long ago left Kabul. He is now a fighter in the equally so-called Northern Alliance.

"The next target was a mile to the north of Kabul in a small valley where the 015 Battalion looks after food storage for the Taliban. The Americans bombed and destroyed all the stocks of food. They used six heavy bombs which exploded at short intervals and the nearest houses - their windows, doors and roofs were all blown off." The Doctor shakes his head repeatedly. He is not going back to Kabul until the war ends.

"Some people in Kabul, some of my friends, think that the Americans will invade. Other people believe - hope - that if (the former king) Zahir Shah comes, he can do something and this will be the end of the war. The more educated people think the Americans will stay a long time in Afghanistan. As for me, I see the Pakistanis and the Americans and the Taliban and Osama as all the same.

"If Osama acted like a terrorist, then so are the Americans, acting like terrorists now. So what if Zahir Shah comes, don't you think American advisors will be behind him? My own feeling is that the Americans are being very stupid. Watch - and you will see."

30 October 2001

KILLED BY A CRUISE MISSILE

The Americans have killed Saifullah of Turangzai, MA in Arabic and MA in Islamic Studies (Peshawar University), BSc (Islamia College), BEd Certificate of Teaching, MPhil student and scholarship winner to Al-Azhar in Cairo, the oldest university in the Arab world.

He spoke fluent English as well as Persian and his native Pashtu, and loved poetry and history and was, so his family say, preparing a little reluctantly to get married. His father, Hedayatullah, is a medical doctor, his younger brother a student of chartered accountancy.

Of course, no one outside Pakistan - and few inside - had ever heard of Saifullah. In these Pashtun villages of the Northwest Frontier, many families do not even have proper names. Saifullah was not a political leader; indeed his 50-year-old father says that his eldest son was a humanitarian, not a warrior. His brother Mahazullah says the same. "He was always a peaceful person, quiet and calm, he just wanted to protect people in Afghanistan whom he believed were the victims of terrorism." But everyone agrees how Saifullah died.

He was killed on 22 October when five US Cruise missiles detonated against the walls of a building in the Darulaman suburb of Kabul, where Saifullah and 35 other men were meeting. His family now call him the shahid, the martyr. Hedayatullah embraces each visitor to the family home of cement and mud walls, offers roast chicken

and mitha, sweets and pots of milk and tea, and insists he be "congrat-
ulated" on being the proud father of a man who died for his beliefs.
Hens cluck in the yard outside and an old, coloured poster, depicting
a Kalashnikov rifle with the word jihad (holy struggle) above it, is
pasted to the wall. But "peace" is the word the family utters most.

Saifullah had only gone to take money to Kabul to help the suffering Afghans, says Mahazullah, perhaps no more than 20,000 rupees -
a mere $3.50 - which he had raised among his student friends.

That's not the way the Americans tell it, of course. Blundering
through their target maps and killing innocent civilians by the day, the
Pentagon boasted that the Darulaman killings targeted the Taliban's
"foreign fighters", of whom a few were Pakistanis, Saifullah among
them.

In Pushtu, his Arabic name means "Sword of God". Mahazullah
dismisses the American claims. Only when I suggest that it might not
be strange for a young Muslim with Saifullah's views to have taken a
weapon to defend Afghanistan does Mahazullah say, briefly, that his
brother "may have been a fighter".

Saifullah's best friend, a smiling, beardless young man with
bright blue eyes, says he telephoned the doomed man on 16 October,
two days before he left for Afghanistan, six days before his death. "I
asked him if he was going to Afghanistan and he said he was - but just
to take money to the Afghans. He said: 'If God wills it, I will be back
after 10 days.' I told him it would be very dangerous. I pleaded with
him not to go, but he said he just wanted to take the money. He said to
me: 'I know my life will be in danger but I'm not going to fight. What
can I do? The Americans are out of range.' He said he just wanted to
give moral support."

Mahazullah never imagined his brother's death. "We never expected his martyrdom. I never thought he would die," he says. A phone
call prepared the family for the news, a friend with information that
some Pakistanis had been killed in Kabul. "It has left a terrible vacuum
in our family life," Mahazullah says.

"You cannot imagine what it is like without him. He was a person
who respected life, who was a reformer. There was no justification for
the war in Afghanistan. These people are poor. There is no evidence,
no proof. Every human being has the right to the basic necessities of
life.

"The family - all of us, including Saifullah - were appalled by the carnage in New York and Washington on 11 September. Saifullah was very regretful about this - we all watched it on television." At no point does the family mention the name of Osama bin Laden.

Turangzai is a village of resistance. During the Third Afghan War in 1919, the British hunted down Hadji Turangzai, one of the principal leaders of the revolt, and burnt the village bazaar in revenge for its insurgency. Disconcertingly, a young man enters Saifullah's family home, greets me with a large smile and announces that he is the grandson of the Hadji, scourge of the English. But this is no centre of Muslim extremism. Though the family pray five times a day, they intend their daughters to be educated at university.

Saifullah spent hours on his personal computer and apparently loved the poetry of the secular Pakistani national poet Allam Mohamed Iqbal of Surqhot - Sir Mohamed Iqbal after he had accepted a British knighthood - and, according to Mahazullah, was interested in the world's religions.

"He would talk a lot about the Northern Ireland problem and about Protestants and Catholics," he says. "He believed that Islam was the religion which most promotes peace in the world. He used to say that the Prophet, peace be upon him, tells us that we can't even attack a person who is engaged in war with us if he has his gun over his shoulder.

"You can only fight a person who is actually attacking you. He thought that every civilian should help the Afghans because they are being attacked. But we are not extremists or terrorists as all the media say we are."

Saifullah, at 26 the oldest of three brothers and two sisters, was unmarried. "Our father told him: 'We are going to marry you,' " Mahazullah says. "But my brother said no, he would only marry after he had finished his studies. His father was trying to see which girls might be suitable for him. It is our duty to follow our parents' wishes because they have an experience we don't have." But Saifullah left for Afghanistan. "Trust me," were the last words he said to his father.

Perhaps he was remembering one of Iqbal's most famous verses: "Of God's command, the inner meaning do you know? To live in constant danger is a life indeed."

NOVEMBER 2001: 'WE WILL DIE TO DEFEND OUR LAND'

Muslim fighter

8 November 2001

COALITION?

"Air Campaign"? "Coalition forces"? "War on terror"? How much longer must we go on enduring these lies? There is no "campaign" - merely an air bombardment of the poorest and most broken country in the world by the world's richest and most sophisticated nation. No MiGs have taken to the skies to do battle with the American B-52s or F-18s. The only ammunition soaring into the air over Kabul comes from Russian anti-aircraft guns manufactured around 1943.

Coalition? Hands up who's seen the Luftwaffe in the skies over Kandahar, or the Italian air force or the French air force over Herat. Or even the Pakistani air force. The Americans are bombing Afghanistan with a few British missiles thrown in. "Coalition" indeed.

Then there's the "war on terror". When are we moving on to bomb the Jaffna peninsula? Or Chechnya - which we have already left in Vladimir Putin's bloody hands? I even seem to recall a massive terrorist car bomb that exploded in Beirut in 1985 - targeting Sayed Hassan Nasrallah, the spiritual inspiration to the Hezbollah, who now appears to be back on Washington's hit list - and which missed Nasrallah but slaughtered 85 innocent Lebanese civilians. Years later, Carl Bernstein revealed in his book, Veil, that the CIA was behind the bomb after the Saudis agreed to fund the operation. So will the US President George Bush be hunting down the CIA murderers involved? The hell he will.

So why on earth are all my chums on CNN and Sky and the BBC rabbiting on about the "air campaign", "coalition forces" and the "war on terror"? Do they think their viewers believe this twaddle?

Certainly Muslims don't. In fact, you don't have to spend long in Pakistan to realise that the Pakistani press gives an infinitely more truthful and balanced account of the "war" - publishing work by local intellectuals, historians and opposition writers along with Taliban comments and pro-government statements as well as syndicated Western analyses - than The New York Times; and all this, remember, in a military dictatorship.

You only have to spend a few weeks in the Middle East and the subcontinent to realise why Tony Blair's interviews on al-Jazeera and Larry King Live don't amount to a hill of beans. The Beirut daily As-Safir ran a widely-praised editorial asking why an Arab who wanted to express the anger and humiliation of millions of other Arabs was forced to do so from a cave in a non-Arab country. The implication, of course, was that this - rather than the crimes against humanity on 11 September - was the reason for America's determination to liquidate Osama bin Laden. Far more persuasive has been a series of articles in the Pakistani press on the outrageous treatment of Muslims arrested in the United States in the aftermath of the September atrocities.

One such article should suffice. Headlined "Hate crime victim's diary", in The News of Lahore, it outlined the suffering of Hasnain Javed, who was arrested in Alabama on 19 September with an expired visa. In prison in Mississippi, he was beaten up by a prisoner who also broke his tooth. Then, long after he had sounded the warden's alarm bell, more men beat him against a wall with the words: "Hey bin Laden, this is the first round. There are going to be 10 rounds like this." There are dozens of other such stories in the Pakistani press and most of them appear to be true.

Again, Muslims have been outraged by the hypocrisy of the West's supposed "respect" for Islam. We are not, so we have informed the world, going to suspend military operations in Afghanistan during the holy fasting month of Ramadan. After all, the 1980-88 Iran-Iraq conflict continued during Ramadan. So have Arab-Israeli conflicts. True enough. But why, then, did we make such a show of suspending bombing on the first Friday of the bombardment last month out of our "respect" for Islam? Because we were more respectful then than now? Or because - the Taliban remaining unbroken - we've decided to forget about all that "respect"?

"I can see why you want to separate bin Laden from our religion," a Peshawar journalist said to me a few days ago. "Of course you want to tell us that this isn't a religious war, but Mr Robert, please, please stop telling us how much you respect Islam."

There is another disturbing argument I hear in Pakistan. If, as Mr Bush claims, the attacks on New York and Washington were an assault on "civilisation", why shouldn't Muslims regard an attack on Afghanistan as a war on Islam?

The Pakistanis swiftly spotted the hypocrisy of the Australians. While itching to get into the fight against Mr bin Laden, the Australians have sent armed troops to force destitute Afghan refugees out of their territorial waters. The Aussies want to bomb Afghanistan - but they don't want to save the Afghans. Pakistan, it should be added, hosts 2.5 million Afghan refugees. Needless to say, this discrepancy doesn't get much of an airing on our satellite channels. Indeed, I have never heard so much fury directed at journalists as I have in Pakistan these past few weeks. Nor am I surprised.

What, after all, are we supposed to make of the so-called "liberal" American television journalist Geraldo Rivera who is just moving to Fox TV, a Murdoch channel? "I'm feeling more patriotic than at any time in my life, itching for justice, or maybe just revenge," he announced this week. "And this catharsis I've gone through has caused me to reassess what I do for a living." This is truly chilling stuff. Here is an American journalist actually revealing that he's possibly "itching for revenge".

Infinitely more shameful - and unethical - were the disgraceful words of Walter Isaacson, the chairman of CNN, to his staff. Showing the misery of Afghanistan ran the risk of promoting enemy propaganda, he said. "It seems perverse to focus too much on the casualties or hardship in Afghanistan ... we must talk about how the Taliban are using civilian shields and how the Taliban have harboured the terror-ists responsible for killing close up to 5,000 innocent people."

Mr Isaacson was an unimaginative boss of Time magazine but these latest words will do more to damage the supposed impartiality of CNN than anything on the air in recent years. Perverse? Why per-verse? Why are Afghan casualties so far down Mr Isaacson's compassion? Or is Mr Isaacson just following the lead set down for him a few days earlier by the White House spokesman Ari Fleischer, who portentously announced to the Washington press corps that in times like these "people have to watch what they say and watch what they do".

Needless to say, CNN has caved in to the US government's de-mand not to broadcast Mr bin Laden's words in toto lest they contain "coded messages". But the coded messages go out on television every hour. They are "air campaign", "coalition forces" and "war on terror".

11 November 2001

BIN LADEN IS THE TARGET

So far, he hasn't put a foot wrong. If Osama bin Laden did plan the 11 September attack in America - and still we wait to see the "over-whelming" proof Tony Blair has talked about, not the seven paragraphs of inference attached to British evidence about the earlier US embassy and warship bombings - then things are unfolding pretty much as he wanted.

President Bush vows revenge and enrages the Islamic world by bombing Afghanistan, the poorest Muslim nation on earth. More than 1,000 Muslims are secretly arrested by US police officers, some of them brutally beaten in detention. The United States - unable to bomb the Taliban into submission - cosies up to the murderers and rapists of the Northern Alliance, ensuring that the largest ethnic group in Af-ghanistan - the Pashtuns - remain loyal to their obscurantist masters.

True, the Alliance's bloodiest commander, Rashid Dostum - who first visited Washington in 1996 - has just captured Mazar-i-Sharif. But this is far from Mr bin Laden's mountain fastness, and Dostum's victory will instill rage and fear among millions of non-Taliban Pash-tun Afghans.

Here for example is how Pakistani journalist Ahmed Rashid first met the man: "The first time I arrived at the fort to meet Dostum there were bloodstains and pieces of flesh in the muddy courtyard. The guards told me that an hour earlier Dostum had punished a soldier for stealing. The man had been tied to the tracks of a Russian-made tank which then drove around the courtyard crushing his body into mince-meat as Dostum watched." America's hero perhaps but not the sort of guy to raise popular support against Mr bin Laden.

Surely now the Americans will send in ground troops. For that - if Mr bin Laden is behind the American attack - is what he must all along have intended. First came the hopeless raid on Mullah Omar's office in Kandahar. Then the reported dispatch of US Special Forces to the ruthless thugs of the Northern Alliance. Surely the US 10th Mountain Division cannot be far behind.

If the Taliban had anyone to fear, it was the Alliance's Shah Massoud. But he was murdered by two Arab suicide bombers on 9 September. Then Abdul Haq - a US favourite who opposed the Taliban - was hanged while trying to arrange a regional coup in Pashtun areas of southern Afghanistan.

Messrs Bush and Blair may adopt Churchillian poses in Washington but Arab Gulf leaders are shivering in their golden palaces. For they know - as the others apparently do not - that Saudi Arabia is the principal target of Mr bin Laden's fury. We may overlook the fact that more than half the 11 September hijackers were Saudis - but the Saudi regime has not. How can it? The Saudi "masses" will not storm onto the streets of Riyadh and Jeddah to overthrow the kingdom's rulers. The danger comes from within the royal family, from the disaffected royal princes who regard Mr bin Laden as an inspiration rather than a state enemy, from the senior ulema (Muslim scholars) who hear in his words the authentic voice of conservative Wahhabi Sunni Islam rather than the effete and corrupt edicts of King Fahd.

Prince Turki al-Faisal, the former head of Saudi intelligence, was the man who helped to choose Mr bin Laden to lead the "Arab brigade" against the Soviets in 1979.

Hear now what the Good Prince had to say about him on the Arab MBC TV channel last week. He was, according to Turki al-Faisal, "a gentle, enthusiastic young man, not talkative and who did not raise his voice while talking. Bin Laden was generally a 'nice guy'". When the "Holy War" against the Soviets began, Prince Turki said, he would travel to Pakistan to keep in touch with events. "It was there that I met him. Once or twice he was invited to the Saudi embassy ... He was in the area supporting jihad."

Mr bin Laden's error - or so says Prince Turki - was to think, back in 1990, that he could lead an Arab army against the Iraqi occupiers of Kuwait. King Fahd of Saudi Arabia preferred American troops for this onerous task. It was then that Prince Turki "saw radical changes in his personality ... From a calm, peaceful gentleman interested in helping Muslims, into a person who believed that he would be able to amass and command an army to liberate Kuwait. It revealed his arrogance and haughtiness".

How Mr bin Laden must have smiled at this description. Any Arab nationalist would regard the desire to use his own people to free Kuwait - rather than an "infidel" army of Westerners - as heroic rather than arrogant. For Mr bin Laden, it is the Americans who are arrogant. And watching the contrails of the B-52s in the skies over Afghanistan last week and the pitiful groups of wounded Afghan civilians hobbling over the border into Pakistan, what Arab would disagree with him?

So far, then, Mr bin Laden is winning, and the Taliban - the "protectors of terrorism" - have turned into "tenacious warriors" according to the Pentagon's own rear admiral spokesman. And the "mastermind of world terror" is too busy making videos to be "smoked" out of the cave in which he is supposedly hiding.

As for the US 10th Mountain Division, what does Mr bin Laden have in store for them? A ripe old guerrilla war of the kind that drove the Soviet conscripts out of Afghanistan's moonscape? Or an explosion to put even the World Trade Centre apocalypse in the shade?

Only on Friday morning, Mr bin Laden was telling his Pakistani biographer, Hamid Mir, that if "America used chemical or nuclear weapons against us then we may retort with chemical or nuclear weapons. We have the weapons as deterrents". True or false, these are not the words of a man who thinks he is losing the war.

14 November 2001

WHAT WILL THE NORTHERN ALLIANCE DO IN OUR NAME?

It wasn't meant to be like this. The nice, friendly Northern Alliance, our very own foot-soldiers in Afghanistan, is in Kabul. It promised - didn't it? - not to enter the Afghan capital. It was supposed to capture, at most, Mazar-i-Sharif and perhaps Herat, to demonstrate the weakness of the Taliban, to show the West that its war aims - the destruction of the Taliban and thus of Osama bin Laden's al-Qa'ida movement - were inevitable.

The corpse of the old man in the centre of Kabul, executed by our heroes in the Alliance, was not supposed to be on television. Only two days ago, Alastair Campbell's 24-hour Washington-London-Islamabad "communication centre" was supposed to counter Taliban propaganda. Now Mr Campbell must set up his team of propagandists in Kabul to fight the lies of our very own foot-soldiers of the Northern Alliance.

Was it not the US Secretary of State Colin Powell who assured General Musharraf of Pakistan the Alliance would be kept under control, that the United Nations' envoy, Lakhdar Ibrahimi, would be allowed to construct a truly representative government in Kabul to replace the Taliban?

General Musharraf had promised his support to the United States - at the risk of his nation and his life - in return for American promises that Afghanistan would be governed by a truly representative coalition. Pakistan's air bases, it's very support for the "war on terrorism", was contingent on Washington's word that the Northern Alliance would not take over Kabul and impose its own diktat on Afghanistan.

Yesterday, the pictures from Kabul were almost identical to the videotapes of April 1992 when the pro-Russians and Communists were defeated. We saw the same jubilation by the non-Pushtu population. And within two days, Hekmatyar Gulbeddin began to bomb the city. The division of ethnic groups plunged the Afghan capital into civil war. Yesterday, the Alliance was supposed to wait on the outskirts of the city while the Americans attempted to construct a workable coalition. But for the present, Afghanistan - without the Taliban - is a country without a government.

What on earth is going on? And what, for that matter, has happened to Mr bin Laden? Are we driving him into the mountains - always supposing he is not already there - or are we pushing him into the tribal areas of the North-West Frontier Province of Pakistan? For without a city, the Taliban themselves will melt back into their birthplace, the madrassa schools along the Pakistan border which created the puritan, obscurantist spirit which has inspired the rulers of Afghanistan these past five years.

The Northern Alliance is advancing, meanwhile, with all its baggage of massacres and looting and rape intact. We have so idolised these gunmen, been so infatuated with them, supported them so unquestioningly, pictured them on television so deferentially that we are now immune to their history. So, perhaps, are they.

General Rashid Dostum, our hero now that he has recaptured Mazar-i-Sharif, is in the habit of punishing his soldiers by tying them to tank tracks and then driving the tanks around his barracks' square to turn them into mincemeat. You wouldn't have thought this, would you, when you heard the jubilant reports of General Dostum's victory on Monday night (12 November)?

Nor would you have thought, listening to the reports from Afghanistan yesterday, that the Northern Alliance was responsible for more than 80 per cent of the drug exports from the country in the aftermath of the Taliban's prohibition of drug cultivation. I have a ghostly memory of writing this story before, not about the Taliban but about the KLA in Kosovo, a guerrilla army which was partly funded by drugs and which, once its political aspirations had been met by Nato's occupation of the Serbian province went on to become "terrorists" (our former Foreign Secretary's memorable description) inside Macedonia. True, Nato's wheel of fortune moves in mysterious ways but it's not difficult to understand how our allies - praised rather than controlled - follow their own agenda.

Why, I wonder, do we always have this ambiguous, dangerous relationship with our allies? For decades, we accepted the received wisdom that the "B" specials were a vital security arm of the Northern Ireland authorities on the grounds that they "knew the territory" - just as, I fear, we rely upon the Northern Alliance because it "knows the land".

The Israelis relied upon their Phalangist militia thugs in Lebanon because the Christian Maronites hated the Palestinians. The Nazis approved of their Croatian Ustashi murderers in 1941 because the Ustashi hated the Serbs.

Is this, I ask myself, why the Northern Alliance is our friend? Not because it is a loyal ally but because it hates the Taliban? Not because it opposes poverty and destitution and the destruction of Afghanistan under an Islamic regime but because it says it loathes Osama bin Laden?

There are brave men in the Alliance, true. Its murdered leader, Ahmed Shah Massoud, was an honourable man. It's not difficult to turn our allies into heroes.

But it remains a fact that from 1992 to 1996, the Northern Alliance was a symbol of massacre, systematic rape and pillage. Which is why we - and I include the US State Department - welcomed the Taliban when they arrived in Kabul. The Northern Alliance left the city in 1996 with 50,000 dead behind it. Now its members are our foot soldiers. Better than Mr bin Laden, to be sure. But what - in God's name - are they going to do in our name?

15 November 2001

KANDAHAR BROODS IN THE RUBBLE

Kandahar last night looked much as it did when the Taliban turned Alexander the Great's timeworn city into their political capital seven years ago: ruined, mined and deserted, most of its inhabitants already in the refugee middens of Pakistan.

The Taliban paid around £1.04m in 1996 to take Kandahar without firing a shot (those were the days when you could buy cities as well as warlords with hard cash), and most of the money came from Saudi Arabia, along with taxes on roads and drugs.

The spiritual role in the Taliban life of the city declared the first capital of Afghanistan in 1747, in the reign of Ahmed Shah Durani, was consecrated on 4 April, 1996 when the Pushtu Kandaharis entered the marble-walled da Kherqa Sherif Ziarat, the Shrine of the Cloak of the Prophet, and brought forth the very robe worn by Mohamed. They took it to the rooftop from which the Taliban leader Mullah Mohamed Omar was speaking, and laid it across his shoulders. Wrapping it around him in the high wind, Omar waited as the crowd proclaimed him Amir al-Momineen, Leader of all Pious Muslims. In just such a way had the Caliph Omar proclaimed himself leader of all Muslims in Arabia after the Prophet's death. Mullah Omar had used this moment to declare a holy war against the regime of President Burhan-uddin Rabbani and his mujahedin government, the very forces which were last night at the gates of Kandahar.

It was ever a place of righteousness and courage. I visited the city in 1980, only days after the first Soviet troops had occupied Kandahar province. Afghan communists patrolled the city by night, Soviet soldiers by day. Yet they vanished each evening when the people of Kandahar emerged onto their rooftops to scream Allahu Akbar, God is great, to the skies. It was a cry of defiance. I spent more than two hours listening to this long declaration-lament which echoed across streets and parks and gardens in an unusual lyrical pattern, one section of the city taking up the call from another.

In the months and years that followed the Taliban takeover, Kandahar was beloved of the Taliban and loathed by the people of Kabul whose pulverised and sepulchral streets no longer merited the status of a decision-making city. To Kandahar came diplomats and statesmen and bootleggers, arms-dealers and drug-runners. Oil company chiefs from Argentina and, yes, from the United States turned up to pay court to Mullah Omar's odd, bearded government. Pakistani embassy staff from Kabul and senior generals in the Pakistani Interservices Intelligence arrived in Kandahar. So did executives of the American oil company Unocal. So did Russian diplomats and senior Saudi intelligence officers.

Under the Taliban's rule, the outward manifestations of crime and pillage finished, often at the end of a rope, while those most ferocious of Islamic punishments for which the Taliban were to become notorious were first practised in Kandahar. The city famous for its gardens and mosques thus became synonymous with the amputation of feet and hands, the urban wearing of the burqa and the prohibition of television and women's education.

That Mullah Omar, untutored and of peasant offspring, should have worn the cloak of the Prophet was an affront to many Afghans and his declaration to be Leader of all Pious Muslims was unprecedented. When King Dost Mohamed Khan adopted the title in 1834, he was fighting foreigners in what is today Pakistan. Mullah Omar declared war against his own Afghan people. Under his rule, Kandahar prospered. His modest offices and home lay alongside the palace of Osama bin Laden - all destroyed in US air and special forces raids over the past month - but the beauty of Kandahar had been torn out during the Soviet occupation when the mujahedin attacked Russian troops in the city.

The Afghan fighters mined the gardens and irrigation ditches and the Soviets used their Hind helicopters to blast away large sections of the old city along with its civilian inhabitants. Nor was Kandahar the haven of peace and legitimacy that the Taliban would later claim. Within a year of their takeover, there were gun battles in surrounding villages as Afghan Pashtuns objected to conscription. The Taliban later executed 18 army deserters in Kandahar jail. The city's Ulema, the religious leaders who surrounded Mullah Omar, one of whom taught him Islamic jurisprudence, became the effective theological power in a land whose internationally recognised capital was only once visited by the man who claimed to be the Prophet's successor.

Arms supplies were regularly flown from Saudi Arabia and Pakistan into Kandahar's newly-equipped airport whose telephone and wireless communications systems had been provided by Islamabad. This same airport was last night reported to be in the hands of the Northern Alliance.

But many Muslims will be more anxious to know if the Cloak of the Prophet remains safe inside its museum of marble and gilded archways. Even more of the city's Pashtun population will be living in fear of the revenge of the Northern Alliance. It would be pleasant to believe that the Alliance's gunmen were in the gardens around Kandahar last night, mulling over Tony Blair's calls for restraint. But, somehow, that does not seem likely.

19 November 2001

THE WAR HAS ONLY JUST BEGUN

When the Iranian army massed on the western border of Afghanistan in 1998 and prepared to storm across the frontier to avenge the Taliban slaughter of its diplomats - and its Afghan allies - in Mazar-i-Sharif, it received a message from the Taliban leadership in Kandahar.

"You will decide the date of your invasion," came the two-sentence communique from Mullah Omar's men. "We will decide the date of your departure." The Iranians wisely held their fire. It may have been a reply from the Taliban - but it was a very Afghan reply. The US and Britain - or the "coalition" as we are constrained to call them - are now getting similar treatment. The Northern Alliance watched the American bombers clear the road to Kabul. They were grateful. Then they drove into Kabul and now they are asking the British to leave. Poor old Jack Straw had trouble contacting the Afghan foreign minister to sort things out. The Afghan satellite phone was not switched on. You bet it wasn't.

The mystery is why we ever expected these people to obey us. Afghan rules don't work that way. Ethnic groups and tribes and villagers don't take orders from foreigners. They do deals. The West wanted to use the Northern Alliance as its foot-soldiers in Afghanistan. The Alliance wanted to use the American bombers to help it occupy the capital. For the Tajiks and Uzbeks and Hazaras, it was all very straightforward. They destroy the Taliban - and then take over Afghanistan, or as much as they can swallow. And if they indulge in a little revenge here and there - 500 or 600 Pakistani fighters massacred in a bloodbath at Mazar, a possible human rights atrocity in the making in Kunduz - what's so surprising?

Even now, faced with the bitter fruits of our coalition with the Northern Alliance, we are reacting with an odd replay of our Bosnian adventure: calling for restraint while at the same time reminding the world that the Afghans are a warlike, cruel people.

As the Alliance gunmen prepare to storm into Kandahar, Mr Blair calls for "restraint". Yet the western media are now set upon informing their readers and viewers that nothing more than a massacre could have been expected of our foot -soldiers. An Irish journalist came on the line to me last week with a familiar complaint. Wasn't I being a bit finicky, getting upset about a little slaughter in Mazar? Weren't the Afghans steeped in age-old traditions of warfare? Wasn't it a bit much to be asking the Afghans to behave in a civilised way?

I tried to remind my interviewer that Afghanistan's civilisation predated Ireland's - and indeed much of Europe's - and that the missiles, tanks, artillery pieces and rocket-propelled grenades with which the Afghans were destroying each other had been provided by the civilised outside powers. Hadn't I listened to this same nonsense about "age old traditions of warfare" peddled by the British foreign secretary Malcolm Rifkind when he was trying to wash his hands of Bosnia?

The real point, however, is that we cannot adopt someone's army as our own and then deny responsibility for its behaviour. We didn't allow the Germans to do that after the Second World War. And when our Northern Alliance boys go on a killing spree, we have to take responsibility for the bloodshed that results.

Take the case of Kunduz. More than 50 US planes have been bombarding the Taliban lines around the area in a deliberate attempt to break the morale of the defenders and allow the Northern Alliance gunmen to capture the district.

The Alliance has given the Taliban a deadline. It's pretty clear what will happen if the Taliban ignore that deadline. They are going to be killed in cold blood. I hope this is not true. I fear it is. But are we going to shrug our shoulders when the knives come out? Are we going to admit we helped the Alliance to gain the upper hand but then eschew all interest in the results? Isn't there even a faint, horrible parallel with Osama bin Laden? If he merely inspired murderers to commit the crimes against humanity of 11 September, surely he was guilty of the death of 5,000 people. But if we facilitate Alliance murderers, it seems we are innocent of the crime.

Meanwhile, outside Kabul, the familiar Northern Alliance anarchy is falling into place. The warlords of Jalalabad are feuding over who rules which part of Nangahar province. The Pashtu tribal leaders around Kandahar are threatening to fight the Northern Alliance. Hazara elements of the alliance are threatening their Tajik and Uzbek comrades if they do not receive a sufficient share of power in Kabul.

Amid all this, in clops the poor old UN donkey, dragged into the pit to undertake the most impossible task ever faced by statesmen in the history of the modern world: to sort out Afghanistan. Would the Alliance please be kind enough to allow the Pashtuns to have a proportionate share in the government? Could we have a few moderate Taliban - perhaps with shorter beards - in a broad-based administration? I can just see the Afghan delegates to these talks when they hear the phrase broad-based. Broad-based?

The only broad-based phenomenon the Afghans know about are ceasefires. And even then, only for Afghans. The most sinister element of the Kunduz ceasefire offer is that it only applies to Pashtuns - not to foreign (ie Arab) fighters - trapped in the area. They, presumably, are to be massacred or - in the chilling words of a BBC reporter with the Alliance yesterday - "given no quarter".

My own experience of armies that give no quarter is that they intend to commit war crimes - as has already happened in Mazar - and that this will only stiffen the resolve of those men who escape the bloodbath. For it is worth remembering the moral basis upon which we are prosecuting this war. This is, remember, a war "for civilisation". It is a war for "democracy". It is a war of "good against evil". It is a war in which "you are either for us or against us".

So when we see the pictures of the next massacre, let's ask ourselves whose side we are on. On the side of the victims or the murderers? And if the side of good happens to coincide with the side of the murderers, what does that make us? We're hearing a lot about the Allied success in the war. But the war has only just begun.

29 November 2001

WHAT WENT WRONG WITH OUR MORAL COMPASS AFTER 9/11?

We are becoming war criminals in Afghanistan. The US Air Force bombs Mazar-i-Sharif for the Northern Alliance, and our heroic Afghan allies - who slaughtered 50,000 people in Kabul between 1992 and 1996 - move into the city and execute up to 300 Taliban fighters. The report is a footnote on the television satellite channels, a "nib" in journalistic parlance. Perfectly normal, it seems. The Afghans have a "tradition" of revenge. So, with the strategic assistance of the USAF, a war crime is committed.

Now we have the Mazar-i-Sharif prison "revolt", in which Taliban inmates opened fire on their Alliance jailers. US Special Forces - and, it has emerged, British troops - helped the Alliance to overcome the uprising and, sure enough, CNN tells us some prisoners were "executed" trying to escape. It is an atrocity. British troops are now stained with war crimes. Within days, The Independent's Justin Huggler has found more executed Taliban members in Kunduz.

The Americans have even less excuse for this massacre. For the US Secretary of Defence, Donald Rumsfeld, stated quite specifically during the siege of the city that US air raids on the Taliban defenders would stop "if the Northern Alliance requested it". Leaving aside the revelation that the thugs and murderers of the Northern Alliance were now acting as air controllers to the USAF in its battle with the thugs and murderers of the Taliban, Mr Rumsfeld's incriminating remark places Washington in the witness box of any war-crimes trial over Kunduz. The US were acting in full military co-operation with the Northern Alliance militia.

Most television journalists, to their shame, have shown little or no interest in these disgraceful crimes. Cosying up to the Northern Alliance, chatting to the American troops, most have done little more than mention the war crimes against prisoners in the midst of their reports. What on earth has gone wrong with our moral compass since 11 September?

Perhaps I can suggest an answer. After both the First and Second World Wars, we - the "West" - grew a forest of legislation to prevent further war crimes. The very first Anglo-French-Russian attempt to formulate such laws was provoked by the Armenian Holocaust at the hands of the Turks in 1915; The Entente said it would hold personally responsible "all members of the (Turkish) Ottoman government and those of their agents who are implicated in such massacres". After the Jewish Holocaust and the collapse of Germany in 1945, article 6 (C) of the Nuremberg Charter and the Preamble of the UN Convention on genocide referred to "crimes against humanity". Each new post-1945 war produced a raft of legislation and the creation of evermore human rights groups to lobby the world on liberal, humanistic Western values.

Over the past 50 years, we sat on our moral pedestal and lectured the Chinese and the Soviets, the Arabs and the Africans, about human rights. We pronounced on the human-rights crimes of Bosnians and Croatians and Serbs. We put many of them in the dock, just as we did the Nazis at Nuremberg. Thousands of dossiers were produced, describing - in nauseous detail - the secret courts and death squads and torture and extra judicial executions carried out by rogue states and pathological dictators. Quite right too.

Yet suddenly, after 11 September, we went mad. We bombed Afghan villages into rubble, along with their inhabitants - blaming the insane Taliban and Osama bin Laden for our slaughter - and now we have allowed our gruesome militia allies to execute their prisoners. President George Bush has signed into law a set of secret military courts to try and then liquidate anyone believed to be a "terrorist murderer" in the eyes of America's awesomely inefficient intelligence services. And make no mistake about it, we are talking here about legally sanctioned American government death squads. They have been created, of course, so that Osama bin Laden and his men should they be caught rather than killed, will have no public defence; just a pseudo trial and a firing squad.

It's quite clear what has happened. When people with yellow or black or brownish skin, with Communist or Islamic or Nationalist credentials, murder their prisoners or carpet bomb villages to kill their enemies or set up death squad courts, they must be condemned by the United States, the European Union, the United Nations and the "civilised" world. We are the masters of human rights, the Liberals, the great and good who can preach to the impoverished masses. But when our people are murdered - when our glittering buildings are destroyed - then we tear up every piece of human rights legislation, send off the B-52s in the direction of the impoverished masses and set out to murder our enemies.

Winston Churchill took the Bush view of his enemies. In 1945, he preferred the straightforward execution of the Nazi leadership. Yet despite the fact that Hitler's monsters were responsible for at least 50 million deaths - 10,000 times greater than the victims of 11 September - the Nazi murderers were given a trial at Nuremberg because US President Truman made a remarkable decision. "Undiscriminating executions or punishments," he said, "without definite findings of guilt fairly arrived at, would not fit easily on the American conscience or be remembered by our children with pride."

No one should be surprised that Mr Bush - a small-time Texas Governor-Executioner - should fail to understand the morality of a statesman in the Whitehouse. What is so shocking is that the Blairs, Schroders, Chiracs and all the television boys should have remained so gutlessly silent in the face of the Afghan executions and East European-style legislation sanctified since 11 September.

There are ghostly shadows around to remind us of the consequences of state murder. In France, a general goes on trial after admitting to torture and murder in the 1954-62 Algerian war, because he referred to his deeds as "justifiable acts of duty performed without pleasure or remorse". And in Brussels, a judge will decide if the Israeli Prime Minister, Arial Sharon, can be prosecuted for his "personal responsibility" for the 1982 massacre in Sabra and Chatila.

Yes, I know the Taliban were a cruel bunch of bastards. They committed most of their massacres outside Mazar-i-Sharif in the late 1990s. They executed women in the Kabul football stadium. And yes, let's remember that 11 September was a crime against humanity.

But I have a problem with all this. George Bush says that "you are either for us or against us" in the war for civilisation against evil. Well, I'm sure not for bin Laden. But I'm not for Bush. I'm actively against the brutal, cynical, lying "war of civilisation" that he has begun so mendaciously in our name and which has now cost as many lives as the World Trade Centre mass murder.

At this moment, I can't help remembering my dad. He was old enough to have fought in the First World War. In the third Battle of

Arras. And as great age overwhelmed him near the end of the century, he raged against the waste and murder of the 1914-1918 war. When he died in 1992, I inherited the campaign medal of which he was once so proud, proof that he had survived a war he had come to hate and loathe and despise. On the back, it says: "The Great War for Civilisation." Maybe I should send it to George Bush.

30 November 2001

'WE'LL FIGHT TO THE END, MARTYRDOM IS OUR VICTORY'

He sat on the floor of a large, cold, wooden-ceilinged room, back against the wall, an embroidered grey shawl wound over his black turban, eyes wearily surveying his visitor.

"An adviser to the Taliban elders of Kandahar" was how he asked to be described. I could call him Mullah Abdullah, although the 32-year-old graduate of Sheikh Hassanjan's madrassah (religious school) in Kohat is known by a different name and holds a far more important post in the Taliban hierarchy. The great mud-walled hujra (guest room) in the family home below the mountains was blasted by a vicious little wind that had given the mullah a bout of flu. Defeat is hard.

So are words in this cold climate. "The people think we are defeated because we have lost many of our men," Mullah Abdullah conceded. "But our men lost their lives in martyrdom and therefore they were successful. So we don't think we have been defeated. We have given up some land to Mr Rabbani (of the Northern Alliance) who was there before (between 1992 and 1996). But when the Americans go home, we'll have the land back." It was the authentic voice of Kandahar. And who knows - given the murder and pillage already re-emerging in Northern Alliance areas - if it may not prove to be true.

The mullah had just arrived from the Taliban's besieged little caliphate, trekking six hours into the desert to avoid the American air raids around Takhta-Pul, resting in his family home overnight before returning to Kandahar, a man in denial or a man who has already decided to go into the mountains. The Americans had secured only a humble airstrip more than 60 miles from Kandahar, he added, a place of no importance. "But the Americans didn't come here for Osama bin Laden - that's not their main reason. They are here because they don't want a country run under an Islamic system of law. They want a government which will do what they want."

Mullah Abdullah seems almost disinterested in the strategy of war. He held a post in the Taliban defence ministry in Kabul, but every military question receives a theological reply. "Even now the Americans have not succeeded in finding Osama bin Laden and his al-Qa'ida. They haven't achieved this mission of theirs for us, Osama is a Muslim and a Muslim from another country is a brother. As for us, we will fight on in the mountains as guerrillas if we lose Kandahar - and if we achieve martyrdom, this is victory."

I was beginning to understand. Victory comes with success and victory comes with defeat. "The Afghans," Lt Col Alexander Burns observed in 1841, "are not deficient in the imaginative faculties, and they may be quoted as a proof that invention precedes judgement."

Yet for Mullah Abdullah, history and politics and defeat appeared part of a religious text. "A hadith (saying) of the Holy Prophet says that it is the right of Muslims to perform jihad," he said. "It was not necessary for us to rule the whole of Afghanistan when the Taliban started its existence from a tiny village. There were only a few Talibans who began all this. At the start, we stated that this was enough. We never cared that we succeeded in gaining 95 per cent of the land of Afghanistan. So we don't care about the land we've lost.

"The Taliban doesn't want the land as such, our main purpose is to convey Islam to the people. If our people return and take back this lost land, it's a success. If we are killed trying to do so, we have received martyrdom and this will be a great success for us too."

This circular argument can have a dizzying effect. The Taliban had operated an "Islamic system" in Kabul - they can say that again - but even if this only applied in Kandahar, it would be a success. Only occasionally did that little worm of doubt creep into the mullah's conversation. "Only time can tell if we can hold Kandahar or not - we are doing our best." It could have been an editorial from a Taliban newspaper - always supposing they hadn't banned newspapers and television. "If we are thrown out of Kandahar, we will go to the mountains and start the guerrilla war as we did with the Russians."

I tried to argue that the Americans were not the Russians, that this was not a simple repeat performance, that the Taliban had been fighting their fellow Afghans this time rather than fighting US forces. But it was no use. "We will die to defend our land," Mullah Abdullah kept repeating. Which is what the Taliban said before the fall of

Mazar-i-Sharif and Kabul and Kunduz. And now they say it before Kandahar.

DECEMBER 2001: SURRENDER OF KANDAHAR

Routine searches in Kandahar Province

7 December 2001

MULLAH MOHAMMED OMAR

The surrender of Kandahar by Mullah Mohammed Omar may, as far as the West is concerned, mark the end of militant Islam in Afghanistan.

His own rise and fall, from village cleric to ruler of the world's most obscurantist state and back to his mud-walled home, took only five years. Reluctant at first, later tinged with a country boy's ambition, it tells in miniature the story of the rise and fall of the world's most implacable Islamic movement.

Was Mullah Omar the protector of Osama bin Laden, his Muslim brother in a Muslim land, as he claimed? Or did the well-educated Mr bin Laden broaden the international perspective of the humble priest from Noudi, suggesting to him that the corruption which Omar fought in Afghanistan existed in - and was the fault of - the Western world, which had supported and then blithely abandoned the mujahedin once the war against the Soviet Union was over?

Journalists like to talk about Mullah Omar as a "shadowy", "secretive" figure, but much is known about the Taliban's spiritual leader.

Far from being a messianic, arrogant preacher, Mullah Omar remains a revered figure among the Pashtuns, not just for his piety but for the courage he showed as he grew up among the dirt and poverty of Kandahar province, working as both a schoolteacher and anti-Soviet partisan.

He lost his eye in battle against the Soviet army but went on to fight the Najibullah communist regime that took over Afghanistan after the Russians retreated. As a guerrilla in the ranks of Younis Khalis' brigade of the Hizb al Islam (the Islamic Party), he was wounded four times.

Mohammed Omar was born in 1959 in the tiny village of Noudi, near Kandahar, the son of a poor farmer of the Pashtun Houtak tribe who died after the family moved to Tarinket, in the province of Arouzagan, leaving Omar, still a boy, to care for his relatives.

He did so by starting a small school near the mosque at Sangasar where he also preached. He never completed his studies, remaining a mullah rather than a mawlawi - one who has graduated from a religious college.

Around him, Afghanistan was disintegrating into anarchy, Pashtuns and Tajiks and Uzbeks and Hazaras fighting each other as the Northern Alliance - our "allies" in our "war for civilisation" today - raped and pillaged Kabul. Mullah Omar called them, "a criminal and treacherous group who sold themselves and their country to foreign colonialists". He would say the same today.

The murder and rape of women - and boys - in Kandahar enraged the young cleric. The opium trade had corrupted the city.

The first incident in which he became actively involved, the crucible in the foundation of the Taliban, followed the kidnap of two teenage girls who had their heads shaved and were then gang-raped in the barracks of a local militia leader. With 30 of his students and just 16 rifles, he rescued the girls and hanged one of the rapists from a tank.

His fame spread, especially among the Pakistani religious schools of Mawlana Fadlurahman, who led the Jamiyat Ullama Islami (Congregation of Islamic Scholars) and who was an ally of Benazir Bhutto, Pakistan's Prime Minister at the time. In 1996, his Taliban membership grew by the day as provinces fell to the austere but law-enforcing young men - some only 14 years old - who followed the still-youthful 37-year-old cleric.

But he remained a shy, reclusive man, reportedly spending hours in contemplation on his prayer mat, a cleric who initially appeared to be a social reformer but who - once the Taliban had captured most of Afghanistan - adopted an extreme version of the Hanafi Sunni religious sect, believing the duty of a Muslim was to create the ideal society that supposedly existed under the Prophet. Amusement, the social role of women, distraction and leisure were all to be erased. A literal interpretation of Islam, which laid down that a man's beard must be the length of two fists, suddenly dominated Afghanistan. Rather than plan a future for the country - the economic rebuilding of the world's most bombed nation with its 20 million mines, its wrecked roads, bridges and dams - he regarded individual and group morality as the focus of human society.

Hence the Department for the Suppression of Vice and Promotion of Virtue was busier than the ministries of economy or defence. Punishment was an educative process - and a brutal one.

No one is certain how the relationship between Mullah Omar and Osama bin Laden developed. Mr bin Laden's arrival followed shortly after the Taliban's 1996 victory and, in the years that followed, the Taliban's political statements, such as they were, became increasingly anti-Western and anti-American.

Mr bin Laden's "War against Crusaders and Jews" may not have been encouraged by Mullah Omar, but his desire to bring down the "treacherous Muslims" running the pro-American regimes of the Gulf must have seemed uncannily similar to Mullah Omar's earlier campaign against the "criminal and treacherous group" of Afghans who were the Taliban's original enemy.

Now that "treacherous" group is at the gates of Kandahar, how true his claim that they had sold themselves to "foreign colonialists" must seem to Mullah Omar today. Back on 24 September, he announced that handing over Mr bin Laden "would mean we were no longer Muslims and that Islam was finished".

Now Mullah Omar is reported to be in the city he made great, but his Taliban appears almost finished. Unless, of course, he decides to keep his word and fight to the end, "to the last breath", as he put it, against the Americans and the "traitors" of the Northern Alliance.

8 December 2001

PREVENTION OF JOY AND PLEASURE

There was always something distinctly odd, as well as frightening, about the Taliban. Take the young immigration officer who stamped my passport at Jalalabad airport in 1997. Why hadn't I obtained an exit visa, he asked. He must have been 14 years old and was wearing a kind of mascara beneath his eyes, eye make-up just as he imagined the Prophet had once worn it.

When I protested that there was no one in his 8th-century statelet to give me an exit visa, he raised his head and tut-tutted at me. "Tut-tut-tut-tut," he went. On and on, shaking his head from side to side. I was an errant schoolboy and he, the child, was the Islamic elder, admonishing the untutored Westerner.

Admonishment, in a sense, was what the Taliban were about. The prevention of joy and pleasure fitted perfectly with their literalist view of Islam. The minister of justice spent much of his time touring Afghanistan to check the length of beards: each had to be "two fists" in length. The darker side of this tomfoolery, of course, was performed in the Kabul sports stadium: the public execution of men and women, the amputation of hands. If God was merciful, the Taliban's interpretation of mercy was more than strained.

And yet - and here there must be an "and yet" - they were a perfect product of the rapine and pillage of the Northern Alliance's years of terror. Yes, the Taliban were in many ways the creation of our very own friends in the Northern Alliance. After 50,000 men and women had been slaughtered in Kabul between 1992 and 1996, accompanied by the creation of a drugs and prostitution mafia, Afghans of every ethnic group sought peace at any price. And when the Taliban arrived, they were welcomed in a dark, fearful kind of way. Thieves may have their hands cut off but at least there were no more thieves. You could drive from Jalalabad to Kandahar in the certainty that you would arrive safely and untouched. As journalists know all too well now, you cannot do that today.

And the drug production was erased. The UN praised the Taliban's prohibition of hashish and heroin production - it was left to the Northern Alliance boys to keep the reefers smoking in the West - and Mullah Omar toured Kandahar, warning the Pashtun tribes of the consequences if they disobeyed his orders.

The rules were those of the refugee camps in Pakistan in which many of the Taliban had grown up. No drugs. Knowledge of the Koran by rote. Women in the tent, unseen, uneducated, serving their men. This was what life was in those camps and this is what the Taliban reproduced inside Afghanistan in 1996: they turned the whole country into one refugee camp, complete with the rules of penury that they learnt in exile during the Afghan-Russian war.

But they were rules that had about them a kind of obscenity. A Scandinavian friend of mine, a diplomat visiting Kabul, was telephoned in his hotel room by a Taliban official. "We are going to execute a murderer by firing squad. Do you want to witness this?" he was asked. The diplomat carefully explained that his country opposed capital punishment for any crime. Hours later the man rang back. The Taliban would no longer execute the condemned man by firing squad, he said. Instead, they would kill him by pushing down a wall on top of him. And in any case, he added, the punishment had been postponed for several days.

And so it went on. No music, no kites, no pigeons, no television, no films, no education for women, no jobs for women. The Taliban said they respected women but, as with so many obscurantists, there was always a suspicion that they feared them.

And so the Ministry for the Prevention of Vice and Promotion of Virtue would use its canes on women who left home without a male relative or dressed without appropriate modesty in full burqa. We in the West clucked our liberal teeth at this with the same disapproval shown to me by that immigration officer at Jalalabad airport.

We chose, naturally enough, to ignore the Wahabi obscurantists in Saudi Arabia whose rules were almost as vicious and equally insensitive to the outside world. Our allies in Saudi can cloak their women in black, prevent them from driving and chop off heads outside mosques in front of baying crowds every Friday. And they got away with it; scarcely a whimper from the West. And thus the Americans, while crowing at the Taliban's overthrow, have carefully avoided any reference to the Taliban's tutors in Saudi Arabia, whose theology is equally literalist and whose mutawa religious police were the very inspiration for the Vice and Virtue men in the Taliban. Certainly, we are free to forget that most of the pilot-murderers of 11 September were Saudis. None of them was a Taliban, though you might be forgiven for thinking, given the venom we express, that it was the other way round.

For we did not go to war in Afghanistan to make the world free for kite flyers or cinema lovers or women in veils. We went after the Taliban because of their protection for Osama bin Laden. Does this mean the end of militant Islam? Will the Americans now turn on Hamas and Islamic Jihad - via their Israeli friends - and the Hizbollah in Lebanon and just about any man with a beard who objects to the United States? I rather suspect that Muslim "extremism" has more tenacity than that, indeed more tenacity than the Taliban. For they were always an unworldly version of their co-religionists in the rest of the Islamic world, more interested in applying sharia law than in resisting the more obvious manifestations of Western oppression.

The Taliban never volunteered to fight for Iraq or for the Palestinians or for the Lebanese. They did not even have a military strategy to fight anybody, just a theological strategy. They ruled Afghanistan in the way they did because it was all they knew.

And so they forgot the principle of power: that you must at least pretend to protect and nurture and show compassion towards your own people. The Taliban disappeared because they cared about morality but not about life, about absolutism rather than human dignity, about rules rather than logic, a world in which challenge was always treachery.

In their territory a few days ago, another boy immigration officer studied my latest entry visa to the Islamic Emirate of Afghanistan - the last the Taliban was to issue, stamped into my passport by their officials in Islamabad after their embassy had been officially closed. The teenager brought down his immigration stamp on my entry visa. It said "Exit". Wrong stamp. But it pretty much symbolised the Taliban.

8 December 2001

PART TWO OF THE WAR FOR CIVILISATION

It needed my old Irish journalist colleague, Vincent Browne, to point out the obvious to me. With a headache as big as Afghanistan, reading through a thousand newspaper reports on the supposed "aftermath" of the Afghan war, I'd become drugged by the lies. Afghan women were free at last, "our" peacekeeping force was on its way, the Taliban were crushed. Anti-American demonstrations in Pakistan had collapsed - we'll forget my little brush with some real Afghans there a couple of weeks ago. Al-Qa'ida was being "smoked out" of its cave. Osama bin Laden was - well, not captured or even dead; but - well, the Americans had a videotape, incomprehensible to every Arab I've met, which "proves" that our latest monster planned the crimes against humanity on New York and Washington.

So it needed Vincent, breathing like a steam engine as he always does when he's angry, to point to the papers in Gemma's, my favourite Dublin newsagents. "What in Christ's sake is going on, Bob?" he asked. "Have you seen the headlines of all this shite?" and he pulled Newsweek from the shelf. The headline: After The Evil.

"What is this biblical bollocks?" Vincent asked me. Osama bin Laden's overgrained, videotaped face stared from the cover of the magazine, a dark, devilish image from Dante's circles of hell. When he captured Berlin, Stalin announced that his troops had entered "the lair of the fascist beast". But the Second World War has nothing on this.

So let's do a "story-so-far". After Arab mass-murderers crashed four hijacked aircraft into the World Trade Centre, the Pentagon and Pennsylvania, a crime against humanity which cost more than 4,000 innocent lives, President Bush announced a crusade for infinite "justice" - later downgraded to infinite freedom - and bombed Afghanistan. Using the gunmen and murderers of the discredited Northern Alliance to destroy the gunmen and murderers of the discredited Taliban, the Americans bombed bin Laden's cave fortresses and killed hundreds of Afghan and Arab fighters, not including the prisoners executed after the Anglo-US-Northern Alliance suppression of the Mazar prison revolt.

The production of the bin Laden videotape - utterly convincing evidence of his guilt to the world's press, largely, if willfully, ignored by the Muslim world - helped to obscure the fact that Mr Evil, seemed to have disappeared. It also helped to airbrush a few other facts away. We could forget that US air strikes, according to statistics compiled by a Chicago University professor, have now killed more innocent Afghans than the hijackers killed westerners and others in the World Trade Centre. We could forget that Mullah Omar, the mysterious leader of the Taliban, has also got away.

We could ignore the fact that, save for a few brave female souls, almost all Afghan women in Kabul continued to wear the burqa. We could certainly close our eyes to the massive preponderance of Northern Alliance killers represented in the new UN-supported, pro-western Government in Kabul. We could clap our hands when a mere 50 Royal Marines arrived in Afghanistan this weekend to support a UN-mandated British-led "peace" force of only a few thousand men who will need the Kabul government's permission to operate in the city and which, in numbers, will come to about one -third of the complement of the British Army destroyed in the Kabul Gorge in 1842.

The "peace" force thinks it will have to defend humanitarian aid convoys from robbers and dissident Taliban. In fact, it will have to fight off the Northern Alliance mafia and drug-growers and warlords, as well as the vicious guerrillas sent out to strike them by bin Laden's survivors. If nothing else, the Taliban made the roads and villages of Afghanistan safe for Afghans and foreigners alike. Now, you can scarcely drive from Kabul to Jalalabad.

Presumably, the CIA will let us pay the Alliance mobsters for their war in Afghanistan. One of the untold stories of this conflict is the huge amount of money handed out to militia leaders to persuade them to fight for the US. When Taliban members changed sides for an Alliance payment of $250,000 and then attacked their benefactors, we all dwelt on their treachery. None of us asked how the Alliance - which didn't have enough money to pay for bullets a few weeks earlier - could throw a quarter of a million bucks at the Taliban in the middle of a fire site. Nor how the Pashtun tribal leaders of Kandahar province are now riding around in brand-new four-wheel drives with thousands of dollars to hand out to their gunmen. I wasn't surprised to read that a Somali warlord is now offering his cash-for-hire services to the US for the next round of the War on Civilisation.

Fortunately for us, the civilian victims of America's B52s will remain unknown in their newly dug graves. Even before the war ended, around 3,700 of them - not counting Mullah Omar's and bin Laden's gunmen - had been ripped to pieces in our War for Civilisation. A few scattered signs of discontent - the crowd that assaulted me two weeks ago, for example, outraged at the killing of their families - can be quickly erased from the record.

It is obviously perverse to note that I haven't met a single ordinary Muslim or, indeed many westerners - Pakistani, Afghan, Arab, British, French, American - who actually believe all this guff. Let's just remember that the new Kabul government is as committed to support

"Islam, democracy, pluralism (sic) and social justice" as Mr Bush is to Good (sic) and the Destruction of Evil. Roll on next year, and don't worry about bin Laden - he may be back just in time to participate in Part Two of the War for Civilisation.

28 December 2001

'WE ARE AT THE START OF OUR MILITARY ACTION ON AMERICA'

The first time I met Osama bin Laden inside Afghanistan, it was a hot, humid night in the summer of 1996. Huge insects flew through the night air, settling like burrs on his Saudi robes and on the clothes of his armed followers. They would land on my notebook until I swatted them, their blood smearing the pages. Bin Laden was always studiously polite: each time we met, he would offer the usual Arab courtesy of food for a stranger: a tray of cheese, olives, bread and jam. I had already met him in Sudan and would spend a night, almost a year later, in one of his mountain guerrilla camps, so cold that I awoke in the morning with ice in my hair.

I had been given a rough blanket and my shoes were left outside the tent. Whenever we met, he would interrupt our interviews to say his prayers, his armed followers - from Algeria, Egypt, the Gulf Arab states, Syria - kneeling beside him, hanging on his every word as if he were a messiah.

On 20 March, 1997, I would meet him again. Although only 41 at the time, his ruggedly groomed beard had white hairs, and he had bags under his eyes; I sensed some infirmity, a stiffness of one leg that gave him the slightest of limps. I still have my notes, scribbled in the frozen semi-darkness as an oil lamp sputtered between us. "I am not against the American people," he said. "Only their government." I told him I thought the American people regarded their government as their representatives. Bin Laden listened to this in silence. "We are still at the beginning of our military action against the American forces," he said.

I remembered those words as I watched those aeroplanes scything into the World Trade Centre towers. And I remembered, too, how in that last meeting he had seized on the Arabic-language newspapers I was carrying in my satchel (a schoolbag I use in rough countries) and scurried to a corner of the tent to read them for 20 minutes, ignoring both his fighters and myself.

The first time we met, in Sudan, I persuaded bin Laden - much against his will - to talk about those days. And he recalled how, during an attack on a Russian firebase not far from Jalalabad, a mortar shell had fallen at his feet. He had waited for it to explode. And in those milliseconds of rationality, he had - so he said - felt a great sense of tranquillity, a sense of calm acceptance, which he ascribed to God.

One of his armed followers in Afghanistan took me up the "bin Laden trail", a terrifying two-hour odyssey along fearful ravines in rain and sleet, the windscreen misting as we climbed the cold mountain. "When you believe in jihad (holy war), it is easy," the gunman informed me, fighting with the steering wheel as stones scuttered from the tyres, bouncing down the valleys into the clouds below. It was two hours more - this was in 1997 - before we reached bin Laden's old wartime camp, the jeep skidding backwards towards sheer cliffs, the headlights illuminating frozen waterfalls above.

Bin Laden is a tall, slim man and towers over his companions. He has narrow, dark eyes that stared hard at me when he spoke of his hatred of Saudi corruption. Indeed, in my long conversation with bin Laden in 1996 - on that hot night of mosquitoes - the Saudi kingdom and its apparatchiks probably consumed more time than his views of America.

History - or his version of it - was the basis of almost all his remarks. And the pivotal date was 1990, the year in which Saddam Hussein invaded Kuwait. "When the American troops entered Saudi Arabia, the land of the two holy places, there was a strong protest from the ulema (religious authorities) against the interference of American troops.

"This big mistake by the Saudi regime of inviting the American troops revealed their deception. They had given their support to nations that were fighting against Muslims. After it insulted and jailed the ulema... the Saudi regime lost its legitimacy."

Bin Laden paused to see whether I had listened to his careful, if frighteningly exclusive, history lesson. "I believe that sooner or later the Americans will leave Saudi Arabia, and that the war declared by America against the Saudi people means war against Muslims everywhere..."

He also told me that "swift and light forces working in complete secrecy" would be needed to oust America from Saudi Arabia. In the following two years, bin Laden was to form his al-Qa'ida movement and declare war on the American people - not just the government and army of the United States.

30 December 2001

TALIBAN DEMISE WAS INEVITABLE

The Taliban made Afghanistan safe for Afghans and helped others make the world unsafe for just about everyone else. And now they are gone - maybe. It's not just the men who've swapped their black turbans for brown ones, or the Taliban who have changed sides - only, perhaps, to re-emerge in their original colours at a later date. It's that the very lawlessness which brought them to power in 1996 - the anarchy and war crimes of the Northern Alliance - may yet produce another Taliban in the years to come.

Theirs was a most odd little emirate, a 12th-century state in which the minister for justice measured morality according to a man's beard - it had to be two fists in length - and the ministry for the prohibition of vice could outlaw pigeons, kites and television sets. If it was heavy with learning - or at least Koranic recitation - it lacked all the social and industrial skills needed in a modern nation. The Taliban outlawed drug production while the Northern Alliance went into heroin overdrive - a fact which forces those leading the "war for civilisation" into quite a few verbal dexterities - and it ended the banditry that the Northern Alliance had produced.

But its demise was inevitable. Self-righteousness did not gain the Taliban popularity and while its prohibition of women - in almost every form - was approved by village elders, it helped to isolate the movement from the outside world. The pathetic wall paintings around Mullah Omar's Kandahar home showed just how sad was the Taliban's world view: childish and simplistic and, at one and the same time, vicious in punishment. Amputations, hangings, a woman's execution and mass killings in the north gave a barbarous edge to the Taliban's supposed "purity".

Nor is Afghanistan a forgiving place. When they were needed to impose law and order, the Taliban were welcomed. When they fell back before US bombing, they were treated with derision. Iranians, who understood the organisation long before the rest of us, always called them the "Black Taliban". Their contempt for the rest of the world prompted the Taliban to give shelter to Osama bin Laden - there was much talk of "brother Muslims" and "traditional hospitality". But it was the Arabs who put up the stiffest fight in the face of the Americans, the Taliban sometimes ready to leave their Arab "brothers" to the mercy of the Alliance.

Will they just be an opaque memory in Afghan history, a bizarre footnote to a ferocious country, village preachers with guns who thought that God was stronger than the US? Back in 1880, the British Army - according to its official report on the Battle of Ahmed Khel - recorded how it suddenly faced savage fighting from Afghan tribesmen, including "a contingent of talibs from Kandahar". Given the Afghan wheel of fortune, it just may be that the Taliban will return once more.

WINTER 2002: AFGHAN TRAP

War on terror

22 January 2002

WE HAVE MADE BIN LADEN A HAPPY MAN

Shackled, hooded, sedated. Taken to a remote corner of the world where they may be executed, where the laws of human rights are suspended. Sounds to me like the Middle East. Shackled, hooded, threatened with death by "courts" that would give no leeway to defence or innocence. In fact, it sounds like Beirut in the 1980s.

I've written this story before. Last time, I remember writing about the threats to my kidnapped journalist friend Terry Anderson of the Associated Press, tied up, hooded, always threatened by his "Islamist" captors in Lebanon. That was between 1986 and 1991 and Terry - let us remember this distinction - was no man of violence. He was a journalist, a comrade, a friend. But he was most cruelly treated, allowed no contacts with his family, held in cold confinement, threatened with death every bit as absolute as the American military courts that know they hold the fate of al-Qa'ida's men in their hands.

And then I remember the revolting prison of Khiam where Israel locked up its Lebanese adversaries - real and presumed, none tried by a court - and where prisoners were brought, shackled, hooded, sedated, for questioning. Their interrogation included electric torture - electrified metal attached to penis and nipples (there were women prisoners, too) - which could never happen at Guantanamo Bay, as America's Israeli allies taught their Lebanese militia men in 1980. They in turn taught it to their Lebanese Shia militia enemies who used electricity on their captives.

America, Israel's friend, could have closed down this sick, disgusting prison if it had insisted. But Washington remained silent. The Lebanese Shia prisoners were left to face the men who applied electrodes to their testicles. The nation that would later declare a war of good against evil didn't see much wrong at Khiam.

And now, a trip down memory lane. In the 1980s, when I was covering the war in Afghanistan between the brave mujahedin guerrillas and the Soviet occupiers, Arab fighters - armed by the Americans, paid by the Saudis and the West - would occasionally be captured by the Russians or by their Afghan communist satrap allies. For the most part, the Arabs were Egyptians. They would be paraded on Kabul television and then executed as "terrorists". We called them "freedom fighters". President Reagan claimed that their masters were not unlike the Founding Fathers.

From time to time, these revolutionary forces would sally forth across the Amu Darya river to attack the Soviet Union itself. The "Arab" Afghans would attack a foreign country from Afghanistan. They would do so in their war against occupation. We supported them. For, yes, they were "freedom fighters". Now, having opposed America, having dared to oppose US forces inside Afghanistan, in order to destroy US forces "occupying" part of the Arab world - in Saudi Arabia, in Kuwait - they have become "unlawful combatants", "battlefield detainees". That, in essence, is what the Russians called them in the 1980s. It justified their detention in the hideous Pol e-Chowkri prison outside Kabul, their incarceration like animals - partly exposed to the elements - before their appearance in front of unfair, drumhead courts.

Minus the torture, the United States is now doing what most Arab regimes have been doing for decades: arresting their brutal "Islamist" enemies, holding them incommunicado, chained and hooded, while preparing unfair trials. President Mubarak of Egypt would approve. So would King Abdullah of Jordan. So would the Saudis, whose grotesque, hopelessly unfair system of Islamic "justice" would be familiar to America's prisoners. The jails of Saddam would be far worse - let us keep things in proportion - but in most of the Arab world and Israel, al-Qa'ida would receive similar treatment.

And whether we like it or not, many Saudis believe that American troops are occupying their country, that the very presence of US soldiers in the Kingdom is a crime. King Fahd, of course, invited the Americans into Saudi Arabia in 1990, after Iraq's invasion of Kuwait. President Bush senior promised the Arabs they would leave when the threat of Iraqi occupation was over. But they are still there. Several years ago, I reported in The Independent that Crown Prince Abdullah - the effective ruler now that the King is so badly incapacitated - wanted the Americans to leave. Much jeering there was from American commentators. But now the Washington Post, no less, has reported that the Saudis want the Americans to quit and the commentators are silent. Not so US Secretary of State Colin Powell. For him, the American presence in Saudi Arabia may last until the world turns into "the kind of place we dreamed of". American troops in Saudi are not only a deterrent to Saddam, he said at the weekend, they are a "symbol" of American influence.

Could al-Qa'ida have a more potent reason for continued resistance? The "occupation" of Saudi Arabia remains the cornerstone of Osama bin Laden's battle against the United States, the original raison d'etre of his merciless struggle against America. And here is Mr Powell proving, in effect, that Washington had ulterior motives for sending him into the Gulf. When he added that "we shouldn't impose ourselves on the Government beyond the absolute minimum requirement that we have", the phrase "beyond the absolute minimum" tells it all. The United States will decide how long it stays in Saudi Arabia - not the Saudis; which is exactly what Mr bin Laden has been saying all along.

Now we learn that US troops arrested six Arabs when they were released from a prison in Bosnia. The Bosnians announced that, since the Americans would not disclose the evidence that might be used against them in a trial - to protect US "intelligence sources" - the men should be released from their Bosnian prison. Which they were - only to be seized by the Americans. And what did the Washington Post tell us in all seriousness? That, the operation was reportedly conducted by US troops acting independently of the Nato-led force (in Bosnia)."

Really? Is the Washington Post that stupid? Are we? Is that what law and order is all about? Yes, the West is fighting a cruel enemy. Anyone who has read the full video statement by Osama bin Laden in December must realise that the war against him - indeed the conflict in Afghanistan - has only just begun. But already we are turning ourselves into the kind of deceitful, ruthless people whom Mr bin Laden imagines us to be. Shackled, hooded, sedated. Prepared for a trial without full disclose of evidence. With a possible death sentence at the end, we are now the very model of the enemies Mr bin Laden wants to fight. He must be a happy man.

23 January 2002

JOURNALISTS ARE NOW DELIBERATE TARGETS

The murder of Daniel Pearl of The Wall Street Journals was as revolting as it was outrageous. But why was he killed? Because he was a Westerner, a "Kaffir"? Because he was an American? Or because he was a journalist? And if he was killed because he was a reporter what has happened to the protection which we in our craft used to enjoy? In Pakistan and Afghanistan, we can be seen as Kaffirs, as unbelievers. Our faces, our hair, even our spectacles, mark us out as Westerners. The Muslim cleric who wished to talk to me in an Afghan refugee village outside Peshawar last October was stopped by a man who pointed at me and asked: "Why are you taking this Kaffir into our mosque?" Weeks later, a crowd of Afghan refugees, grief-stricken at the slaughter of their relatives in a US B-52 bomber air raid, tried to kill me because they thought I was an American.

But over the past quarter century I have witnessed the slow, painful, dangerous erosion of respect for our work. We used to risk our lives in wars - we still do - but journalists were rarely deliberate targets. We were impartial witnesses to conflict, often the only witnesses, the first writers of history. Even the nastiest militias understood this. "Protect him, look after him, he is a journalist," I recall a Palestinian guerrilla ordering his men when I entered the burning Lebanese town of Bhamdoun in 1983.

But in Lebanon, in Algeria and then in Bosnia, the protection began to disintegrate. Reporters in Beirut were taken hostage - the

Associated Press's Terry Anderson disappeared for almost seven years - while Algerian journalists were hunted down and beheaded by Islamist groups throughout the Nineties. Olivier Quemener, a French cameraman, was cruelly shot down in the Casbah area of Algiers as his wounded colleague lay weeping by his side. Pasting "TV" stickers on your car in Sarajevo was as much an invitation to the Serb snipers above the city to shoot at journalists as it was a protection.

Where did we go wrong? I suspect the rot started in Vietnam. Reporters have identified themselves with armies for decades. In both World Wars, journalists worked in uniform. Dropping behind enemy lines with US commandos did not spare an AP reporter from a Nazi firing squad. But these were countries in open conflict, reporters whose nations had officially declared war. Wearing a uniform enabled journalists to claim the protection of the Geneva Convention; in civilian clothes they could be shot as spies. It was in Vietnam that reporters started wearing uniforms and carrying weapons - and shooting those weapons at America's enemies - even though their country was not officially at war and even when they could have carried out their duties without wearing soldiers' clothes. In Vietnam, reporters were murdered because they were reporters.

This odd habit of journalists to be part of the story, to play an almost theatrical role in wars, slowly took hold. When the Palestinians evacuated Beirut in 1982, I noticed that several French reporters were wearing Palestinian kuffiah scarves. Israeli reporters turned up in occupied southern Lebanon with pistols. Then in the 1991 Gulf war, American and British television reporters started dressing up in military costumes, appearing on screen - complete with helmets and military camouflage fatigues - as if they were members of the 82nd Airborne or the Hussars. One American journalist even arrived in boots camouflaged with painted leaves although a glance at any desert suggests that this would not have served much purpose. In the Kurdish flight into the mountains of northern Iraq more reporters could be found wearing Kurdish clothes. In Pakistan and Afghanistan last year, the same phenomenon occurred, Reporters in Peshawar could be seen wearing Pushtun hats. Why? No one could ever supply me with an explanation. What on earth was CNN's Walter Rodgers doing in US Marine costume at the American camp outside Kandahar? Mercifully, someone told him to take it off after his first broadcast. Then Geraldo Rivera of Fox News arrived in Jalalabad with a gun. He fully intended, he said, to kill Osama bin Laden. It was the last straw. The reporter had now become combatant.

Perhaps we no longer care about our profession. Maybe we're all too quick to demean our own jobs, to sneer at each other, to adopt the ridiculous title of "hacks" when we should regard the job as foreign correspondent as a decent, honourable profession. I was astounded last December when an American newspaper headline announced that I had deserved the beating I received at the hands of that Afghan crowd. I had almost died but the article, by Mark Steyn, carried a headline that a "multiculturalist (me) gets his due". My sin, of course, was to explain that the crowd had lost relatives in America's B-52 raids, that I would have done the same in their place. That shameful, unethical headline, I should add, appeared in Daniel Pearl's own newspaper, The Wall Street Journal.

Can we do better? I think so. It's not that reporters in military costume - Rodgers in his silly Marine helmet, Rivera clowning around with a gun, or even me in my gas cape a decade ago - helped to kill Daniel Pearl. He was murdered by vicious men. But we are all of us - dressing up in combatant's clothes or adopting the national dress of people - helping to erode the shield of neutrality and decency which saved our lives in the past. If we don't stop now, how can we protest when next our colleagues are seized by ruthless men who claim we are spies?

7 March 2002

'THE WAR AGAINST TERROR COMES FIRST'

In Afghan fields, the poppies blow. Yes, even as the Americans are moving deeper into the Afghan trap, the warlords and gangsters running much of the western-supported Afghan government are ensuring a bumper new crop of heroin for the world's markets.

The UN have warned of this, of course, but nothing is being done. The "war against terror" comes first. The broken roads and highways of Afghanistan are now ribbons of anarchy and brigandage and murder across the country. The pathetic little force of peace-keepers in Kabul cannot control all of the capital, let alone the rest of the country. The Interim President, Hamid Karzai, can scarcely control the street outside his office. But the "war against terror" comes first.

Locked into their "war against terror" - and now discovering that their enemies want to fight them - the Americans remain equally indolent when confronted by the infinitely more dangerous conflict 2,000 miles to the west of Kabul, in the streets of Jerusalem, Ramallah, Tel Aviv, Nablus, Jenin and Gaza. When the Israeli army goes on a shooting spree in the refugee camps and kills 16 Palestinians, among them two children, the US calls for "restraint". When a Palestinian suicide bomber murders a crowd of Israelis in Jerusalem, including two babies and a 10-year old, the US boldly blames Yasser Arafat for not "stopping terrorism" by locking up the bad guys. And Ariel Sharon? Why, he's busy destroying the police stations and prisons to make sure Mr Arafat can't do what he's been ordered to do.

And when Mr Sharon actually announces that Israel must "inflict greater losses" - in other words, kill more Palestinians - Washington is silent. Maybe it's not indolence. Maybe the Bush administration actually believes that the man held "personally responsible" by an Israeli commission of inquiry for the murder of 1,700 Palestinian civilians in Beirut in 1982 really is fighting America's "war on terror". Maybe America's moral compass has become so skewed by the crimes against humanity on 11 September that President Bush simply no longer cares what Mr Sharon does.

It's as if all the lessons of history - in Afghanistan as well as the Middle East - have been tossed into a bin. Take ex-President Clinton. He arrives in Israel and what does he do? He blames Mr Arafat. And what does his preposterous wife say when she does the same thing? "Yasser Arafat bears the responsibility for the violence that has occurred; it rests on his shoulders ..." She says that her role as a US Senator is "to support the Israeli people". Really? What's wrong with supporting innocent Palestinians as well? Wrong religion? Back-to-front writing? Wrong eye colour?

So a war against colonial occupation has been transformed into an offshoot of the "war on terror", the language of this war ever more infantile. We now have to learn by rote the following words: tit-for-tat, cycle-of-violence, axis of evil, bunker-buster, daisy-cutter ... Is there no end to this childishness? No, there is not. For the latest little killer is the word "transfer" or "resettlement". As in "the simple answer... would be to create a vast separation from Israel, resettling the Palestinians in Jordan, where 80 per cent of the population is Palestinian." This comes from an article published in USA Today. In Israel itself, an opinion poll asks Israelis how many of them would support "transfer" - of Arabs out of their homes, of course, not Jewish settlers off Arab land - as a solution to the war.

This is incredible. "Transfer" is ethnic cleansing and ethnic cleansing is a war crime. If American newspapers are prepared to print such an option and if Israelis are asked to give their opinion on it, what is Mr Milosevic doing in The Hague? The moral collapse is already underway. Take the watering down of the US government's latest report on human rights. In 2000, it said that Egypt's hopelessly unfair military courts "do not ensure civilian defendants due process before an independent tribunal". In the 2001 report, however, that sentence has been censored out. It has to be, of course, because Mr Bush is now setting up his own military courts to try his prisoners at Guantanamo Bay without due process.

And while the Americans are distorting the nature of the war between Israel and the Palestinians, they are lying about Afghanistan. General Tommy Franks, the head of the US Central Command, refers in the following words to the mistaken killing of 16 innocent Afghans at Hazar Qadam: "I will not characterise it as a failure of any type." Sorry? Either General Franks - who on Tuesday managed to refer to his newly killed soldiers as dying "in Vietnam" - didn't read the facts or he is a very disreputable man.

His boss, Donald Rumsfeld, refuses to use the word "mistake" or even "investigation" after thousands of innocent Afghans died under US bombs because the word "sometimes has the implication of more formality or a disciplinary action". When Washington's top military men are so dishonest, is it any surprise that Israeli tanks can open fire on refugee camps without any serious response from the US or blast cars carrying children because they want to kill their father?

It is surely time that Europe became involved. It is surely time that the EU held a summit about these terrible conflicts and involved itself directly. We should be expanding the peace force in Kabul to remove the weapons of Afghanistan and let America move into the swamp of semi-occupation and guerrilla warfare if that is what it wishes. We should be asking Israel to repay the EUR17.29m (£10.5m) of European taxpayers' money that has been destroyed by the Israeli army in its vandalisation of EU-funded Palestinian infrastructure.

Since the Americans won't talk to Yasser Arafat, we should take over from them. If Washington is too slovenly to halt this terrible war between Arab and Israeli, we must try to do so. We're asked to fund America's bankrupt policies with our euros. So now it's time to demand that we have a say in them. Instead of that, Downing Street, which over Christmas castigated those journalists who predicted chaos and blood in Afghanistan - myself included, I'm glad to say - feeds Mr Bush's fantasies by supporting yet another war with Iraq.

I'm beginning to suspect that 11 September is turning into a curse far greater than the original bloodbath of that day, that America's absorption with that terrible event is in danger of distorting our morality. Is the anarchy of Afghanistan and the continuing slaughter in the Middle East really to be the memorial for the thousands who died on 11 September?

SPRING - SUMMER 2002: 'NO QUARREL WITH THE PEOPLE OF AFGHANISTAN'

Afghan farmer

10 June 2002

NATION BUILDING

Washington wants the loya jirga to succeed. True, far too many of its pliant warlords - the Pashtun and Tajik gangsters whom the Americans paid in thousands of dollars for their sometimes loyal alliance against Osama bin Laden - have been trying to bribe and bamboozle their own candidates into power once they realised that the "grand assembly" of Afghans would actually be held today. And true, there has been intimidation and delegates murdered.

But a successful interim government - whatever its chances of producing fair parliamentary elections - is vital for the United States. Firstly, it will allow President Bush, despite his failure to capture either Mr bin Laden or the Pimpernel-like Mullah Omar, to claim that America has fulfilled its promise to bring "democracy" to Afghanistan. Secondly - and more importantly - because it is America's ticket out of the country. As an article in the Wall Street Journal, the President's best friend in his "war on terror", put it last week, nation-building "certainly beats keeping crack (sic) US troops on the Afghan-Pakistan border for the next 10 to 15 years".

But even if the democrats and the killers and murderers of Afghanistan - let us not be squeamish about some of the "delegates" - bring off their tribal rites today, it's by no means certain that Afghanistan's central authority will be able to do any more than they have already: rule the streets of Kabul while regional warlords - including one of their own vice-ministers - battle with rival mafiosi in the rest of the country.

Hamid Karzai, the head of the present interim government, has only one popular mandate in Afghanistan. It doesn't come from the thugs of the Northern Alliance who "liberated" Kabul from the Taliban last November.

Nor does it come from his own Pashtun people, with whom his prestige has rested only upon his personal integrity. It comes from his friends in the West, those who advised him, dressed him in his stunning green robes and paid for his advancement. It comes from those Western nations - stand up, all of us - who have promised to fund, through him, the regeneration of Afghanistan.

The gang leaders of Afghanistan have agreed to let Mr Karzai remain leader of the next interim government. But at present, those same mafia bosses are running many of the major cities of Afghanistan. Humanitarian organisations and charities are, in many cases, still forced to funnel their aid through these ruthless men, in Mazar-i-Sharif, in Nangahar province, in Khost. Voters in the forthcoming elections know that their humanitarian aid comes via the warlords.

So who will they vote for in parliamentary elections? Mr Karzai is trying to form the country's first non-sectarian political group - allegedly with the brother of Ahmed Shah Masood, the Tajik leader murdered two days before the 11 September atrocities in the United States. And loya jirgas have their uses. While by no means pliant, the British used them to maintain their control of Afghanistan in the late 19th and early 20th centuries. The wretched President Nadjibullah - he who was emasculated and then strangled by the Taliban in 1996 - persuaded two loya jirgas to keep him in power.

So with American money behind him, Mr Karzai may have a good chance to go on leading Afghanistan - at least for the moment.

15 July 2002

'DISTRACTION' IN KASHMIR HELPS AL-QA'IDA

How better to distract Pakistan's army from supporting America's "war on terror" than by promoting - yet again - a war in Kashmir?

Whether or not the mysterious "Hindu" holy men who turned into mass murderers in the slums of Jammu on Saturday night (13 July) were Islamist gunmen, a suspicion is growing in Pakistan that supporters of Osama bin Laden would be happy to provoke another crisis with India if it relieved the pressure on Al-Qa'ida along the Pakistan-Afghan frontier.

In the past two weeks, two major gun battles have been fought in the tribal territories along the Afghan border between Pakistani troops and Al-Qa'ida men, in the last of which four Islamists, all apparently from Chechnya, were shot dead near the Jarma Bridge in Kohat.

A Pakistani policeman and a soldier were also killed. The authorities in Islamabad have been boasting that their para-military forces have penetrated some areas of the semi-autonomous tribal territories along the frontier for the first time in 100 years - a claim which probably says as much about the last days of the British Empire as it does about modern Pakistan.

But Al-Qa'ida knows that these battles are being encouraged by the American FBI, whose officers are urging the Pakistanis to move ever deeper into the hitherto untouchable Pashtun tribal zones whose rule has always been entrusted to local village chieftains. In recent days, credible reports have described how some local Pakistani tribal elements have been seized by US special forces inside Pakistan, in effect, kidnapping them then taking them for interrogation in Kandahar.

Little wonder, therefore, that Al-Qa'ida might want to hit back. By indulging in a new round of guerrilla warfare and killing along the old Line of Control in Kashmir, Islamists can achieve several objectives. They can force President Pervez Musharraf to withdraw his troops from the Afghan border to reinforce the Pakistan army opposite the Indian front line. They can once more force the world's eyes away from the guerrilla battles in Afghanistan.

Most of all, they can force Washington to pay more attention to the dangers of a nuclear confrontation between India and Pakistan than to its continuing and still far-from-successful campaign in Afghanistan.

At the same time, a resurgence of violence in Kashmir reminds 150 million Pakistanis that it is the nation's most important wound and the source of constant humiliation. General Musharraf's latest tinkering with the constitution - along with his continued support for the US - is creating renewed anger in the country's cities. The massacre of 24 civilians by attackers dressed as holy men can only concentrate the minds of those who are losing faith in General Musharraf, not to mention those Muslim religious extremists who always opposed him.

It was surely not by coincidence that the attack came at the moment when US and Indian intelligence officers were concluding two days of talks on "counter -terrorism" in Washington, a conference - the fifth of its kind - which ended with a joint statement that "the two sides agreed to further intensify intelligence sharing and co-ordinate action in pursuit of the remains sic of Al-Qa'ida members and associated terrorist groups".

In reality, any militant Islamic group can regard itself as part of Al-Qa'ida if it wishes - bin Laden's "foundation" is not a formal institution with card -carrying members - although this is still not apparent to the US.

Saturday's killings will therefore serve to recreate all the old ambiguities.

India and Pakistan will have to pretend to be more interested in crushing "terrorism" far from Afghanistan than ending the Kashmir dispute, while the Americans - anxious to encourage the continued assistance of both sides against Al-Qa'ida - will have to pretend to be more interested in Kashmir than in their "war on terror". All of which will be good news for Osama bin Laden.

21 July 2002

PAKISTANI INTELLIGENCE LINKS TO AL-QA'IDA

The FBI is becoming almost as distrustful of its Pakistani counterpart as the CIA is of the warlords across the border in Afghanistan.

During the trial of journalist Daniel Pearl's murderers - which ended with the conviction of the British public schoolboy Omar Sheikh - one small but disturbing fact never made its way into the headlines: that one of the co-accused was a former Pakistani police officer. The final testimony of the trial - released only yesterday morning - must owe something to his evidence.

It revealed, for example, that Mr Pearl made two escape attempts from his captors and that it was this which prompted them to murder him. Three Yemenis were brought in to perform his throat-cutting. But all we know of the ex-cop is that - even at the time of his arrest - he was still working for the Pakistan Special Branch.

Pakistan's Inter-Services Intelligence (ISI), the powerful state institution which helped arm Afghan fighters against the Soviets and then supported the Taliban, was supposedly reformed once the Pakistani President, General Pervez Musharraf, joined President George Bush's "war on terrorism".

Few in Pakistan believe it. There are rumours, for example, that intelligence officers helped to hide three al-Qa'ida members after a gun battle in a village in Waziristan, in the border tribal territories on 25 June in which 10 soldiers were killed. US agents in Pakistan suspect that several of their raids on remote villages in Waziristan were betrayed to al-Qa'ida operatives in advance. Since then, both the FBI and the Pakistan army have preferred not to inform local police officers of their activities.

Although authorities in Islamabad insist that US forces cannot operate alone inside Pakistani territory, recent reports suggest the contrary. Last week, for example, three Pakistani tribesmen were apparently picked up by US troops from the border town of Angoor Adda and flown across the frontier to the US base at Birmal in Afghanistan. It also appears that American forces have been using their old Afghan device of handing out wads of cash in return for local tribal loyalty.

If Pakistan can deny America is waging an undercover war on its territory, it is far more difficult to conceal the involvement of a police Rangers inspector, Waseem Akhtar, in the conspiracy to murder General Musharraf during his visit to Karachi on 26 April. And there is evidence that the explosives to be used in the failed attack were subsequently employed in the suicide bombing of the US consulate in Karachi on 14 June.

Because of the past co-operation between the Taliban - and by extension al-Qa'ida and Pakistan's intelligence services - many Pakistan Special Branch and Field Security Wing officers are working blind, forced to build up entirely new files on militants who remain well known to elements of the ISI. Only patient police work in Karachi, for instance, uncovered hitherto unknown connections between Islamist and secular groups, leading to a series of arrests.

All in all, the civil police and the Americans might learn more by talking to the ISI. But no one is sure for whom their individual members work.

6 August 2002

COLLATERAL DAMAGE

The first anniversary is approaching of the attacks of 11 September and the subsequent war on terror'. To mark the date, The Independent today launches a major new series of special reports by our Middle East correspondent Robert Fisk. In his first dispatch from Afghanistan, he relates the untold story of Hajibirgit, a tiny village in the south-west of the country, where a raid by US Special Forces left a tribal elder and a three-year-old girl dead . . .

President George Bush's "war on terror" reached the desert village of Hajibirgit at midnight on 22 May. Haji Birgit Khan, the bearded, 85-year-old Pushtu village leader and head of 12,000 local tribal families, was lying on a patch of grass outside his home. Faqir Mohamed was sleeping among his sheep and goats in a patch of sand to the south when he heard "big planes moving in the sky". Even at night, it is so hot that many villagers spend the hours of darkness outside their homes, although Mohamedin and his family were in their mud-walled house. There were 105 families in Hajibirgit on 22 May, and all were woken by the thunder of helicopter engines and the thwack of rotor blades and the screaming voices of the Americans.

Haji Birgit Khan was seen running stiffly from his little lawn towards the white-walled village mosque, a rectangular cement building with a single loudspeaker and a few threadbare carpets. Several armed men were seen running after him. Hakim, one of the animal herders, saw the men from the helicopters chase the old man into the mosque and heard a burst of gunfire. "When our people found him, he had been killed with a bullet, in the head," he says, pointing downwards. There is a single bullet hole in the concrete floor of the mosque and a dried bloodstain beside it. "We found bits of his brain on the wall."

Across the village, sharp explosions were detonating in the courtyards and doorways of the little homes. "The Americans were

throwing stun grenades at us and smoke grenades," Mohamedin recalls. "They were throwing dozens of them at us and they were
shouting and screaming all the time. We didn't understand their language, but there were Afghan gunmen with them, too, Afghans with
blackened faces. Several began to tie up our women - our own women
- and the Americans were lifting their burqas, their covering, to look
at their faces. That's when the little girl was seen running away." Abdul Satar says that she was three years old, that she ran shrieking in
fear from her home, that her name was Zarguna, the daughter of a man
called Abdul-Shakour - many Afghans have only one name - and that
someone saw her topple into the village's 60ft well on the other side
of the mosque. During the night, she was to drown there, alone, her
back apparently broken by the fall. Other village children would find
her body in the morning. The Americans paid no attention. From the
description of their clothes given by the villagers, they appeared to
include Special Forces and also units of Afghan Special Forces, the
brutish and ill-disciplined units run from Kabul's former Khad secret
police headquarters. There were also 150 soldiers from the US 101st
Airborne, whose home base is at Fort Campbell in Kentucky. But Fort
Campbell is a long way from Hajibirgit, which is 50 miles into the desert from the south-western city of Kandahar. And the Americans
were obsessed with one idea: that the village contained leaders from
the Taliban and Osama bin Laden's al-Qa'ida movement.

A former member of a Special Forces unit from one of America's
coalition partners supplied his own explanation for the American behaviour when I met him a few days later. "When we go into a village
and see a farmer with a beard, we see an Afghan farmer with a beard,"
he said. "When the Americans go into a village and see a farmer with
a beard, they see Osama bin Laden."

All the women and children were ordered to gather at one end
of Hajibirgit. "They were pushing us and shoving us out of our homes,"
Mohamedin says. "Some of the Afghan gunmen were shouting abuse
at us. All the while, they were throwing grenades at our homes." The
few villagers who managed to run away collected the stun grenades
next day with the help of children. There are dozens of them, small
cylindrical green pots with names and codes stamped on the side. One
says "7 BANG Delay: 1.5 secs NIC-01/06-07", another "1 BANG, 170
dB Delay: 1.5s." Another cylinder is marked: "DELAY Verzagerung ca.
1,5s." These were the grenades that terrified Zarguna and ultimately

caused her death. A regular part of US Special Forces equipment, they are manufactured in Germany by the Hamburg firm of Nico-Pyrotechnik - hence the "NIC" on several of the cylinders. "dB" stands for decibels.

Several date stamps show that the grenades were made as recently as last March. The German company refers to them officially as "40mm by 46mm sound and flash (stun) cartridges". But the Americans were also firing bullets. Several peppered a wrecked car in which another villager, a taxi driver called Abdullah, had been sleeping. He was badly wounded. So was Haji Birgit Khan's son.

A US military spokesman would claim later that US soldiers had "come under fire" in the village and had killed one man and wounded two "suspected Taliban or al-Qa'ida members". The implication - that 85-year-old Haji Birgit Khan was the gunman - is clearly preposterous.

The two wounded were presumably Khan's son and Abdullah, the taxi driver. The US claim that they were Taliban or al-Qa'ida members was a palpable lie - since both of them were subsequently released. "Some of the Afghans whom the Americans brought with them were shouting Shut up!' to the children who were crying," Faqir Mohamed remembers.

"They made us lie down and put cuffs on our wrists, sort of plastic cuffs. The more we pulled on them, the tighter they got and the more they hurt. Then they blindfolded us. Then they started pushing us towards the planes, punching us as we tried to walk."

In all, the Americans herded 55 of the village men, blindfolded and with their hands tied, on to their helicopters. Mohamedin was among them. So was Abdul-Shakour, still unaware that his daughter was dying in the well. The 56th Afghan prisoner to be loaded on to a helicopter was already dead: the Americans had decided to take the body of 85-year-old Haji Birgit Khan with them.

When the helicopters landed at Kandahar airport - headquarters to the 101st Airborne - the villagers were, by their own accounts, herded together into a container. Their legs were tied and then their handcuffs and the manacle of one leg of each prisoner were separately attached to stakes driven into the floor of the container. Thick sacks were put over their heads. Abdul Satar was among the first to be taken from this hot little prison. "Two Americans walked in and tore my clothes off," he said. "If the clothes would not tear, they cut them off with scissors. They took me out naked to have my beard shaved and to have my photograph taken. Why did they shave off my beard? I had my beard all my life."

Mohamedin was led naked from his own beard-shaving into an interrogation tent, where his blindfold was removed. "There was an Afghan translator, a Pushtun man with a Kandahar accent in the room, along with American soldiers, both men and women soldiers," he says. "I was standing there naked in front of them with my hands tied. Some of them were standing, some were sitting at desks. They asked me: What do you do?' I told them: I am a shepherd - why don't you ask your soldiers what I was doing?' They said: Tell us yourself.' Then they asked: What kind of weapons have you used?' I told them I hadn't used any weapon.

"One of them asked: Did you use a weapon during the Russian occupation period, the civil war period or the Taliban period?' I told them that for a lot of the time I was a refugee." From the villagers' testimony, it is impossible to identify which American units were engaged in the interrogations. Some US soldiers were wearing berets with yellow or brown badges, others were in civilian clothes but apparently wearing bush hats. The Afghan interpreter was dressed in his traditional salwah khameez. Hakim underwent a slightly longer period of questioning; like Mohamedin, he says he was naked before his interrogators.

"They wanted my age and my job. I said I was 60, that I was a farmer. They asked: Are there any Arabs or Talibans or Iranians or foreigners in your village?' I said No.' They asked: How many rooms are there in your house, and do you have a satellite phone?' I told them: I don't have a phone. I don't even have electricity.' They asked: Were the Taliban good or bad?' I replied that the Taliban never came to our village so I had no information about them. Then they asked: What about Americans? What kind of people are Americans?' I replied: We heard that they liberated us with President Hamid Karzai and helped us - but we don't know our crime that we should be treated like this.' What was I supposed to say?"

A few hours later, the villagers of Hajibirgit were issued bright-yellow clothes and taken to a series of wire cages laid out over the sand of the airbase - a miniature version of Guantanamo Bay - where they were given bread, biscuits, rice, beans and bottled water. The younger boys were kept in separate cages from the older men. There was no more questioning, but they were held in the cages for another five days. All the while, the Americans were trying to discover the identity of the 85-year-old man. They did not ask their prisoners - who could have identified him at once - although the US interrogators may not have wished them to know that he was dead. In the end, the Americans gave a photograph of the face of the corpse to the International Red Cross. The organisation was immediately told by Kandahar officials that the elderly man was perhaps the most important tribal leader west of the city.

"When we were eventually taken out of the cages, there were five American advisers waiting to talk to us," Mohamedin says. "They used an interpreter and told us they wanted us to accept their apologies for being mistreated. They said they were sorry. What could we say? We were prisoners. One of the advisers said: We will help you.' What does that mean?" A fleet of US helicopters flew the 55 men to the Kandahar football stadium - once the scene of Taliban executions - where all were freed, still dressed in prison clothes and each with a plastic ID bracelet round the wrist bearing a number. "Ident-A-Band Bracelet made by Hollister" was written on each one. Only then did the men learn that old Haji Birgit Khan had been killed during the raid a week earlier. And only then did Abdul-Shakour learn that his daughter Zarguna was dead.

The Pentagon initially said that it found it "difficult to believe" that the village women had their hands tied. But given identical descriptions of the treatment of Afghan women after the US bombing of the Uruzgan wedding party, which followed the Hajibirgit raid, it seems that the Americans - or their Afghan allies - did just that. A US military spokesman claimed that American forces had found "items of intelligence value", weapons and a large amount of cash in the village. What the "items" were was never clarified. The guns were almost certainly for personal protection against robbers. The cash remains a sore point for the villagers. Abdul Satar said that he had 10,000 Pakistani rupees taken from him - about $200 (£130). Hakim says he lost his savings of 150,000 rupees - $3,000 (£1,900). "When they freed us, the Americans gave us 2,000 rupees each," Mohamedin says. "That's just $40 £25. We'd like the rest of our money."

But there was a far greater tragedy to confront the men when they reached Hajibirgit. In their absence - without guns to defend the homes, and with the village elder dead and many of the menfolk prisoners of the Americans - thieves had descended on Hajibirgit. A group of men from Helmand province, whose leader is Abdul Rahman Khan - once a brutal and rapacious "mujahid" fighter against the Russians, and now a Karzai government police commander - raided the village once the Americans had taken away so many of the men. Ninety-five of the 105 families had fled into the hills, leaving their mud homes to be pillaged.

The disturbing, frightful questions that creep into the mind of anyone driving across the desert to Hajibirgit today are obvious. Who told the US to raid the village? Who told them that the Taliban leadership and the al-Qa'ida leadership were there? Was it, perhaps, Abdul Rahman Khan, the cruel police chief whose men were so quick to pillage the mud-walled homes once the raid was over? For today, Hajibirgit is a virtual ghost town, its village leader dead, most of its houses abandoned. The US raid was worthless. There are scarcely 40 villagers left. They all gathered at the stone grave of Zarguna some days later, to pay their respects to the memory of the little girl. "We are poor people - what can we do?" Mohamedin asked me. I had no reply. President Bush's "war on terror", his struggle of "good against evil" descended on the innocent village of Hajibirgit.

And now Hajibirgit is dead.

8 August 2002

FAMILIES OF THE DISAPPEARED DEMAND ANSWERS

They came for Hussain Abdul Qadir on 25 May. According to his wife, there were three American agents from the FBI and 25 men from the local Pakistani CID. The Palestinian family had lived in the Pakistani city of Peshawar for years and had even applied for naturalisation.

But this was not a friendly visit to their home in Hayatabad Street. "They broke our main gate and came into the house without any respect," Mrs Abdul Qadir was to report later to the director of human rights at Pakistan's Ministry of Law and Justice in Islamabad.

"They blindfolded my husband and tied his hands behind his back. They searched everything in the house - they took our computer, mobile phone and even our land-line phone. They took video and audio cassettes. They took all our important documents - our passports and other certificates and they took our money too," she said.

Where, Mrs Abdul Qadir asked Ahsan Akhtar, the director of human rights, was her husband? The Independent has now learnt exactly where he is - he is a prisoner in a cage on the huge American air base at Bagram in Afghanistan. He was kidnapped - there appears to be no other word for it - by the Americans and simply flown over the international frontier from Pakistan. His "crime" is unknown. He has no lawyers to defend him. In the vacuum of the US "war on terror", Mr Abdul Qadir has become a non-person.

His wife has now received a single sheet of paper from the Red Cross which gives no geographical location for the prisoner but lists his nationality as "Palastainian" (sic) and the following message in poorly written Arabic: "To the family and children in Peshawar. I am well and need, first and foremost, God's mercy and then your prayers. Take care of your faith and be kind to the little ones. Could you send me my reading glasses? Your father: Hussain Abdul Qadir."

The sheet of paper is dated 29 June and the Red Cross has confirmed that the prisoner - ICRC number AB7 001486-01 - was interviewed in Bagram.

Needless to say, the Americans will give no information about their prisoners or the reasons for their detention. They will not say whether their interrogators are Afghan or American - there are increasing rumours that Afghan interrogators are allowed to beat prisoners in the presence of CIA men - or if, or when they intend to release their captives. Indeed, the Americans will not even confirm that prisoners have been seized in Pakistan and taken across the Afghan border.

Fatima Youssef has also complained to the Pakistani authorities that her Syrian husband, Manhal al-Hariri - a school director working for the Saudi Red Crescent Society - was seized on the same night as Mr Abdul Qadir from their home in Peshawar, again by three Americans and a group of Pakistani CID men.

"I have the right to ask where my husband is and to know where they have taken him," she has written to the Pakistani authorities. "I have the right to ask for an appeal to release him now, after an interrogation, I have the right to ask for the return of the things which they took from my house."

An Algerian doctor, Bositta Fathi, was also taken that same night by two Americans and Pakistani forces, according to his wife. "I don't have any support and I am not able to go anywhere without my husband," she has told Mr Akhtar in Islamabad. Both Mr al-Hariri and Dr Fathi are believed to be held at Bagram, which is now the main American interrogation centre in Afghanistan. "From there," one humanitarian worker told The Independent, "you either get released or packed off to Guantanamo. Who knows what the fate of these people is or what they are supposed to have done? It seems that it's all outside the law."

Many Arabs moved to Peshawar during the war against the Russians in Afghanistan and remained there as doctors or aid workers. The Abdul Qadirs, for example, asked for naturalisation in January 1993 - Mr Abdul Qadir holds a Jordanian passport - long before Osama bin Laden returned to Afghanistan and founded his al-Qa'ida movement.

"I don't know why all this happened to us because we are Muslims and Arabs," Mrs Abdul Qadir says. "I want to know about my husband. We will leave Pakistan if the government wants us to leave. We will do anything the government wants but in a human and civilised manner."

w At least 15 people were killed in a shoot-out between Afghan police and what witnesses said was a group of Arabs and Pakistanis south of Kabul yesterday. Omar Samad, a foreign ministry spokesman described the gang as "determined and suicidal".

11 August 2002

AL-QA'IDA GRAVEYARD

In Kandahar, the locals come in their thousands to the graves of Osama bin Laden's fallen warriors

They are honoured as saints. Beneath the grey mounds of dust and dried mud lie the "martyrs" of al-Qa'ida.

Here, among these 150 graves, lie the three men who held out to the end in the Mirweis hospital, shooting at the Americans and their Afghan allies until they died amid sewage and their own excrement. Other earth hides the bodies of the followers of Osama bin Laden who fought at Kandahar airport in the last battle before the fall of the Taliban.

They are Arabs and Pakistanis and Chechens and Kazakhs and Kashmiris and all - if you believe the propaganda - are hated and loathed by the native Pashtun population of Kandahar.

Not true. For while the US special forces cruise the streets of this brooding, hot city in their 4x4s, the people of Kandahar visit this bleak graveyard with the reverence of worshippers. They tend the graves in their hundreds. On Fridays, they come in their thousands, travelling hundreds of miles.

They bring their sick and dying. For word has it that a visit to the graveyard of Mr bin Laden's dead will cure disease and pestilence. As if kneeling at the graves of saints, old women gently wash the baked-mud sepulchres, kissing the dust upon them, looking up in prayer to the spindly flags which snap in the dust storms. The Kandahar Ku-brestan - the place of graves - is a political as well as a religious lesson for all who come here.

"Foreigners are advised to stay away from the al-Qa'ida grave-yard," a Western aid worker announces with ceremony. "You may be in danger there." But when I visited the last resting place of Mr bin Laden's men, there was only the fine, gritty winds of sand to fear. It crept into my eyes, my nose, my mouth, my ears. Many of the men around the graves kept their scarves around their faces, dark eyes staring at the foreigner in their midst. The local authorities have put two Afghan soldiers on duty to control the crowds, but all they do is watch the visitors as they put bowls of salt on the graves and take pieces of mud from the graves to touch with their tongues.

An old man from Helmand was there. He had put stones and salt and mud on the tombs - he shook hands with me with salt on his fingers - and he had come because he was sick. "I have pain in my knee and I have polio and I heard that if I came here I would be cured," he said. "I put salt and grain on the graves. Later I collect the grain and eat the salt, and take the mud from the grave home." Khurda, the Pashtuns call this, bringing salt to the tombs of saints.

A second, older man had travelled from Uruzgan with his mother. "My mother had leg and back pains and I brought her to Kandahar so she could see the doctors. But when I heard the stories about these martyrs' graves - and that they might cure her - I also brought my mother here. She is happier here than going to the doctor's." I watched his elderly mother on her knees, scraping dust from the mud tombs, praying and crying.

The two soldiers at the graveyard appear to have succumbed to the same visionary trance as the worshippers. "I've seen for myself people who get healed here," a young, unbearded man with a Kalashnikov rifle on his shoulder told me with a smile. "It's true. People get well after visiting the graves. I've seen deaf men who could hear again and I've seen the dumb speak. They were cured."

This is not the time - and definitely not the place - to contradict such conviction. The sand blasts over this graveyard with a ruthlessness worthy of Osama bin Laden. The city cemetery is much larger - there are square miles of tribal graveyards within the perimeter. But it is the al-Qa'ida dead who attract most mourners. Attracted by what, the foreigner wonders? By the rumours and legend of healing? By the idea that these men resisted the foreigners to the end, preferred to die rather than surrender, that the non-Afghan "martyrs" had fought like Afghans?

Perhaps it's as well the American special forces boys don't drop by for a visit. They might see something that would - and should - worry them.

13 August 2002

THE MANTRA THAT MEANS THIS TIME IT'S SERIOUS

How small he looked in the high-backed chair. You had to sit in the auditorium of the UN General Assembly yesterday to realise that George Bush Jnr - threatening war in what was built as a house of peace - could appear such a little man. But then again Julius Caesar was a little man and so was Napoleon Bonaparte. So were other more modern, less mentionable world leaders. Come to think of it so was General Douglas MacArthur, who had his own axis of evil, which took him all the way to the Yalu river.

But yesterday, two-thirds of the way through his virtual declaration of war, there came a little, dangerous, tell-tale code, which suggested that President Bush really does intend to send his tanks across the Tigris river. "The United States has no quarrel with the Iraqi people," he said. In the press gallery, nobody stirred. Below us, not a diplomat shifted in his seat. The speech had already rambled on for 20 minutes but the speechwriters must have known what this meant when they cobbled it together.

Before President Reagan bombed Libya in 1985, he announced that America "had no quarrel with the Libyan people." Before he bombed Iraq in 1991, Bush the Father told the world that the United States "had no quarrel with the Iraqi people". Last year Bush the Son, about the strike at the Taliban and al-Qa'ida, told us he "had no quarrel with the people of Afghanistan". And now that frightening mantra was repeated. There was no quarrel, Mr Bush said - absolutely none - with the Iraqi people. So it's flak jackets on.

Perhaps it was the right place to understand just how far the Bush administration's obsession with Iraq might take us. The green marble fittings, the backcloth wall of burnished gold and the symbol of that dangerous world shielded by the UN's palm trees gave Mr Bush the furnishings of an emperor, albeit a diminutive one. Just a day earlier, he told us, America had commemorated an attack that had "brought grief to my country".

But he didn't mention Osama bin Laden, not once. It was Saddam Hussein to whom we had to be reintroduced - he used Saddam's name seven times in his address, with countless references to the "Iraqi regime".

Riding that veil of American tears which bin Laden's killers had created, it was also clear that the Bush plans for the Middle East were on a far greater scale than the mere overthrow of the Iraqi leader who once regarded himself as America's best friend in the Gulf. There must be a democratic Afghanistan - President Hamid Karzai vigorously nodded his approval - and there must be democracy in Palestine; and this would lead to "reforms throughout the Muslim world". Reforms? In Saudi Arabia? In Jordan? In Iran? We were not told.

The Bush theme, of course, was an all too familiar one, of Saddamite evil, lashed with the usual caveats, conditional clauses and historical distortions. We all know Saddam Hussein is a vicious, cruel dictator - we knew that when he was our friend - but the President insisted on telling us again. Saddam had repeatedly flouted UN Security Council resolutions; no mention here, of course, of Israel's flouting of resolutions 242 and 338 demanding an end to the occupation of Palestinian land.

Mr Bush spoke of the tens of thousands of opponents of Saddam Hussein who had been arrested and imprisoned and summarily executed and tortured - "all of these horrors concealed from the world by the apparatus of a totalitarian state".

But there was no mention, unfortunately, that all these beatings and burnings and electric shocks and mutilations and rapes were being merrily perpetrated when America was on very good terms with Iraq before 1990, when the Pentagon was sending intelligence information to Saddam to help him kill more Iranians.

Indeed one of the most telling aspects of the Bush speech was that all the sins of which he specifically accused the Iraqis - a good proportion of which are undoubtedly true - began in the crucial year of 1991. There was no reference to Saddam's flouting of UN resolutions when the Americans were helping him. There were a few reminders by Mr Bush of the gas attacks against Iran - without mentioning that this very same Iran is now supposed to be part of the "axis of evil".

Then there were the little grammatical problems, the slight of hand historians use when they cannot find the evidence to prove that Richard III really did kill the princes in the tower. If it wasn't for the 1991 Gulf War, Iraq "would likely" have possessed a nuclear weapon by 1993. Iraq "retains the physical infrastructure need to build" a nuclear weapon - which is not the same thing as actually building it. The phrase "should Iraq acquire fissile material" doesn't mean it has. And being told that Iraq's enthusiasm for nuclear scientists "leaves little doubt" about its appetite for nuclear weapons isn't quite the same having it proved.

Maybe this supposition is true - but is that the evidence upon which America will go to war? The UN - for this was the emperor's message to the delegates sitting before him - could take it or leave it, join America in war or end up like that old donkey, the League of Nations. Believe it or not, Mr Bush actually mentioned the League, dismissing it as a talking shop without adding that the US had refused to join.

But it was clear how Mr Bush would sell his war on the back of 11 September. "Our greatest fear is that terrorists will find a shortcut to their mad ambitions when an outlaw regime supplies them with the technologies to kill on a massive scale," he said. And there you have it. Osama bin Laden equals Saddam Hussein and - who knows - Iran or Syria or anyone else. What was the name of that river which Julius Caesar crossed? Was it not called the Rubicon? Yesterday, Mr Bush may have crossed the very same river.

AUTUMN 2002: TERRIFYING NEW AGE

Flag of Al-Qa'ida

8 October 2002

TANKER ATTACK FITS BIN LADEN'S ECONOMIC WAR

To look at those images of the French oil tanker Limburg, scorched and holed off Yemen, you had to remember the very last sermon Osama bin Laden gave before he disappeared in Afghanistan last December.

The American economy, he said, would be destroyed. "Oil tankers," a Palestinian friend told me later. "If he goes for the oil tankers, the Americans will have to escort every tanker round the Gulf with a warship. Think what that would do to the price of oil."

Yesterday - as the world mulled over the Limburg captain's report of a small explosives-laden boat ramming itself against the side of his 300,000 ton double-hulled supertanker - the price of a barrel of oil duly broke the $30 envelope.

First we had the USS Cole two years ago, almost sunk by suicide bombers at the cost of 17 US sailors' lives. Then we had the al-Qa'ida men arrested in Morocco this year for allegedly planning to sink an

American or British warship off the Straits of Gibraltar. And now the Limburg.

The oil markets were yesterday studying the announcement from Yemen's Prime Minister, Abdul-Kader Bajammal, that "terrorism" was not involved. A senior State Department official seemed to back up the Yemeni contention that it was an accident. The French government did not rule out an attack.

Captain Peter Raes, speaking on behalf of Compagnie Maritime Belge, which owns the ship's operators Euronav, said: "Another vessel colliding with the tanker would never have had the energy to break through to the cargo hold tank."

Captain Raes said the force tore a very large hole 26 feet by 19 across the hull of the ship which was unlikely to have been made by any gas leakage.

"On top of that the explosion occurred on the water line - There is absolutely nothing which can trigger an explosion at that height," he said.

In Bahrain yesterday, US military sources indicated that the 5th Fleet was now examining the security of oil tanker fleets throughout the Gulf.

During the 1980-88 Iran-Iraq war, US warships were forced to accompany Kuwait-bound tankers up the Gulf to protect them from Iranian attack. One more tanker attack and the American navy could be back in the convoy business again, vulnerable to the same small killer boats that assaulted the Cole.

The price of oil would go on rising - giving Washington even greater reason to invade Iraq and lower the price of crude by seizing Saddam's oil fields.

Osama bin Laden is alive, living in Afghanistan and plotting more attacks, according to a satellite telephone conversation reportedly intercepted over the weekend. Be he on earth or in the netherworld, he must be smiling today.

14 October 2002

SLAUGHTER IN PARADISE

Why? Yesterday's crime against humanity in Bali provoked an almost identical reaction to the atrocities of 11 September 2001. Everyone wanted to know who had planted the bombs - almost certainly a satellite of Al-Qa'ida - and everyone wanted to know how the killers planned their massacre.

But no one - neither the Australian Prime Minister, John Howard, nor Tony Blair nor Jack Straw - wanted to talk about motives. "Terrorism" was the all-important word (an accurate one too), which was used to smother any discussion about what lay behind the crime.

Australians were the principal victims and their murderers must have known they would be. So why were they targeted? John Howard has been among President Bush's toughest supporters. Australia lined up to join the "war on terror" within 24 hours of the attacks on New York and Washington last year. Australian special forces have been operating with American troops in the Afghan mountains against al-Qa'ida. It's a fair bet that yesterday's savagery was al-Qa'ida hitting back.

The French have already paid a price for their initial support for Mr Bush. The killing of 11 French submarine technicians in Karachi has been followed by the suicide attack on the French oil tanker Limburg off the coast of Yemen. Now, it seems, it is the turn of Australia.

If the group which set off the three bombs in Bali is one of the "Islamist" movements on the edge of al-Qa'ida, the choice of target was familiar: a nightclub, a place associated in the mind of Islamists with sex, alcohol and immorality - the same type of target Palestinian suicide bombers have struck in Israel.

If millions of Muslims are revolted at the Bali massacre, few will approve of nightclubs. The usual moral slippage can be employed; the bombing was terrible, but ... Or so the murderers will hope.

The victims were largely young civilians, just as innocent as the thousands who died in the World Trade Centre. Civilians get no quarter in this war, whether they are investment brokers in New York, Afghan families or Australian honeymooners.

So who is next? When is Britain's turn? Where are Britons most at risk? Alas, they are scattered across the globe in embassies, on holidays, on every airline of the world. Our support for the United States - an infinitely closer alliance than any support from France - makes Britain the most likely candidate for attack after the US. Then there are the small, more vulnerable nations that give quiet assistance to the American military; Belgium, which hosts Nato HQ; Canada, whose special forces have also been operating in Afghanistan; Ireland, which allows US military aircraft to refuel at Shannon.

Bali only emphasises what the last year should have taught us: that individual innocence no longer protects us, that we are living - whether we know it or not - in a terrifying new age.

6 December 2002

AL-QA'IDA ADJUSTS TO OUR METHODS

The Americans take them shackled and hooded on to transport aircraft to Kandahar. They live in pens of eight or 10 men. They are given cots with blankets but no privacy. They are forced to urinate and defecate publicly because the Americans want to watch their prisoners at all times.

But United States forces have not only failed to hunt down Osama bin Laden while they are preparing for war in Iraq: they are finding it almost impossible to crack the al-Qa'ida network because Bin Laden's men have resorted to primitive methods of communication that cut individual members of al-Qa'ida off from all information.

This extraordinary, grim scenario comes from an American intelligence officer just back from Afghanistan who agreed to talk to The Independent - and to supply his own photographs of prisoners - on condition of anonymity. His prognoses were chilling and totally at variance with the upbeat briefings of the US Defence Secretary, Donald Rumsfeld. Even in Pakistan, he says, middle-ranking Pakistani army officers are tipping off members of al-Qa'ida to avoid American-organised raids.

"We didn't catch whom we were supposed to catch," the officer told me. "There was an over-expectation by us that technology could do more than it did. Al-Qa'ida are very smart. They basically found out how we track them. They realised that if they communicated electronically, our Rangers would swoop on them. So they started using couriers to hand-carry notes on paper or to repeat messages from their memory and this confused our system. Our intelligence is hi-tech - they went back to primitive methods that the Americans cannot adapt to."

The American officer said there were originally "a lot of high-profile arrests". But the al-Qa'ida cells didn't know what other members were doing. "They were very adaptive and became much more decentralised. We caught a couple of really high-profile, serious al-Qa'ida leaders but they couldn't tell us what specific operations were going to take place. They would know that something big was being planned but they would have no idea what it was."

The officer, who spent at least six months in Afghanistan this year, was scathing in his denunciation of General Abdul Rashid Dostam, the Uzbek warlord implicated in the suffocation of up to a thousand Taliban prisoners in container trucks. "Dostam is totally culpable and the US believes he's guilty but he's our guy and so we won't say so."

Gen Dostam uses Turkish military intelligence men as bodyguards. "There was concern in the Isaf International Security Assistance Force that the Turks who run it would create ethnic problems, which is one reason the Turkish army does not share the Kabul Isaf compounds with other Isaf troops. But one of the things we failed to do was create a real government. We let the warlords firmly entrench themselves and now they can't be dislodged," he said.

According to the same officer, American security agents in Karachi were looking for the murderers of US journalist Daniel Pearl but there, as in many other cases, they would find their arrest "targets" had fled because of secret support within middle ranks of the Pakistani army. "We would go with the Pakistanis to a location but there would be no one there because once the middle level of the Pakistani military knew of our plans, they would leak the information. In the North-West Frontier province, the frontier corps is a second-rate army - they are a lot more anti-Western in sentiment than the main Pakistani army. In the end we had to co-ordinate everything through Islamabad."

As for the hundreds of prisoners taken in Afghanistan, the American officer insisted that none were beaten "now" although he claimed ignorance about earlier evidence that soldiers based in Kandahar had broken the bones of captives after their initial arrest. "Only prisoners who were likely to be violent or unco-operative are hooded and their hands are tied behind their backs with plastic restraint bands. Sometimes we would take the hoods off prisoners when they were travelling in our helicopters, at other times not," he said.

"In Kandahar, in what we call their living areas, the prisoners are given cots with blankets and Adidas suits and runners, but they have no privacy. There are no sides to their living areas because we have to see them all the time. They have no privacy in the bathroom. Some of them masturbate when they are looking at the female guards.

Our guards had no reaction to this. They are soldiers. When the interrogations take place, the prisoners are allowed to sit. I don't want to
get into specifics about the questions we ask them.

"There was non-co-operation at the beginning. But they had a
misconception that they were going to be treated the way they treated
each other. When they're not tortured, I think this has a lot to do with
changing their opinion."

But the Americans were even short of translators. "We recruited
Farsi-speakers who can speak the local version of Persian in Afghanistan, Dari. They would be civilians hired in the US. But they had to go
through full security procedures and out of every five, only one or two
would be given security clearance."

The American officer also had a low opinion of the Western journalists he met at Bagram. "They just hung around our base all day.
Whenever we had some special operation, we'd offer the journalists
some facility to go on patrol with our special forces and off they'd go -
you know, we're on patrol with the special forces' - and they wouldn't
realise we were stringing them along to get them out of the way."

28 December 2002

HANG ON, I THOUGHT THE ENEMY WAS BIN LADEN

Who would have believed, a year ago, that it would be the beardless features of Saddam Hussein we'd have to hate rather than the
unshaven Osama bin Laden? When did it take place, this transition
from "the evil one" (Newsweek) to the Beast of Baghdad?

As usual, our newspaper and television journalists connived at
it all. Wasn't it their job to point out that something funny was going
on? Wasn't it the task of reporters to say: hang on, I thought the enemy
was Bin Laden - you've just changed the picture?

But no; Osama faded from our screens, to be replaced by Saddam. Our enemy no longer lived in Afghan caves, but on the banks of
the Tigris. And instead of graphics of Afghan mountains and Al-Qa'ida
networks, we got stories of weapons of mass destruction and human
rights abuses in Iraq.

I recall a similar phenomenon more than a decade ago. Saddam
had been our hate figure ever since he invaded Kuwait, but we had
driven the Iraqis out of our favourite emirate and, all of a sudden, General Colin Powell turned up in northern Iraq - the Kurdish bit we had

decided to save rather late in the day - talking about "Iraqi officials". I was at Mr Powell's press conference that day, and I asked him why he no longer mentioned Saddam. And he just shrugged his shoulders and went on talking about "Iraqi officials". Saddam had been airbrushed out of the US administration's script - just as he was written back in, centre stage, earlier this year.

So I owe it to Professor Robert Alford of the City University of New York Graduate Centre, who enlightened me about the mystical transition the Americans accomplished. A series of tables he has drawn up show something remarkable: that the "Iraq" story started growing - and the Osama saga diminishing - just as the Enron scandal broke. Back in January, Enron was receiving 1,137 "mentions" in The New York Times, The Washington Post and The Los Angeles Times, and Iraq only 200. Iraq stories grew almost 100 per cent by early spring as Enron mentions declined by 50 per cent to 618. After a dip in early summer, Iraq soared to 1,529 mentions, with Enron down to 310. Remarkable, isn't it, how you can clear a messy economic scandal off the front pages by renaming your hate figure?

Of course, it's also a good idea to change hate figures when your closest ally, Israel, is in danger of producing one in the form of Ariel Sharon. If we hadn't had Bin Laden and Saddam to worry about, we might all have been taking a closer look at Mr Sharon, the man who greeted the slaughter of one Hamas man and nine children in Gaza as "a great success". We might also have been taking a closer look at his involvement in the Sabra and Chatila massacre in 1982 when - as is now clear - more than a thousand male survivors of the original massacre were handed back by the Israeli army to the Phalangist mass murderers. But the failure of a few survivors to prosecute Mr Sharon in Brussels scarcely made a headline.

Then there was the Middle East peace conference that was going to take place this summer. Colin Powell announced just that in the spring. But it never happened. The "peace" conference vanished, just like Bin Laden. And we never even asked why. In a new world of secrecy, we don't bother to do that. And oddly, that's what this past year has produced: a kind of lethargy about the tragedy of the Middle East, a failure to respond to real injustice and occupation and misery. Instead, we are allowing ourselves to wander off to war in Iraq.

So let's go back - post-Enron - to the UN arms inspectors. They got into Iraq and - horror - didn't find a single microbe. Then we had to get our hands on Iraq's weapons manifesto. And when it arrived - all 12,000 pages - we complained there was too much of it.

The Americans - who would have screamed foul if Saddam had handed over a mere 10 pages - announced that it was a "blizzard", a deliberate attempt to obscure what we all knew to be true but couldn't actually find out; that Saddam had weapons of mass destruction. At which point, the Americans simply hijacked the whole document because - so we were informed - they had better security with photocopying machines and faster translators. This, remember, from the country that failed to warn us about September 11 because - yes - the interpreters couldn't translate Arabic fast enough.

It was also the year of "regime change". Not just Saddam's, but Yasser Arafat's too. Arafat must go, his corrupt regime replaced by a state-of-the-art democracy amid the ruins left by Israel's air raids. Or so we were told. Bush's decision that Arafat had to pack up ensured that the dreadful old man would be re-elected the following month. But when the Secretary of Defence, Donald Rumsfeld, referred to the "so-called" occupied territories - presumably thinking that the soldiers all over the West Bank were Swiss - it looked as if the US administration had lost its grip on Middle East reality.

So let's talk oil. Bush was an oil man. Vice-president Cheney was an oil man. Condoleezza Rice was an oil lady. And we owe it to The New York Times's most right-wing columnist, William Safire - well connected to both the Bush administration and, personally, to Ariel Sharon - to learn what all this means. In a remarkable article in October, he gave the game away about our forthcoming war in Iraq. "The government of New Iraq," he wrote, "... would reimburse the United States and Britain for much of their costs in the war and transitional government out of future oil revenues and contracts..." The evolving democratic government of New Iraq "would repudiate the corrupt $8bn debt' Russia claims was run up by Saddam..."

Far more disturbing for President Putin of Russia, according to Safire, would be "the heavy investment to be made by the US and British companies that will sharply increase the drilling and refining capacity of the only nation Iraq whose oil reserves rival those of Russia, Saudi Arabia and Mexico". I wonder if we will remember that when we go to war in the next month or so? Certainly we won't be talking about Enron.

2003: IRAQ WAR

War in Iraq

5 February 2003

DON'T MENTION THE WAR IN AFGHANISTAN

There's one sure bet about the statement to be made to the UN Security Council today by the US Secretary of State, Colin Powell - or by General Colin Powell as he has now been mysteriously reassigned by the American press: he won't be talking about Afghanistan.

For since the Afghan war is the "successful" role model for America's forthcoming imperial adventure across the Middle East, the near-collapse of peace in this savage land and the steady erosion of US forces in Afghanistan - the nightly attacks on American and other international troops, the anarchy in the cities outside Kabul, the warlordism and drug trafficking and steadily increasing toll of murders - are unmentionables, a narrative constantly erased from the consciousness of Americans who are now sending their young men and women by the tens of thousands to stage another "success" story.

This article is written in President George Bush's home state of Texas, where the flags fly at half-staff for the Columbia crew, where the dispatch to the Middle East of further troops of the 108th Air Defence Artillery Brigade from Fort Bliss and the imminent deployment from Holloman Air Force Base in neighbouring New Mexico of undisclosed numbers of F-117 Nighthawk stealth bombers earned a mere 78-word down-page inside "nib" report in the local Austin newspaper.

Only in New York and Washington do the neo-conservative pundits suggest - obscenely - that the death of the Columbia crew may well have heightened America's resolve and "unity" to support the Bush adventure in Iraq. A few months ago, we would still have been asked to believe that the post-war "success" in Afghanistan augured well for the post-war success in Iraq.

So let's break through the curtain for a while and peer into the fastness of the land that both President Bush and Prime Minister Blair promised not to forget. Hands up those who know that al-Qa'ida has a radio station operating inside Afghanistan which calls for a holy war against America? It's true. Hands up again anyone who can guess how many of the daily weapons caches discovered by US troops in the country have been brought into Afghanistan since America's "successful" war? Answer: up to 25 per cent.

Have any US troops retreated from their positions along the Afghan-Pakistan border? None, you may say. And you would be wrong. At least five positions, according to Pakistani sources on the other side of the frontier, only one of which has been admitted by US forces. On 11 December, US troops abandoned their military outpost at Lwara after nightly rocket attacks which destroyed several American military vehicles. Their Afghan allies were driven out only days later and al-Qa'ida fighters then stormed the US compound and burnt it to the ground.

It's a sign of just how seriously America's mission in Afghanistan is collapsing that the majestically conservative Wall Street Journal - normally a beacon of imperial and Israeli policy in the Middle East and South-west Asia - has devoted a long and intriguing article to the American retreat, though of course that's not what the paper calls it.

"Soldiers still confront an invisible enemy," is the title of Marc Kaufman's first-class investigation, a headline almost identical to one which appeared over a Fisk story a year or so after Russia's invasion of Afghanistan in 1979-80. The soldiers in my dispatch, of course, were Russian. Indeed, just as I recall the Soviet officer who told us all at Bagram air base that the "mujahedin terrorism remnants" were all that was left of the West's conspiracy against peace-loving (and Communist) Afghans, so I observed the American spokesmen - yes, at the very same Bagram air base - who today cheerfully assert that al-Qa'ida "remnants" are all that are left of Bin Laden's legions.

Training camps have been set up inside Afghanistan again, not - as the Americans think - by the recalcitrant forces of Gulbuddin Hekmatyar's anti-American Afghans, but by Arabs. The latest battle between US forces and enemy "remnants" near Spin Boldak in Kandahar province involved further Arab fighters, as my colleague Phil Reeves reported. Hekmatyar's Hezb-i-Islami forces have been "forging ties" with al-Qa'ida and the Taliban; which is exactly what the mujahedin "terrorist remnants" did among themselves in the winter of 1980, a year after the Soviet invasion.

An American killed by a newly placed landmine in Khost; 16 civilians blown up by another newly placed mine outside Kandahar; grenades tossed at Americans or international troops in Kabul; further reports of rape and female classroom burnings in the north of Afghanistan - all these events are now acquiring the stale status of yesterday's war.

So be sure that Colin Powell will not be boasting to the Security Council today of America's success in the intelligence war in Afghanistan. It's one thing to claim that satellite pictures show chemicals being transported around Iraq, or that telephone intercepts prove Iraqi scientists are still at their dirty work; quite another to explain how all the "communications chatter" intercepts which the US supposedly picked up in Afghanistan proved nothing. As far as Afghanistan is concerned, you can quote Basil Fawlty: "Whatever you do, don't mention the war.

18 May 2003

SO WHAT WAS THE WAR FOR?

More than 50 dead in a week. Thanks for the Iraq war. Thank you, Mr Bush and Mr Blair, for making our world safer by ridding us of the one tyrant - Saddam Hussein - who never had any connection with 11 September 2001, or with the Riyadh bombings or with the bombings in Casablanca. The "liberation" of Iraq was supposed to free us from the bombers of al-Qa'ida.

So said Mr Blair. So said Mr Straw. Could you talk to us, please, Messrs Blair and Straw? What was Iraq for? No, we don't have any "claim of responsibility" for the Casablanca massacre, but the nature of the cold calculation behind the Casablanca bombings is sufficient. One suicide bomber kills himself by blowing open the doors of the Jewish community centre. Then his surviving comrade blows himself up inside.

Weren't the Jews - like the Christians - "people of the Book", honoured by Islam? But then - and there's always a "but then" - wasn't Morocco a "friend" of the West, a country that has resorted to torture again over the past year in its pro-American battle against "terrorism", yet another country in which human rights have taken second place to President Bush's war on terror? Osama bin Laden always said that his intention was to overthrow "the corrupt monarchies of the Arab world". It was Saudi Arabia at the beginning of the week, Morocco at the end.

So, back to the point. Ten suicide bombers killed the innocent of Casablanca - that's more than half the total killers of 11 September 2001. And only five days after al-Qa'ida struck Riyadh.

Was it not President Bush who boasted to us of how America had struck a devastating blow in the "war on terror" in Iraq? Was it not Vice-President Cheney who informed us that al-Qa'ida was reeling from America's bombardment of Afghanistan? Was it not Defence Secretary Rumsfeld who would have us believe that half of al-Qa'ida's leadership was eliminated - either through capture or murder (let us speak frankly) at America's hands? So take a look at the terrain.

Afghanistan is in a state of anarchy, its pathetic government scarcely ruling over Kabul. Iraq is in an even more incipient state of anarchy, largely without electricity, money or petrol. And this is a war of good against evil? Casablanca is a sorry and pertinent page in the history of America's folly in the Arab world.

So what comes next? More boasts by President Bush that he is winning the "war against terror" or more claims - yes, he told you so - that the "war on terror" is eternal? Heaven spare us all.

11 September 2003

ALL IN THE NAME OF THE DEAD OF 11 SEPTEMBER

When the attacks were launched against the World Trade Centre and the Pentagon two years ago today, who had ever heard of Fallujah or Hillah? When the Lebanese hijacker flew his plane into the ground in Pennsylvania, who would ever have believed that President George Bush would be announcing a "new front line in the war on terror" as his troops embarked on a hopeless campaign against the guerrillas of Iraq?

Who could ever have conceived of an American president calling the world to arms against "terrorism" in "Afghanistan, Iraq and Gaza"? Gaza? What do the miserable, crushed, cruelly imprisoned Palestinians of Gaza have to do with the international crimes against humanity in New York, Washington and Pennsylvania?

Nothing, of course. Neither does Iraq have anything to do with 11 September. Nor were there any weapons of mass destruction in Iraq, any al-Qa'ida links with Iraq, any 45-minute timeline for the deployment of chemical weapons nor was there any "liberation".

No, the attacks on 11 September have nothing to do with Iraq. Neither did 11 September change the world. President Bush cruelly manipulated the grief of the American people - and the sympathy of the rest of the world - to introduce a "world order" dreamed up by a clutch of fantasists advising the Secretary of Defence, Donald Rumsfeld.

The Iraqi "regime change", as we now know, was planned as part of a Perle-Wolfowitz campaign document to the would-be Israeli prime minister Benjamin Netanyahu years before Bush came to power. It beggars belief that Tony Blair should have signed up to this nonsense without realising that it was no more nor less than a project invented by a group of pro-Israeli American neo-conservatives and right-wing Christian fundamentalists.

But even now, we are fed more fantasy. Afghanistan - its American-paid warlords raping and murdering their enemies, its women still shrouded for the most part in their burqas, its opium production now back as the world's number one export market, and its people being killed at up to a hundred a week (five American troops were shot dead two weekends ago) is a "success", something which Messrs

Bush and Rumsfeld still boast about. Iraq - a midden of guerrilla hatred and popular resentment - is also a "success". Yes, Bush wants $87bn to keep Iraq running, he wants to go back to the same United Nations he condemned as a "talking shop" last year, he wants scores of foreign armies to go to Iraq to share the burdens of occupation - though not, of course, the decision-making, which must remain Washington's exclusive imperial preserve.

What's more, the world is supposed to accept the insane notion that the Israeli-Palestinian conflict - the planet's last colonial war, although all mention of the illegal Jewish colonies in the West Bank and Gaza have been erased from the Middle East narrative in the American press - is part of the "war on terror", the cosmic clash of religious will that President Bush invented after 11 September. Could Israel's interests be better served by so infantile a gesture from Bush?

The vicious Palestinian suicide bombers and the grotesque implantation of Jews and Jews only in the colonies has now been set into this colossal struggle of "good" against "evil", in which even Ariel Sharon - named as "personally" responsible for the 1982 Sabra and Chatila massacre by Israel's own commission of inquiry - is "a man of peace", according to Mr Bush.

And new precedents are set without discussion. Washington kills the leadership of its enemies with impunity: it tries to kill Osama bin Laden and Mullah Omar and does kill Uday and Qusay Hussein and boasts of its prowess in "liquidating" the al-Qa'ida leadership from rocket-firing "drones". It tries to kill Saddam in Baghdad and slaughters 16 civilians and admits that the operation was "not risk-free". In Afghanistan, three men have now been murdered in the US interrogation centre at Bagram. We still don't know what really goes on in Guantanamo.

What do these precedents mean? I have a dark suspicion. From now on, our leaders, our politicians, our statesmen will be fair game too. If we go for the jugular, why shouldn't they? The killing of the UN's Sergio Vieira de Mello, was not, I think, a chance murder. Hamas's most recent statements - and since they've been added to the Bush circus of evil, we should take them seriously - are now, more than ever, personally threatening Mr Sharon. Why should we expect any other leader to be safe? If Yasser Arafat is driven into exile yet again, will there be any restraints left?

Of course, America's enemies were a grisly bunch. Saddam soiled his country with the mass graves of the innocents, Mullah Omar allowed his misogynist legions to terrify an entire society in Afghanistan. But in their absence, we have created banditry, rape, kidnapping, guerrilla war and anarchy. And all in the name of the dead of 11 September. The future of the Middle East - which is what 11 September was partly about, though we are not allowed to say so - has never looked bleaker or more bloody. The United States and Britain are trapped in a war of their own making, responsible for their own appalling predicament but responsible, too, for the lives of thousands of innocent human beings - cut to pieces by American bombs in Afghanistan and Iraq, shot down in the streets of Iraq by trigger-happy GIs.

As for "terror", our enemies are closing in on our armies in Iraq and our supposed allies in Baghdad and Afghanistan - even in Pakistan. We have done all this in the name of the dead of 11 September. Not since the Second World War have we seen folly on this scale. And it has scarcely begun.

THE FIGHT CONTINUES

2004-2007: BIN LADEN IS STILL HERE

MURDER OF U.S. NATIONALS OUTSIDE THE UNITED STATES; CONSPIRACY
TO MURDER U.S. NATIONALS OUTSIDE THE UNITED STATES; ATTACK ON A
FEDERAL FACILITY RESULTING IN DEATH

USAMA BIN LADEN

Aliases: Usama Bin Muhammad Bin Ladin, Shaykh Usama Bin Ladin, The Prince, The
Emir, Abu Abdallah, Mujahid Shaykh, Hajj, The Director

DESCRIPTION

Date of Birth Used:	1957	Hair:	Brown
Place of Birth:	Saudi Arabia	Eyes:	Brown
Height:	6'4" to 6'6"	Sex:	Male
Weight:	Approximately 160 pounds	Complexion: Olive	
Build:	Thin	Citizenship: Saudi Arabian	
Language:	Arabic (probably Pashtu)		
Scars and Marks:	None known		
Remarks:	Bin Laden is left-handed and walks with a cane.		

CAUTION

Usama Bin Laden is wanted in connection with the August 7, 1998, bombings of the United
States Embassies in Dar es Salaam, Tanzania, and Nairobi, Kenya. These attacks killed over
200 people. In addition, Bin Laden is a suspect in other terrorist attacks throughout the world.

REWARD

The Rewards For Justice Program, United States Department of State, is offering a reward of
up to $25 million for information leading directly to the apprehension or conviction of Usama
Bin Laden. An additional $2 million is being offered through a program developed and
funded by the Airline Pilots Association and the Air Transport Association.

SHOULD BE CONSIDERED ARMED AND DANGEROUS

FBI wanted poster

8 May 2004

BEASTIALISING OUR ENEMIES

Less than six months before the outbreak of the First World War,
my grandmother, Margaret Fisk, gave my father William a 360-page

book of imperial adventure, Tom Graham VC, A Story of the Afghan War. "Presented to Willie by his Mother," she wrote in thick pencil inside the front cover. "Willie" would have been almost 15 years old.

Only after my father's death in 1992 did I inherit this book, with its handsome, engraved hardboard cover embossed with a British Victoria Cross, and only last month did I read the book. An adventure by William Johnston and published in 1900, it tells the story of the son of a British mine-owner who grows up in the northern English port of Seaton and, forced to leave school and become an apprentice clerk because of his father's sudden impoverishment, joins the British Army underage. Tom Graham is posted to a British unit in County Cork in the south-west of Ireland - he even kisses the Blarney stone - and then travels to India and to the Second Afghan War where he is gazetted a Second Lieutenant in a Highland regiment. As he stands at his late father's grave in the local churchyard before leaving for the army, Tom vows that "he would lead a pure, clean and upright life".

The story is typical of my father's generation, a rip-roaring, racist story of British heroism and Muslim savagery. The real-life murder of the British embassy staff in Kabul in 1879 provoked a British military response and Tom Graham marches into Afghanistan with his regiment. Within days, Tom is driving his bayonet "up to the nozzle" into the chest of an Afghan, a "swarthy giant, his eyes glaring with hate". In the Kurrum Valley, Graham fights off "infuriated tribesmen, drunk with lust and plunder". The author notes that whenever British troops fell into Afghan hands, "their bodies were dreadfully mutilated and dishonoured by those fiends in human form". Afghans are a "villainous" lot at one point in the text, "rascals" at another and, of course, "fiends in human form".

The text is not only racist but also anti-Islamic. "Boy readers," the author pontificates, "may not know that it was the sole object of every Afghan engaged in the war of 1878-80 to cut to pieces every heretic he could come across. The more pieces cut out of the unfortunate Britisher the higher his summit of bliss in Paradise." After Graham is wounded in Kabul, the Afghans - in the words of his Irish-born army doctor - have become "murtherin villains, the black niggers". A British artillery officer urges his men to fire at close-packed Afghan tribesmen with the assurance that his cannon fire "will scatter the flies".

It's not difficult to see how easily my father's world of "pure, clean and upright" Britons bestialised its enemies. Though there are a few references to the "boldness" of Afghan tribesmen, no attempt is made to explain their actions. The notion that Afghans do not want foreigners invading and occupying their country does not exist in the story.

But, of course, history is not kind to latter-day liberals. For I have in my library another book of the period, a sensitive and thoughtful biography of Henry Mortimer Durand - the man who drew the "Durand Line" between Afghanistan and the British Raj - which includes a replica of an original letter sent by the real-life Durand to his biographer's sister. On 12 December 1879, he recalls, "Two Squadrons of the 9th Lancers were ordered to charge a large force of Afghans in the hope of saving our guns. The charge failed, and some of our dead were afterwards found dreadfully mutilated by Afghan knives... I saw it all."

The problem is clear. The Afghans really did chop bits off young Englishmen - later historical works would make it quite clear what bits these authors were talking about - just as Iraqis kicked the head off an American mercenary in Fallujah on 30 March this year and hanged his burned remains, along with those of a colleague, from the girder of an old British railway bridge over the Euphrates river. Our enemies are savages. So are we. First we learn to hate our enemies and bestialise them - and then we bellow our wrath and take our revenge when our enemies oblige us by behaving in exactly the way we expect them to. And then we torture them and humiliate them.

The present-day equivalent of Tom Graham VC is Hollywood, with its poisonous, racist portrayal of Arabs and Muslims. True to form, our enemies turned out, on 11 September 2001, to be as terrible as our movies made them out to be. One day, some serious research might be conducted into how far the pilot killers modelled themselves on Hollywood's version of their ruthlessness.

But it's not difficult to see how the American thugs at the Abu Ghraib prison acquired their cruelty. Born-again Christians who no doubt publicly wished to be seen upholding a "pure, clean and upright life" treated the Iraqis as if they were "fiends in human form", as "fanatics", as "flies". Hadn't the US proconsul in Iraq, Paul Bremer, described America's enemies as "dead-enders", "die-hards", "terrorists"? When the young woman involved in this torture expressed her surprise at all the fuss, I immediately understood why. Not because what she did was routine - though it clearly was - but because that is ϟ was told to treat these Iraqi prisoners. Hadn't they been killing American soldiers, setting off car bombs, murdering schoolchildren? Hollywood turned into reality.

Now maybe you don't think that entertainment influences the young, that Tom Graham VC could no more influence a young Englishman than Hollywood could bend the mind of the American guards at Abu Ghraib. Well, you would be wrong. For Bill Fisk - the "Willie" of that dedication almost a century ago - was also taken from school in a northern English seaport because his father Edward could no longer support him. He was apprenticed to a clerk, in Birkenhead. In the few notes he left before his death, Bill recalled that he tried to join the British Army underage; he travelled to Fulwood Barracks in Preston to join the Royal Field Artillery on 15 August 1914, 11 days after the start of the First World War and almost exactly six months after his mother had given him Tom Graham. Successful in enlisting two years later, Bill Fisk, too, was sent to a British battalion in County Cork. I even have a pale sepia snapshot of him then, kissing the Blarney stone. Two years later, in France, my father was gazetted a Second Lieutenant in the King's Liverpool Regiment. Was he not consciously following the life of the fictional Tom Graham?

No, Bill Fisk didn't torture prisoners - at the end of the First World War, with great nobility, he refused to command a firing party ordered to execute an Australian soldier for murder. But don't tell me we aren't conditioned by what we read and what we see as a child. All his life, Bill Fisk talked about "niggers", demeaned the Irish and talked about the "Yellow Peril" - the Chinese - as the world's greatest danger. He was a man of the Victorian age. I fear the American torturers in Iraq are creatures of our century. For if you are taught to despise your enemy as inhuman, you will - if you get the chance - cease to be a human yourself.

30 December 2004

THE MONSTER HAS BEEN BORN

This was the year the 'war on terror' " an obnoxious expression which we all parroted after 11 September 2001 " appeared to be almost as endless as George Bush once claimed it would be. And unsuccessful. For, after all the bombing of Afghanistan, the overthrow of the Taliban, the invasion of Iraq and its appallingly tragic aftermath, can anyone claim today that they feel safer than they did a year ago?

We have gone on smashing away at the human rights we trumpeted at the Russians " and the Arabs " during the Cold War. We have perhaps fatally weakened all those provisions that were written into our treaties and conventions in the aftermath of the Second World War to make the world a safer place. And we claim we are winning.

Where, for example, is the terror? In the streets of Baghdad, to be sure. And perhaps again in our glorious West if we go on with this folly. But terror is also in the prisons and torture chambers of the Middle East. It is in the very jails to which we have been merrily sending out trussed-up prisoners these past three years. For Jack Straw to claim that men are not being sent on their way to torture is surely one of the most extraordinary " perhaps absurd is closer to the mark " statements to have been made in the 'war on terror'. If they are not going to be tortured " like the luckless Canadian shipped off to Damascus from New York " then what is the purpose of sending them anywhere?

And how are we supposed to 'win' this war by ignoring all the injustices we are inflicting on that part of the world from which the hijackers of September 11 originally came? How many times have Messrs Bush and Blair talked about 'democracy'? How few times have they talked about 'justice', the righting of historic wrongs, the ending of torture? Our principal victims of the 'war on terror', of course, have been in Iraq (where we have done quite a bit of torturing ourselves).

But, strange to say, we are silent about the horrors the people of Iraq are now enduring. We do not even know " are not allowed to know " how many of them have died. We know that 1,100 Iraqis died by violence in Baghdad in July alone. That's terror.

But how many died in the other cities of Iraq, in Mosul and Kirkuk and Irbil, and in Amara and Fallujah and Ramadi and Najaf and Kerbala and Basra? Three thousand in July? Or four thousand? And if those projections are accurate, we are talking about 36,000 or 48,000 over the year " which makes that projected post-April 2003 figure of 100,000 dead, which Blair ridiculed, rather conservative, doesn't it?

It's not so long ago, I recall, that Bush explained to us that all the Arabs would one day wish to have the freedoms of Iraq. I cannot think of an Arab today who would wish to contemplate such ill fortune, not least because of the increasingly sectarian nature of the authorities, elected though they are.

The year did allow Ariel Sharon to achieve his aim of turning his colonial war into part of the 'war on terror'. It also allowed al-Qa'ida's violence to embrace more Arab countries. Jordan was added to Egypt. Woe betide those of us who are now locked into the huge military machine that embraces the Middle East. Why, Iraqis sometimes ask me, are American forces " aerial or land " in Uzbekistan? And Kazakhstan and Afghanistan, in Turkey and Jordan (and Iraq) and in Kuwait and Qatar and Bahrain and Oman and Yemen and Egypt and Algeria (there is a US special forces unit based near Tamanrasset, co-operating with the same Algerian army that was involved in the massacre of civilians the 1990s)?

In fact, just look at the map and you can see the Americans in Greenland and Iceland and Britain and Germany and ex-Yugoslavia and Greece " where we join up with Turkey. How did this iron curtain from the ice cap to the borders of Sudan emerge? What is its purpose? These are the key questions that should engage anyone trying to understand the 'war on terror'.

And what of the bombers? Where are they coming from, these armies of suiciders? Still we are obsessed with Osama bin Laden. Is he alive? Yes. But does he matter? Quite possibly not. For he has created al-Qa'ida. The monster has been born. To squander our millions searching for people like Bin Laden is about as useless as arresting nuclear scientists after the invention of the atom bomb. It is with us.

Alas, as long as we are not attending to the real problems of the Middle East, of its record of suffering and injustice, it " al-Qa'ida " will still be with us. My year began with a massive explosion in Beirut, just 400 metres from me, as a bomb killed the ex-prime minister Rafiq Hariri. It continued on 7 July when a bomb blew up two trains back from me on the Piccadilly line. Oh, the dangerous world we live in now. I suppose we all have to make our personal choices these days. Mine is that I am not going to allow 11 September 2001 to change my world. Bush may believe that 19 Arab murderers changed his world. But I'm not going to let them change mine. I hope I'm right.

5 November 2005

A POET ON THE RUN IN FORTRESS EUROPE

Mohamed sits on the chair beside me in Amsterdam and opens his little book of poetry. His verse slopes down the page in delicate Persian script, the Dari language of his native Afghanistan. 'God, why in the name of Islam is there all this killing, why all this anti-people killing ... the only chairs left in my country are chairs for the government, those who want to destroy Afghanistan.' He reads his words of anger slowly, gently interrupted by an old chiming Dutch clock. Outside, the Herengracht canal slides gently beneath the rain. It would be difficult to find anywhere that least resembles Kabul.

'The donkeys came to Afghanistan, Massoud, Rahbani and the rest,' Mohamed reads on. 'All the people were waiting for the donkeys. Gulbudin said these donkeys have no tails " 'only I have a tail, so I shall have a ministry,' he said. The donkeys are now in the government.' Donkeys may be nice, friendly beasts to us, but to call anyone in the Muslim world a khar " a donkey " is as insulting as you can get. Mohamed was talking about the 'mujahedin' guerrilla fighters who moved into Kabul after the Russian withdrawal in 1990, an arrival that presaged years of civil war atrocities which left at least 65,000 Afghans dead. This was the conflict which so sickened the anti-Soviet fighter Osama bin Laden that he left Afghanistan for Sudan.

Mohamed looks at me " a small energetic man with dark, sharp eyes. 'I wanted future generations to know what we went through, to understand our pain,' he says to me. I couldn't stop myself writing this poetry.' This was his mistake. Betrayed to the 'mujahedin', he was thrown into a foul prison in Kabul, rescued only by the intercession of his father. The Taliban came next and Mohamed could not prevent his pen from betraying him again. 'I kept my poetry 'under the table', as we say, but someone at my office found a poem I had written called Out of Work and told the boss who was a mullah.' When he knew that he had been discovered, Mohamed ran in terror from his office to his father's home.

Mohamed seems to spend his life on the run. He and his wife and three children live in the north of Holland, desperate to stay in the land to which they fled six years ago, but the courts " in the new spirit of anti-immigrant, anti-Muslim Europe " have rejected their pleas to stay. Mohamed's papers have expired. Now he waited in fear for the policeman who would demand: 'Your papers please.' A family friend, Hoji Abdul-Rahman, originally arranged for Mohamed and his family to flee Kabul for Jalalabad and then across the Afghan border to Pakistan where 'Hoji' " an honorific title bestowed on those who have made the pilgrimage to Mecca " obtained fake visas and passports that enabled them to fly to Holland. 'I went straight to the police to tell them we were here,' Mohamed said. 'They were very good to us. They told us to register at Zevenaar as asylum-seekers, which we did.'

He was housed in a small Dutch village where the local people treated the Afghan family with great kindness. 'They always came to see us in our flat and gave us food and invited us to their homes,' Mohamed said, producing a sad poem entitled Thank You for Everything in tribute to the Dutch people. But fate struck Mohamed again. Had the last of four court hearings into his case have dated his refugee status from the day he arrived in Holland rather than that of his first visit to Zevenaar in 2000 " which was delayed because the Dutch authorities were enjoying the week-long millennium celebrations " he would probably have qualified for permanent refugee status.

'But the court dated my arrival from the delayed registration at Zevenaar and told me my family had to leave Holland. They said that the Taliban had been defeated and that Afghanistan was now a 'democracy'. But they wouldn't accept that Karzai's government includes many of the 'mujahedin' warlords who locked me up in prison. They will do the same again.' Which is probably true. But now Mohamed, his wife and three children " one of them born in Holland " wait for the police to take them to Schipol airport for the long journey back to their dangerous homeland.

The ferocious murder of film-maker Theo van Gogh and the callous behaviour of his Muslim murderer " who announced in court that he felt no compassion for van Gogh's family " has hardened Dutch government hearts just as the rioting in Clichy-sous-Bois has hardened those of Messrs Sarkozy and Chirac. So what am I to say to Mohamed as he sits hunched in the deep, soft armchair of my hotel room, clutching his poetry book and his sack of expired refugee papers, a mechanical engineer with a foreign language degree from a Ukrainian university who must now clear garbage from Dutch apartment blocks to earn money? I can't help you, I say quietly. I will write about you. I will try to pump some compassion out of the authorities. But the days of such humanity " if they ever existed in Britain " have run out.

Next day, I am giving a lecture in the Belgian city of Antwerp when a man in the audience starts to berate me. 'Why should we help Afghans or Iraqis or other Muslims when their own governments treat them like shit?' he asked. 'Why should we have to save them from their own people. Why do we have to treat them better?' I explain that it was us " we, the West " who armed the 'mujahedin' to fight the Russians and then ignored Afghanistan when it collapsed into civil war, that we nurtured the Taliban via Saudi Arabia and Pakistan when we thought we could negotiate with them for a gas pipeline across Afghanistan, that the current US ambassador in Iraq " that other blood-drenched democratic success story " was once involved with the company Unocal, which negotiated with the Taliban over the pipeline route, that Karzai had also been working for Unocal. To no avail.

Our new moral compass, it seems, is no longer 'Saddam was worse than us' but 'why should we treat Muslims any better than they treat each other?'. And now we know that the CIA is holding other Muslims in bunkers deep beneath the earth of democratic Romania and brave old democratic Poland for a little torture, what hope is there for Mohamed? For him " and for us in Britain soon if Lord Blair of Kut al-Amara gets his way " it will be a familiar story from Europe's dark past. Vos papiers, Monseiur. Arbeitspapiere, bitte schon. Your papers, please.

20 January 2006

STILL HE ELUDES, THREATENS, AND TAUNTS US

So why only on audio? Why no video tape? Is he sick? Yes, say the usual American "intelligence sources". It's the same old story: Osama bin Laden talks to us from the mouth of a cave, from within a cave, from a basement perhaps, from a tape almost certainly recorded down a telephone line from far away. Yesterday's message, broadcast as ever by al-Jazeera television, was a reminder that security - not sickness - decides his method of communication.

We invaded Afghanistan to find Bin Laden and we fight and die in Iraq to kill his supporters - yet still he eludes us, still he threatens us, still he taunts us.

How much longer can this nonsense go on? President Jacques Chirac warns that France - of all countries - might use nuclear weapons, if attacked. On whom, I wonder? America blows Pakistani children to pieces and claims it has killed five wanted men, including a bomb-maker. But there's absolutely no evidence Bin Laden says that America will be attacked again unless it accepts a truce in the wars in Iraq and Afghanistan. Weren't we supposed to be winning the "war on terror"? Oh no, the "experts" tell us, Bin Laden and al-Qa'ida are losing, that's why they want a truce. Some hope.

It's a game. Bin Laden has no intention of calling an end to his own war and nor has George Bush and nor has Tony Blair. The Bin Laden offer, almost certainly, is intended to be rejected. He wants Bush and Blair to refuse it. Then, after the next attack, will come the next audio tape. See what happens when you reject our ceasefire? We warned you. And we'll ask: is it him? So why no video tape? Never before in history have so many wanted men sent pictures and messages and video tapes out of the dark.

The irony, of course, is that Bin Laden is now partly irrelevant. He has created al-Qa'ida. His achievement - that word should be seen in context - is complete. Why bother hunting for him now? It's a bit like arresting the world's nuclear scientists after the invention of the atom bomb. The monster has been born. It's al-Qa'ida we have to deal with.

So we are told that America's security hasn't prevented an attack, that "operations' take time to prepare. "It is better not to fight the Muslims on their land,' Bin Laden says. "We'd not mind offering you a truce that is fair in the long term... so we can build Iraq and Afghanistan," he says. Forget for a moment the deep cynicism behind this message - deconstructing the Shia of Iraq seems to be one of the Iraqi insurgents' aims - it also reveals one of Bin Laden's old themes: the idea that these wars will bankrupt the United States.

"There is no shame in this solution because it prevents the wasting of billions of dollars... to the merchants of war.' These are almost the same words Bin Laden used to me when we last met. "The Americans will be bankrupted," he said, not realising that war primes the pumps of a superpower economy.

It is as if both "sides" in this conflict live on illusions. Mssrs Bush and Blair keep telling us things in Iraq are getting better, when we all know that they are getting worse. Anarchy has seized that entire country. American bodies coming home to the United States? Just don't let the press take photographs of the coffins. Bombs in London? Nothing to do with Iraq, Blair haplessly told us last July.

Now there's a website in Spanish about Iraq on the White House screens. Why? Because the Spaniards are interested in the war their army has left? Or because so many of the American soldiers dying in Iraq are Hispanics? And now we have Paul Bremer, America's equally hapless former pro-consul in Baghdad, telling us that those same Spanish troops contributed to the uprising in Najaf because they weren't performing their tasks in Iraq. More nonsense. What started the uprising was Bremer's own anger at an attack on him in a tiny Shia Muslim newspaper which he ordered to be closed (in an announcement of execrable Arabic). It was this which prompted Muqtada al-Sadr to fight the Americans.

And so we go on. Blame foreign fighters - even if 158,000 of them in Iraq happen to be wearing American uniforms - blame Syria, blame Iran. And blame Spain of course. Blame anyone who is not "with us".

In truth, it will need Iran and Syria to help get the US and Britain out of this shameful adventure. But what do we do? Raise the stakes on Iran by claiming that it intends to make nuclear weapons. And why Iran? Why not that infinitely more unstable Islamic state called Pakistan which has nuclear weapons? Because its dictator, President General Musharraf is on "our side". Why not attack North Korea, whose leader is more unstable than any Iranian cleric? Because he also has nuclear weapons.

In Afghanistan, the Taliban are slowly returning. Outside Kabul every woman wears a burqa. Weren't they supposed to have taken them off? Weren't women now "free" in Afghanistan? US troops are being killed at an increasing rate there. Weren't they supposed to have won? Now Canada has split its troops and sent a battalion to Kandahar to fight the Taliban and al-Qa'ida. What are the Canadians now doing in combat operations? What risks does this now pose for the Canadian nation which kept out of Iraq?

It was only a few months ago that Bin Laden was bombarding us with explanations for his movement's attacks. Why did no one ask, he said, why Sweden was not assaulted? And so, I suppose, we can indeed fear more attacks on the United States, more bombing raids, further chapters in the "war on terror".

And all the time we in the West fail to look for a way to end this "war". How about some justice in the Middle East? How about lifting the blanket of injustice that has lain across the region for so many decades? Muslims there will probably like some of the democracy we say we're trying to export to them. They would also like human rights off our Western supermarket shelves.

But they would also like another kind of freedom - freedom from us. And this, it seems, we are not going to give them. So the war goes on. Stand by for more audio tapes, and more threats, and more death.

8 October 2006

'I AM WAITING FOR THE NEXT EXPLOSION'

A few days after Lebanon's latest war came to an end, I went through many of the reporter's notebooks I have used in my last 30 years in the Middle East. Some contained the names of dead colleagues, others the individual stories of the suffering of Arabs and Kurds and Christians and Jews. One, dated 1991, is even splashed with a dark and viscous substance, the oil that came raining down on us from the skies over the Kuwaiti desert after Saddam blew up the wells of the Emirate. It was only after a few minutes that I realised what I was looking for: some hint, back in the days of dangerous innocence, of what was going to happen on 11 September 2001.

And sure enough, in one notebook, part of a transcript of an interview I gave in Toronto in the late 1990s, I see myself trying to discourage the Middle East optimism of my host. "There is an explosion coming in the Middle East," I tell him. What was this explosion I was talking about? I find myself writing almost the same thing a couple of years later in The Independent - I refer to "the explosion to come" without locating it in the Middle East at all. What was I talking about? And then, most disturbingly, I re-run parts of a film series I made with the late Michael Dutfield for Channel 4 and Discovery in 1993. Called From Beirut to Bosnia, it was billed as an attempt to record "Muslims growing anger towards the West."

In one sequence, I walk into a destroyed mosque in a Bosnian village called Cela. And I hear my voice on the soundtrack, saying: "When I see things like this, I think of the place I work, the Middle East... I wonder what the Muslim world has in store for us... Maybe I should end each of my reports with the words: 'Watch out!' " And when I checked back to my post-production notes, I find the dates of all our film sequences listed. I had walked into that Bosnian mosque, watched by Serb policemen, on 11 September 1993. My warning was exactly eight years too early.

I don't like journalists who, in middle age, start to pontificate morbidly about the wickedness of a world that should be full of love, or who rummage through old notebooks in search of pessimism. So I own up at once. Surely we don't have to be weighed down by the baggage of history, always looking backwards and holding up billboards with the "The End of the World is Nigh" written in black for readers too bored to look at the fine print. Yet when I sit on my seafront balcony today, I am waiting for the next explosion to come.

Beirut is a good place to reflect on the tragedy through which the Middle East is now inexorably moving. After all, the city has suffered so many horrors these past 31 years, it seems haunted by the mass graves that lie across the region, from Afghanistan to Iraq to "Palestine" and to Lebanon itself. And I look across the waters and see a German warship cruising past my home, part of Nato's contribution to stop gunrunning into Lebanon under UN Security Council Resolution 1701. And then, I ask myself what the Germans could possibly be doing when no guns have ever been run to the Hizbollah guerrilla army from the sea. The weapons came through Syria, and Syria has a land frontier with the country and is to the north and east of Lebanon, not on the other side of the Mediterranean.

And then when I call on my landlord to discuss this latest, hopeless demonstration of Western power, he turns to me in some anger and says, "Yes, why is the German navy cruising off my home?" And I see his point. For we Westerners are now spreading ourselves across the entire Muslim world. In one form or another, "we" - "us", the West - are now in Khazakstan, Afghanistan, Pakistan, Iraq, Egypt, Algeria, Yemen, Qatar, Bahrain, Kuwait, Saudi Arabia, Oman and Lebanon. We are now trapped across this vast area of suffering, fiercely angry people, militarily far more deeply entrenched and entrapped than the 12th-century crusaders who faced defeat at the battle of Hittin, our massive forces fighting armies of Islamists, suicide bombers, warlords, drug barons, and militias. And losing. The latest UN army in Lebanon, with its French and Italian troops, is moving in ever greater numbers to the south, young men and women who have already been threatened by al-Qa'ida and who will, in three of four months, be hit by al-Qa'ida. Which is one reason why the French have been palisading themselves into their barracks in southern Lebanon. There is no shortage of suicide bombers here, although it will be the Sunni - not the Hizbollah-Shiite variety - which will strike at the UN.

When will the bombers arrive? After further massacres in Iraq? After the Israelis cross the border again? After Israel - or the US - bombs Iran's nuclear facilities in the coming months? After someone in the northern city of Tripoli, perhaps, or in the Palestinian camps outside Sidon, decides he has seen too many Western soldiers trampling the lands of southern Lebanon, too many German warships off the coast, or heard too many mendacious statements of optimism from George W Bush or Tony Blair or Condoleezza Rice. "There will be no 'new' Middle East, Miss Rice," a new Hizbollah poster says south of Sidon. And the Hizbollah is right. The entire region is sinking deeper into bloodshed and all the time, over and over again, Bush and Blair tell us it is all getting much better, that we can all be heartened by the spread of non-existent democracies, that the dawn is rising on Condi's "new" Middle East. Are they really hoping that they can distort the mirror of the world's reality with their words? There is a kind of new dawn rising in the lands from the old Indian empire to the tides of the Mediterranean. The only trouble is that it is blood red.

It is as if the Bushes and Blairs do not live on this planet any more. As my colleague Patrick Cockburn wrote recently, the enraging thing about Blair's constant optimism is that, to prove it all a pack of lies, a journalist has to have his throat cut amid the anarchy which Blair says does not exist. The Americans cannot protect themselves in Iraq, let alone the Iraqis, and the British have twice nearly been defeated in battles with the Taliban, and the Israeli army - counting it as part of the "West" for a moment - were soundly thrashed when they crossed the border to fight the Hizbollah, losing 40 men in 36 hours. Yet still Blair delayed a ceasefire in Lebanon. And still - be certain of this - when the fire strikes us again, in London or New York or wherever, Blair and Bush will say that the attack has nothing to do with the Middle East, that Britain's enemies hate "our values" or our "way of life".

I once mourned the lack of titans in the modern world, the Roosevelts and the Churchills, blood-drenched though their century was. Blair and Bush, posing as wartime leaders, threatening the midget Hitlers around them, appear to have gone through a kind of "stasis", a psychological inability to grasp what they do not want to hear or what they do not want to be true. And they have lost the thread of history.

In the past, we - the "West" - could have post-war adventures abroad and feel safe at home. No North Korean tried to blow himself up on the London Tube in the 1950s. No Viet Cong ever arrived in Washington to assault the United States. We fought in Kenya and Malaya and Palestine and Suez and Yemen, but we felt safe in Gloucestershire. Perhaps the change came with the Algerian War of Independence when the bombers attacked in Paris and Lyons, or perhaps it came later when the IRA arrived to bomb London.

But it is a fact that "we" cannot take our armies and warships and tanks and helicopter gunships and para battalions foreign wars and expect to be unhurt at home. This is the inescapable logic of history that Bush and Blair will not face, will not acknowledge, will not believe - will not even let us believe. All across the Middle East, we are locked in battle in our preposterous "war on terror" because "the world changed forever" on 11 September, even though I have said many times that we should not allow 19 murderers to change our world. So we live in a darker world of phone-taps and "terror plots" and underground CIA prisoners whose interrogators set about victims in secret, tearing to pieces the Geneva Conventions so painfully constructed after the Second World War.

And in a world betrayed. Remember all those promises we made to the Arabs about creating a wonderful new functioning democracy in Iraq whose example would be followed by other Middle East states? And remember our promise to honour the fledgling democracy of Lebanon, the famous "Cedars Revolution" - a title invented by the US State Department, so the Lebanese should have been suspicious - which brought the retreat of the Syrian army. Lebanon was then held up to be a future model for the Arab world. But once the Hizbollah crossed the frontier and seized two Israeli soldiers, killing three others on 12 July, we stood back and watched the Lebanese suffer. "If there is one thing this last war has convinced me of," a young Lebanese woman put it to me this month, "it is that the Lebanese are on their own. I can never trust a foreign promise again."

And this is true. For the direct result of the disastrous Israeli campaign has been to turn the Hizbollah into heroes of the Arab - indeed the Muslim - world, to break apart the fragile political stability established by the Lebanese prime minister, Fouad Siniora, and to have Hizbollah's leader, Sayed Hassan Nasrallah, declare a "divine victory" and demand a "national unity" government which, if it comes about, will be pro-Syrian. The language now being used in Lebanon by the country's political leaders is approaching the incendiary, lethal grammar of pre-civil war Lebanon.

Samir Geagea, the Christian ex-militia commander, brought out tens of thousands of supporters to jeer at Nasrallah. "They demand a strong state but how can a strong state be built with a statelet in its midst?" Geagea demanded to know after the Hizbollah suddenly announced that it has no intention of handing over its weapons. Indeed, Nasrallah is now boasting that he still has 20,000 missiles in southern Lebanon, a claim which led the Druze leader, Walid Jumblatt, to abuse Nasrallah as a creature of Syria - there is speculation over the depth of his relationship with Damascus but his arms certainly come from Iran - and to say to him: "Sayed Nasrallah, rest your mind, I will not reach an agreement with you. When you separate yourself from the Syrian leadership, I will possibly hold a dialogue with you." Thus two more paper-thin links - between Lebanon's Druze community and the Christians and the larger population of Shiite Muslims - have been broken. And that is how civil wars start.

Had Bush - indeed Blair - denounced Israel's claim that it held the Lebanese government responsible for the kidnapping and killing of its soldiers, and demanded an immediate ceasefire, then the disaster that is destroying Lebanon's democracy would not have happened. But no, Bush and Blair let the bloodshed go on and postponed hopes of a ceasefire for the Lebanese upon whom they had lavished so much praise a year ago. Just last week, the Lebanese recovered the bodies of five more children under the rubble of the Sidon Vocational Training Centre in Tyre. Ali Alawiah identified his children Aya, Zeinab and Hussein and his nephews Battoul and Abbas. All would have been alive if even Blair and Margaret Beckett had demanded a ceasefire. But they are dead. And Blair and Beckett and Bush should have this on their conscience.

The fact they don't speak sorrowfully of our double standard of morality. Almost all Lebanon's 1,300 dead - which comes close to half the total of the World Trade Centre murders - were civilians. But we don't care for them as we do our own "kith and kin". This is the same sickness that pervades our policies in Iraq where we never counted the number of civilians killed, only the tally of our precious soldiers who died there.

How did we come to be infected by this virus of negligence and betrayal? Does it really go back to the Crusades or the ramblings of

Spanish Christians of the 15th century - whose portrayals of the Prophet Mohamed were infinitely more obscene than Denmark's third-rate cartoonist - or to the vicious anti-Muslim ravings of long-forgotten Popes who seem to obsess the present incumbent of the Vatican? I am still uncertain what Benedict meant by his quotation of the old man of Byzantium - while I am equally suspicious of his almost equally insulting remarks at Auschwitz where he blamed Nazi Germany's cruelty on a mere "gang of criminals". But then again, this is a Pope - anti-divorce, anti-homosexual and, once, anti-aircraft - who has signally failed to follow John Paul II's devotions on the need for the seed of Abraham to acknowledge the love they should show to each other.

This failure to see the Other as the same as "us" is now evident across the Middle East. Some months ago, I received letters originally written to his family by a young Marine officer in Iraq who was trying - eloquently, I have to add - to explain how frustrating his work with Iraqis had become. "There is something culturally childish in their understanding of Western governance and management that will require immeasurable education and probably several generations to overcome if they find it of any interest," he wrote. "Our understanding of their tribal governance and its relationship to formal civil management is equally naïve and charges our frustration... The reality is that they cannot, culturally, comprehend our altruism or believe our stated intentions... Liberation will compete with invasion as our legacy but locally we are ideologically irrelevant... I share the American fascination with action and it has consistently betrayed us in our foreign policy."

The reality in Iraq is summed up by the same American Marine officer's description of the building of the Ramadi glass factory, a story that shows just how vacuous all the stories of our "success" there are. "The Division has poured hundreds of thousands of dollars into a glass factory. It does not work. It will take millions of dollars to rehabilitate and modernise. There are supposed to be 2,500 Iraqis employed there but they have nothing to do and no more than 100 arrive on any given day to sit in their offices as new computers and furniture are delivered with our compliments... It is like walking through a fictional business that physically exists. It may be Kafka's revenge. Most rooms are empty but are still preserved as they had been under a layer of dust. Some areas hold a man at a desk in a stark room too large for him. It is like Pompeii being slowly reoccupied, as if nothing had happened. I stood on a tall mound of broken glass outside. Shards of window panes shattered in the process of manufacturing them. The windows of the city were poured and cut here once... This glass was made from sand, desert made invisible until exposed by reflection. The bright sunlight makes little impression on the pile due to a dull coating of dust but the fragments fracture further and slide beneath my feet with the sound of ruin. Walking on windows and unable to see the ground." Could there be a more Conradian description of the failure of the American empire in Iraq?

And does it not echo a remark that TE Lawrence - Lawrence of Arabia - made of Iraq in the 1920s: "Do not try to do too much with your own hands. Better the Arabs do it tolerably than that you do it perfectly... Actually, also, under the very odd conditions of Arabia, your practical work may not be as good as, perhaps, you think."

A different kind of alienation, of course, is reflected in our dispute with Iran. "We" think that its government wants to make nuclear weapons - in six months, according to the Israelis; in 10 years, according to some nuclear analysts. But no one asks if "we" didn't help to cause this "nuclear" crisis. For it was the Shah who commenced Iran's nuclear power programme in 1973 and Western companies were shoulder-hopping each other in their desire to sell him nuclear reactors and enrichment technology. Siemens, for example, started to build the Bushehr reactor. And the Shah was regularly interviewed on Western television stations where he said that he didn't see why Iran shouldn't have nuclear weapons when America and the Soviets had them. And we had no objection to the ambitions of "our" Policeman of the Gulf.

And when Ayatollah Khomeini's Islamic revolution engulfed Iran, what did he do? He called the nuclear programme "the work of the devil" and closed it down. It was only when Saddam Hussein invaded Iran the following year and began showering Iran with missiles and chemical weapons - an invasion supported by "us" - that the clerical regime decided they may have to use nuclear weapons against Iraq and reopened the complex. In other words, it was the West which supported Iran's original nuclear programme and it was closed by the chief divine of George Bush's "axis of evil" and then reopened when the West stood behind Saddam (in the days when he was "our strongman" rather than our caged prisoner in a dying state).

The greater irony, of course, is that if we were really concerned about the spread of nuclear technology among Muslim states, we would be condemning Pakistan, most of whose cities are in a state of almost Iraqi anarchy and whose jolly dictator now says he was threatened with being "bombed back to the Stone Age" by the Americans if he didn't sign up to the "war on terror". Now it happens that Pakistan is infinitely more violent than Iran and it also happens that it was a close Pakistani friend of the Pakistani President-General Pervez Musharraf - a certain scientist called Abdul Qadeer Khan - who actually gave solid centrifuge components to Iran. But all that has been taken out of the story. And so they will remain out of the narrative because Pakistan already has a bomb and may use it if someone decided to create a new Stone Age in that former corner of the British empire.

But all this raises a more complex question. Are we really going to carry on arguing for years - for generation after generation of crisis - over who has or doesn't have nuclear technology or the capacity to build a bomb? Are "we" forever going to decide who may have a bomb on the basis of his obedience to us - Mr Musharraf now being a loyal Pakistani shah - or his religion or how many turbans are worn by ministers in the government. Are we still going to be doing this in 2007 or 2107 or 3006?

What I suspect lies behind much of our hypocrisy in the Middle East is that Muslims have not lost their faith and we have. It's not just that religion governs their lives, it is the fact that they have kept the faith - and that is why we try to hide that we have lost it by talking about Islam's "difficulty with secularism". We are the good liberals who wish to bestow the pleasures of our Enlightenment upon the rest of the world, although, to the Muslim nations, this sounds more like our desire to invade them with different cultures and traditions and - in some cases - different religions.

And Muslims have learnt to remember. I still recall an Iraqi friend, shaking his head at my naivety when I asked if there was not any cup of generosity to be bestowed on the West for ridding Iraqis of Saddam's presence. "You supported him," he replied. "You supported him when he invaded Iran and we died in our tens of thousands. Then, after the invasion of Kuwait, you imposed sanctions that killed tens of thousands of our children. And now you reduce Iraq to anarchy. And you want us to be grateful?"

And I recalled seeing a train load of gassed Iranian soldiers on the way to Tehran, coughing up mucus and blood into stained handkerchiefs and coughing up the gas too because I suddenly smelled a kind of dirty perfume and walked down the train opening all the windows. I saw their vast wobbling blisters upon which ever-smaller blisters would form, one on top of the other. And where did this filthy stuff come from, this real weapon of mass destruction Saddam was using? Components came from Germany and from the US. No wonder US Lieutenant Rick Francona noted indifferently in a report to the Pentagon that the Iraqis had drenched Fao in gas when he visited the battlefield during the war. So do we expect the Iranians to be grateful that we eventually toppled Saddam?

Needless to say, the division between Shias and Sunnis - especially in Iraq - can reach stages of cruelty not seen since the European Protestant-Catholic wars; nor, in this context, should we forget the conflict we are still trying to control in Northern Ireland. Islam as a society, rather than a religion, does have to face the "West"; it must find, in the words of that fine former Iranian president Mohamad Khatami, a "civil society". And it is outrageous that Muslims have not condemned the slaughter in Darfur or, indeed, in Iraq and, one might add, on the battlefields of the Iran-Iraq war where one and a half million Muslims killed each other over almost eight years. Self-criticism is not in great supply across the Muslim world where, of course, our spirited Western political conflicts and elections sometimes look like self-flagellation.

As for our desire to award the Muslim Middle East with "our" democratic systems, it's not just in Lebanon that we have proved to be much less enthusiastic about its existence in the Arab world. The former US ambassador to Iraq - once he realised the Shiites would join the Sunni resistance if they did not have elections, for democracy was originally not going to be America's gift there - accepted a dominant role for Muslim clerics in the government, thus ensuring discrimination against women in marriage, divorce and inheritance.

When Daniel Fried, the US Assistant Secretary of State for European and Eurasian Affairs visited Paris last year, he lectured European and Arab diplomats on what he called "the US-European imperative to support democratic reform and democratic reformers in the Middle East" - forgetting, it seems, that just such a man, Khatami, existed in Iran but had been snubbed by the US. His failure as a genuinely elected president produced his somewhat cracked successor. Fried, however, insisted that bringing democracy to the Middle East "is not for us a question of political theory, but of central strategic importance", something that clearly didn't matter less than a year later in Lebanon and certainly not when the Palestinians participated in genuine elections, of which more later.

Fried took the risky step of quoting the French historian Alexis de Tocqueville to back his claim that democracy, far from being a fragile flower, was "robust, and its applicability is potentially universal". The former French foreign minister, Hubert Védrine, was invited to reply to respond to Fried's words and he cynically spoke of "people who have historical experience, who have seen how past experiences turned out", the subtext of which was: "You Americans have no sense of history." Védrine spoke of meeting with Madeleine Albright when she was the US Foreign Secretary. "I told her we had no problem regarding the objective of democracy, but I asked whether it was a process, or a religious conversion, like Saint Paul on the road to Damascus." And he quoted the Mexican writer, Octavio Pas: "Democracy is not like Nescafé, you don't just add water." For historical reasons, Védrine told Fried, "Because of colonialism, the Middle East is the region of the world where external intervention is most at risk of being rejected."

And when it is imposed, as America says it would like to do in Damascus, what will happen? A nice, flourishing electoral process to put Syrians in power or another descent into Iraqi-style horrors with a Sunni-Muslim regime in place in Damascus?

And so to "Palestine" - the inverted commas are more important than ever today - and its own act of democracy. Of course, the Palestinians elected the wrong people, Hamas, and had to suffer for it. Democratic Israel would not accept the results of Palestine's democratic elections and the Europeans joined with America in placing sanctions against the newly elected government unless it recognised Israel and all agreements signed with Israel since the Camp David accords of the 1970s. Even when Ariel Sharon was staging his withdrawal of 8,500 settlers from Gaza last year, he was shifting 12,000 more settlers into the West Bank, and George W Bush had effectively accepted this illegality by talking of the "realities" of the Jewish settlements still being enlarged there. And that was the end of UN Security Council Resolutions 242 and 338 upon which the "peace process" was supposed to be based - Israeli withdrawal from territories occupied in the 1967 Middle East war, in return for the security of all states in the area.

One of the few honourable American statesmen to grasp what this portends is ex-President Jimmy Carter, who wrote after the Palestinian elections in May this year that "innocent Palestinian people are being treated like animals, with the presumption that they are guilty of some crime. Because they voted for candidates who are members of Hamas, the US government has become the driving force behind an apparently effective scheme of depriving the general public of income, access to the outside world and the necessities of life... The additional restraints imposed on the new government are a planned and deliberate catastrophe for the citizens of the occupied territories, in hopes that Hamas will yield to the economic pressure." Oh, for the years of the Carter administration... And now we have the wall - or the "fence" as too many journalists gutlessly call it. The Palestinians went to the International Court in the Hague to have it declared illegal because much of its course runs through their land. The court said it was illegal. And Israel ignored the court's decision and, once more, the US supported Israel. Here was another lesson for the Palestinians. They went peacefully - without violence or "terrorism" - to our Western institutions to get justice. And we were powerless to help them because Israel rejected this symbol of Western freedoms.

Ehud Olmert, the Israeli prime minister whose Lebanese bombardment was such a catastrophe, still says that the wall is only temporary, as if it might be shifted back to the original frontiers of Israel. But if it is only temporary, it can also be moved forward to take in more Jewish settlements on Arab land, colonies which, it must be noted, are illegal under international law. Olmert says he wants to draw "permanent borders" unilaterally - which is against the spirit of Camp David which Hamas is now supposed to abide by.

And how does US Secretary of State Condoleezza Rice respond to this? Well, try this for wriggle room. "I wouldn't on the face of it just say absolutely we don't think there's any value in what the Israelis are talking about." And if the US does recognise - which it will - unilaterally fixed borders of the kind proposed by Olmert, it will sanction the permanent annexation of up to 10 per cent of the Arab territory seized in 1967, contrary to all previous US policy and to the International Court. All this, of course, is part of the new flouting of international laws which the US - and increasingly Israel - now regards as its right since the world "changed forever" on 11 September, 2001.

Remarkably, however, the US still believes that it is increasingly loathed in the Arab world not because of its policies but because its policies are not being presented fairly. It's not a political problem, it's a public-relations problem. Curiously, that is what Israel thought when accused of killing too many Lebanese during the 1982 invasion of Lebanon. What we do is right. We're just not selling it right. Hence, the appointment of Karen Hughes as US "Undersecretary of State for Public Diplomacy". Her line is straight to the point. "I try to portray the facts in the best light for our country," she said after her appointment. "Because I believe we're a wonderful country and that we are doing things across the world."

The columnist Roger Cohen placed her problem in a nutshell. The problem are the facts. And they include the fact that, in the 65-year period between 1941 and 2006, the US has been at war in some form or another for all but 14 of them. And people around the world have got tired of this. They got tired of America's insatiable need for an enemy - and suspicious of all the talk of democracy, freedom and morality in which every war was cast. They stopped buying the US narrative. Hughes says that the vision followed by bin Laden's followers "is a mission of destruction and death; ours a message of life and opportunity." Well, yes. "If only it were that simple," Cohen wrote.

At that Paris meeting with Fried, Védrine won almost all the arguments, not that Fried realised it. Védrine pleaded with the Americans to exercise caution in the Middle East. "We don't know how things are going to turn out in Afghanistan, Iraq or Egypt," he said presciently. "This is a high-risk process, like transporting nitroglycerine. You talk about an alliance; if there is an alliance, it must not be an ideological alliance, but an alliance of surgeons, of professionals, of chemists specialised in explosive substances. If we set out to do this, it will take 20 or 30 years, far longer than the second Bush administration."

But the US Marines and the 82 Airborne are not surgeons or chemists. They are losing control of lands they thought they had conquered or "liberated". Iraq is already out of control. So is much of Afghanistan. Palestine looks set to go the same way and Lebanon is in danger of freefall. A series of letters in The New York Times in April this year suggested that ordinary US citizens grasp the "democratic"

argument better than their leaders. "Democracy cannot be easily imposed on people who are not prepared to accept it," one wrote.
"Democracy cannot be exported," wrote another. "Changing a political
culture happens only if the people embrace it. Iraqi society is too trau-
matized by the history of Saddam Hussein and the war to do more
than survive both at this point." Spot on.

It may well be that journalists in the "West" should feel a burden
of guilt for much that has happened because they have, with their gul-
libility, helped to sell US actions much more effectively than Karen
Hughes. Their constant references to a "fence" instead of a wall, to
"settlements" or "neighbourhoods" instead of colonies, their description of the West Bank as "disputed" rather than occupied, has a bred
a kind of slackness in reporting the Israeli-Palestinian conflict. Just as
it did Iraq when so many reporters from the great Western newspapers and TV stations used US ambassador Bremer's laughable
description of the ferocious insurgents as "dead-enders" or "remnants" - the same phrase still being used by our colleagues in Kabul in
reference to a distinctly resurgent Taliban which is being helped - despite General Musharraf's denials - by the Pakistani intelligence
service, the ISI.

Much worse, however, is the failure to enquire into the real policies of governments. Why, for example, was there no front-page
treatment of this year's Herzliya conference, Israel's most important
policy-making jamboree? Most of the important figures in the Israeli
government - they had yet to be elected - were in attendance. The conference was the place where Ehud Olmert first suggested handing
over slices of the West Bank: "The choice between allowing Jews to
live in all parts of the land of Israel" - the "land of Israel" in this context
included the West Bank - "and living in a state with a Jewish majority
mandate giving up part of the land of Israel. We cannot continue to
control parts of the territories where most of the Palestinians live."

However, most speakers agreed that the Palestinians would be
given a state on whatever is left after the huge settlements had been
included behind the wall. Benjamin Netanyahu even suggested the
wall should be moved deeper into the West Bank. But the implications
were obvious. A Palestinian state will be allowed, but it will not have
a capital in east Jerusalem nor any connection between Gaza and the
bits of the West Bank that are handed over. So there will be no peace,

and the words "Palestinian" and "terrorist" will, again, be inextricably linked by Israel and the US.

There were articles in the Israeli press about Herzliya, including one by Sergio Della Pergola in which he warned of the "menace" to Israel of Palestinian birth rates and advised that "if the demographic tie doesn't come in 2010, it will come in 2020." Earlier conferences have discussed the possible need for the revoking of the citizenship rights of some Israeli Arabs. Already this year, Haaretz has reported an opinion poll in which 68 per cent of Israeli Jews said they would refuse to live in the same building as an Arab - 26 per cent would agree to do so - and 46 per cent of Israeli Jews said they would refuse to allow an Arab to visit their home. The inclination toward segregation rose as the income level of the respondents dropped - as might be expected - and there was no poll of Palestinian opinion, though the Palestinians might be able to point out that tens of thousands of Israelis already do live on their land in the huge colonies across the West Bank, most of which will remain, illegally, in Israeli hands.

All these details are available in the Arab press - and of course, the Israeli press, but are largely absent from our own. Why? Even when Norman Finkelstein wrote a damning academic report on the way Israel's High Court of Justice "proved" the wall - deemed illegal by the Hague - was legal, it was virtually ignored in the West. So, for that matter, was the US academics' report on the power of the Israeli lobby, until the usual taunts of "anti-Semitism" forced the American mainstream to write about it, albeit in a shifty, frightened way.

There are so many other examples of our fear of Middle Eastern truth. Our soft handling of Hosni Mubarak's increasingly autocratic regime in Egypt is typical. So is reporting of Algeria now that British governments are prepared to deport refugees home on the grounds that they no longer face arrest and torture. But arrest and torture continue in Algeria. Its recent amnesty poll effectively immunises all members of the security services involved in torture and makes it a crime to oppose the amnesty.

Is this really the best that we journalists can do? Save for the indefatigable Seymour Hersh, there are still no truly investigative correspondents in the US press. But challenging authority should not be that difficult. No one is being asked to end the straightforward reporting of Arab tyrannies. We are still invited to ask - and should ask - why the Muslim world has produced so many dictatorships, most of them supported by "us". But there are too many dark corners into which we will not look. Where, for example, are the CIA's secret torture prisons? I know two reporters who are aware of the locations. But they are silent, no doubt in the interests of "national security".

This reluctance to confront unpleasant truths diminishes the reader or viewer for whom Middle East reporting in the US media is almost incomprehensible to anyone who does not know the region. It also has its trickle-down effects even in theatres, universities and schools in America. The case of the play about Rachel Corrie - the young US activist twice run over by an Israeli bulldozer while trying to prevent the demolition of Palestinian homes - taken off the New York stage was one of the more deplorable of these. I was also surprised in the Bronx to find that Fieldston, a private school in Riverdale - was forced to cancel a college meeting with two Palestinian lecturers when parents objected to the absence of an Israeli on the panel. The fact that Israeli speakers were to be invited later made no difference. The school's principal later announced that the meeting would "not be appropriate given the sensitivity and complexity of the issue". Complex problems are supposed to be explained. But this could not be explained because, well, it was too complex and - the truth - would upset the usual Israeli lobbyists.

So there we go again. Freedom of speech is a precious commodity but just how precious I found out for myself when I addressed the American University of Beirut after receiving an honorary degree there this summer. I made my usual points about the Bush administration and the growing dangers of the Middle East only to find that a US diplomat in Beirut was condemning me in front of Lebanese friends for being allowed to criticise the Bush administration in a college which receives US government money.

And so on we go with the Middle East tragedy, telling the world that things are getting better when they are getting worse, that democracy is flourishing when it is swamped in blood, that freedom is not without "birth pangs" when the midwife is killing the baby.

It's always been my view that the people of this part of the Earth would like some of our democracy. They would like a few packets of human rights off our supermarket shelves. They want freedom. But they want another kind of freedom - freedom from us. And this we do not intend to give them. Which is why our Middle East presence is heading into further darkness. Which is why I sit on my balcony and wonder where the next explosion is going to be. For, be sure, it will happen. Bin Laden doesn't matter anymore, alive or dead. Because, like nuclear scientists, he has invented the bomb. You can arrest all of the world's nuclear scientists but the bomb has been made. Bin Laden created al-Qa'ida amid the matchwood of the Middle East. It exists. His presence is no longer necessary.

And all around these lands are a legion of young men preparing to strike again, at us, at our symbols, at our history. And yes, maybe I should end all my reports with the words: Watch out!

4 March 2007

BIN LADEN AT 50

He was 36 when I first met him. Osama bin Laden's beard had no trace of grey in 1993. He was a young man, building a new road for poor villagers in Sudan, a trifle arrogant perhaps, very definitely wary of the Western journalist - 10 years older than him - who had turned up in the cold Sudanese desert one Sunday morning to talk to him about his war against the Soviet Union in Afghanistan.

Was I going to ask him about "terror"? No, I wanted to know what it was like to fight the Russians. A Soviet mortar shell had fallen beside him, Bin Laden said. Nangahar province, maybe 1982. "I felt Seqina as I waited for it to explode," he said. Seqina means an almost religious calmness. The shell - and many must curse it for being a dud - did not explode. Otherwise Osama bin Laden would have been dead at 25.

When I met him again in Afghanistan in 1996, he was 39, raging against the corruption of the Saudi royal family, contemptuous of the West. When Saddam Hussein invaded Kuwait in 1990, Bin Laden told the House of Saud that his Arab legion could destroy the Iraqis; no need to bring the Americans to the land of Islam's two holiest places. The King turned him down. So the Americans were now also the target of Osama's anger.

Has he grown wiser with age? The next year, he told me he sought God's help "to turn America into a shadow of itself ". I wrote "rhetoric" in the margin of my notebook - a mistake. Age was giving Bin Laden a dangerous self-confidence. But as the years after 11 September 2001 went by, I watched the al-Qa'ida leader's beard go grey in the videotapes. He talked about history more and more: the Balfour

Declaration, the Sykes-Picot agreement, the end of the Ottoman Caliphate. His political speeches appealed to Arabs whose pro-American dictators would never have the courage to tell George W Bush to take his soldiers home.

There was no contrition. Age - if it bestows wisdom - did not allow Bin Laden to question his own motives, to express any self-doubt. In the tapes, his robes were embroidered. He appeared like a Mahdi, a seer. But I wondered, as the years went by, if he was any longer relevant. Nuclear scientists invented the atom bomb. What would have been the point of arresting all the scientists afterwards? The bomb existed. Bin Laden created al-Qa'ida. The monster was born. What is the point, any longer, in searching for 50-year-old Bin Laden?

Five years ago, Time magazine offered to buy one of my photographs of Bin Laden in Afghanistan for its front cover. I refused to sell it. Time wanted, so their picture desk told me, to use a computer to "age" him in my snapshot. Again, I refused. "So how much do you want?" the Time picture desk asked. They didn't understand. Bin Laden may have no integrity, but my pictures did: they showed a man in his 30s and 40s, not in his 60s or 70s.

But now he is 50 years old. I don't think he'll be celebrating in his cave. Just reflecting that, white-flecked though his beard now is, he remains the West's target number one, as iconic as any devil, so embarrassing to Mr Bush that the President dare no longer pronounce his name, lest it remind his audience that Bin Laden is the one that got away.

I read the "experts", telling me that Bin Laden has cancer, that he needs medical machines to survive. But we say this about all our enemies. Bin Laden uses now a stick to walk - unusual for a man of 50 - but we know he was wounded in Afghanistan. The truth is - and forget the "experts" who might tell you otherwise - that Bin Laden is still alive. Like the Scarlet Pimpernel, he may be damned and elusive, but he remains on this earth. Aged 50.

2008: WINNING THE WAR AGAINST TERROR

US Rangers on patrol

1 June 2008

ESSENTIALLY DEFEATED

So al-Qa'ida is "almost defeated", is it? Major gains against al-Qa'ida. Essentially defeated. "On balance, we are doing pretty well," the CIA's boss, Michael Hayden, tells The Washington Post. "Near strategic defeat of al-Qa'ida in Iraq. Near strategic defeat for al-Qa'ida in Saudi Arabia. Significant setbacks for al-Qa'ida globally - and here I'm going to use the word 'ideologically' - as a lot of the Islamic world pushes back on their form of Islam." Well, you could have fooled me.

Six thousand dead in Afghanistan, tens of thousands dead in Iraq, a suicide bombing a day in Mesopotamia, the highest level of suicides ever in the US military - the Arab press wisely ran this story head to head with Hayden's boasts - and permanent US bases in Iraq after 31 December. And we've won?

Less than two years ago, we had an equally insane assessment of the war when General Peter Pace, the weird (and now mercifully retired) chairman of the US joint chiefs of staff, said of the American war in Iraq that "we are not winning but we are not losing". At which point,

George Bush's Defence Secretary, Robert Gates, said he agreed with Pace that "we are not winning but we are not losing".

James Baker, who had just produced his own messy report on Iraq then said - reader, please do not laugh or cry - "I don't think you can say we're losing. By the same token, I'm not sure we're winning." Then Bush himself proclaimed, "We're not winning; we're not losing." Pity about the Iraqis. But anyway, now we really, really are winning. Or at least al-Qa'ida is "almost" - note the "almost", folks - defeated. So Mike Hayden tells us.

Am I alone in finding this stuff infantile to the point of madness? As long as there is injustice in the Middle East, al-Qa'ida will win. As long as we have 22 times as many Western forces in the Muslim world as we did at the time of the Crusades - my calculations are pretty accurate - we are going to be at war with Muslims. The hell-disaster of the Middle East is now spread across Pakistan, Afghanistan, Iraq, Gaza, even Lebanon. And we are winning?

Yes, we've bought ourselves some time in Iraq by paying half of the insurgents to fight for us and to murder their al-Qa'ida cousins. Yes, we are continuing to prop up Saudi Arabia's head-chopping and torture-practising regime - no problem there, I suppose, after our enthusiasm for "water-boarding" - but this does not mean that al-Qa'ida is defeated.

Because al-Qa'ida is a way of thinking, not an army. It feeds on pain and fear and cruelty - our cruelty and oppression - and as long as we continue to dominate the Muslim world with our Apache helicopters and our tanks and our Humvees and our artillery and bombs and our "friendly" dictators, so will al-Qa'ida continue.

Must we live this madness through to the very end of the Bush regime in Washington? Is there no one in that magnificent, imperial city who understands what "we" are doing out here in the Middle East? Why on earth does The Washington Post even give room to the fantasies of a functionary from the CIA, the very organisation that failed to prevent 9/11 because - if we are to believe what we are told - a phone call in Arabic about crashing planes into the twin towers hadn't been translated in time? Are we going to bomb Iran? Is this what we are waiting for now? Or is it to be another proxy Iranian-American war in Lebanon, fought out by Hizbollah and the Israelis? And does Mike believe al-Qa'ida is in Iran?

Israel continues to build settlements for Jews - and Jews only - on Arab land. And Washington does nothing. Illegal though these settlements are, George Bush goes along with it. They fuel anger and frustration and a righteous sense of grievance - and Washington will not prevent this outrage from continuing. I open my Arab papers each morning to find new reasons why the Bin Ladens of this world will not go away.

Take the story that came out of Gaza this week. Eight Palestinian students won grants from the Fulbright scholarship programme to study in the United States. You'd think, wouldn't you, that it was in the interest of America to bring these young Muslim people to the land of the free. But no. Israel won't let them leave Gaza. It's all part of the "war on terror" which Israel claims it is fighting alongside America. So the US State Department has cancelled the scholarships. No, it's not worth turning yourself into an al-Qa'ida suicide bomber for such a nonsense. But it would be difficult to find anything meaner, pettier, more vicious than this in yesterday's papers.

Does Mike Hayden read this stuff? Or is he, like most of Washington, so frightened of Israel that he wouldn't say boo to a goose? Doesn't the CIA realise - or imagine - that as long as we allow the Middle East to fester under a cloak of injustice, al-Qa'ida will continue? Why are our forces - and this is a question I was asked in Baghdad - in Pakistan, Afghanistan, Iraq, Jordan, Turkey, Egypt, Algeria (yes, US special forces have a base near Tamanraset), Bahrain, Kuwait, Yemen, Oman, Saudi Arabia, Qatar and Tajikistan? (Yes again, French bomber pilots are based at Dushanbe to fly "close air support" for our lads in Afghanistan.)

And as long as we have stretched this iron curtain across the Middle East, we will be at war and al-Qa'ida will be at war with us. This new iron curtain, by the way, starts up in Greenland and stretches down through Britain and Germany, through Bosnia and Greece to Turkey. What is it for? What's on the other side? Russia. China. India.

These are questions we do not ask; certainly they're not the kind of questions that The Washington Post would dare to put to Mike and his chums at the CIA. Yes, we huff and we puff about democracy and freedom and human rights, though we give little enough of them to the Muslim world. For the kind of freedom they want - the kind of freedom that allows outfits like al-Qa'ida to flourish - is freedom from "us". And this, I fear, we do not intend to give them.

Mike Hayman may think the Muslim world is "pushing back" al-Qa'ida's "form of Islam", but I doubt it. Indeed, I rather suspect al-Qa'ida is growing stronger. Mike says they're defeated in Iraq and Saudi Arabia. But are they defeated in London? And Bali? And in New York and Washington?

21 August 2008

'BONE IN CRUSADERS THROATS'

Al-Qa'ida "in the Maghreb" strikes again. Forty-three dead on Tuesday (19 August), another 11 yesterday. And across the Muslim world, it continues. A suicide bomber in Mersin in Turkey, 23 dead in a hospital complex in Pakistan and - let us not forget how these figures are put together in the Middle East - 10 French soldiers at Salopi in Afghanistan. Yes, I'm sure we're winning the "war against terror". But aren't we losing it?

It was one of al-Qa'ida's most prominent leaders who announced in 2006 - on 11 September, of course - that the Salafist Group for Preaching and Combat and al-Qa'ida would be "a bone in the throat of the American and French crusaders" and they kept their dark word. Tuesday's appalling suicide bombing in Algeria was followed yesterday by car bombs in the city of Bouira. Just as the earlier suicide bombing targeted police cadets, so the Bouira bomb were aimed at foreign nations. Canadians and Frenchmen were said to be among the victims.

If the bombings seem casually crafted to a Western audience, they did not appear that way in the Arab world. "From Asia to the Maghreb - terrorism is coasting along," the Beirut French language newspaper L'Orient Le Jour headlined its front page on Wednesday. It was perfectly correct. The last French military casualties on this scale were at the Drakkar building in Beirut in 1983. The fact that the Taliban could officially announce not only the French dead in the town of Salopi but their own casualties as well showed how sophisticated their attacks have now become.

If it was not clear last night whether the latest Algerian attack was a suicide bomber - the slovenly Algerian press agency declined to say (which probably means it was) - the target, foreigners working on a dam project - spoke for itself. The local police - in Iraq, in Algeria, in

Afghanistan, in Pakistan - are now the men who will pay the price for fighting the West's "war on terror".

Is it worth it? This is the question that the Iraqis and the Algerians and the Afghans and the Pakistanis now have to ask themselves. In answering this question, they will have to ask whether we care about them - we do not, of course - and whether the money they make from working for us is worth their lives. The mere fact that 10 French dead matter so much in Afghanistan - when 10 Afghan villagers matter so little when they are killed off in our anti-Taliban air raids - speaks mountains about our love for the Muslims of this towering, massive landscape.

In reality, we care as much about the Afghans of Afghanistan as we care about the Iraqis of Iraq and the Algerians of Algeria.

I remember well, with great sadness, how we cared nothing for the babies whose throats were slashed by so-called Islamists (some of whom, it turned out, worked for the government) in Algeria, giving the statistics of dead children rather than their names. I printed the names of these poor babies. And it was to the shame of their murderers - and to the government whose savage butchers participated in these outrageous acts - that they cared nothing for them.

20 September 2008

RE-WINNING THE WAR IN AFGHANISTAN

Poor old Algerians. They are being served the same old pap from their cruel government. In 1997, the Pouvoir announced a "final victory" over their vicious Islamist enemies. On at least three occasions, I reported - not, of course, without appropriate cynicism - that the Algerian authorities believed their enemies were finally beaten because the "terrorists" were so desperate that they were beheading every man, woman and child in the villages they captured in the mountains around Algiers and Oran.

And now they're at it again. After a ferocious resurgence of car bombing by their newly merged "al-Qa'ida in the Maghreb" antagonists, the decrepit old FLN government in Algiers has announced the "terminal phase" in its battle against armed Islamists. As the Algerian journalist Hocine Belaffoufi said with consummate wit the other day, "According to this political discourse ... the increase in attacks represents undeniable proof of the defeat of terrorism. The more terrorism collapsed, the more the attacks increased ... so the stronger (terrorism) becomes, the fewer attacks there will be."

We, of course, have been peddling this crackpot nonsense for years in south-west Asia. First of all, back in 2001, we won the war in Afghanistan by overthrowing the Taliban. Then we marched off to win the war in Iraq. Now - with at least one suicide bombing a day and the nation carved up into mutually antagonistic sectarian enclaves - we have won the war in Iraq and are heading back to re-win the war in Afghanistan where the Taliban, so thoroughly trounced by our chaps seven years ago, have proved their moral and political bankruptcy by recapturing half the country.

It seems an age since Donald "Stuff Happens" Rumsfeld declared,"A government has been put in place (in Afghanistan), and the Islamists are no more the law in Kabul. Of course, from time to time a hand grenade, a mortar explodes - but in New York and in San Francisco, victims also fall. As for me, I'm full of hope." Oddly, back in the Eighties, I heard exactly the same from a Soviet general at the Bagram airbase in Afghanistan - yes, the very same Bagram airbase where the CIA lads tortured to death a few of the Afghans who escaped the earlier Russian massacres. Only "terrorist remnants" remained in the Afghan mountains, the jolly Russian general assured us. Afghan troops, along with the limited Soviet "intervention" forces, were restoring peace to democratic Afghanistan.

And now? After the "unimaginable" progress in Iraq - I am quoting the fantasist who still occupies the White House - the Americans are going to hip-hop 8,000 soldiers out of Mesopotamia and dump another 4,700 into the hellfire of Afghanistan. Too few, too late, too slow, as one of my French colleagues commented acidly. It would need at least another 10,000 troops to hope to put an end to these Taliban devils who are now equipped with more sophisticated weapons, better trained and increasingly - sad to say - tolerated by the local civilian population. For Afghanistan, read Irakistan.

Back in the late 19th century, the Taliban - yes, the British actually called their black-turbaned enemies "Talibs" - would cut the throats of captured British soldiers. Now this unhappy tradition is repeated - and we are surprised! Two of the American soldiers seized when the Taliban stormed into their mountain base on 13 July this year were executed by their captors.

And now it turns out that four of the 10 French troops killed in Afghanistan on 18 August surrendered to the Taliban, and were almost immediately executed. Their interpreter had apparently disappeared shortly before their mission began - no prizes for what this might mean - and the two French helicopters which might have helped to save the day were too busy guarding the hopeless and impotent Afghan President Hamid Karzai to intervene on behalf of their own troops. A French soldier described the Taliban with brutal frankness. "They are good soldiers but pitiless enemies."

The Soviet general at Bagram now has his amanuensis in General David McKiernan, the senior US officer in Afghanistan, who proudly announced last month that US forces had killed "between 30 and 35 Taliban" in a raid on Azizabad near Herat. "In the light of emerging evidence pertaining (sic) to civilian casualties in the ... counter-insurgency operation," the luckless general now says, he feels it "prudent" - another big sic here - to review his original investigation. The evidence "pertaining", of course, is that the Americans probably killed 90 people in Azizabad, most of them women and children. We - let us be frank and own up to our role in the hapless Nato alliance in Afghanistan - have now slaughtered more than 500 Afghan civilians this year alone. These include a Nato missile attack on a wedding party in July when we splattered 47 of the guests all over the village of Deh Bala.

And Obama and McCain really think they're going to win in Afghanistan - before, I suppose, rushing their soldiers back to Iraq when the Baghdad government collapses. What the British couldn't do in the 19th century and what the Russians couldn't do at the end of the 20th century, we're going to achieve at the start of the 21 century, taking our terrible war into nuclear-armed Pakistan just for good measure. Fantasy again.

Joseph Conrad, who understood the powerlessness of powerful nations, would surely have made something of this. Yes, we have lost after we won in Afghanistan and now we will lose as we try to win again. Stuff happens.

25 September 2008

SIX YEARS IN GUANTANAMO

Sami al-Haj walks with pain on his steel crutch; almost six years in the nightmare of Guantanamo have taken their toll on the Al Jazeera journalist and, now in the safety of a hotel in the small Norwegian town of Lillehammer, he is a figure of both dignity and shame. The Americans told him they were sorry when they eventually freed him this year - after the beatings he says he suffered, and the force-feeding, the humiliations and interrogations by British, American and Canadian intelligence officers - and now he hopes one day he'll be able to walk without his stick.

The TV cameraman, 38, was never charged with any crime, nor was he put on trial; his testimony makes it clear that he was held in three prisons for six-and-a-half years - repeatedly beaten and force-fed - not because he was a suspected "terrorist" but because he refused to become an American spy. From the moment Sami al-Haj arrived at Guantanamo, flown there from the brutal US prison camp at Kandahar, his captors demanded that he work for them. The cruelty visited upon him - constantly interrupted by American admissions of his innocence - seemed designed to turn al-Haj into a US intelligence "asset".

"We know you are innocent, you are here by mistake," he says he was told in more than 200 interrogations. "All they wanted was for me to be a spy for them. They said they would give me US citizenship, that my wife and child could live in America, that they would protect me. But I said: 'I will not do this - first of all because I'm a journalist and this is not my job and because I fear for myself and my family. In war, I can be wounded and I can die or survive. But if I work with you, al-Qa'ida will eliminate me. And if I don't work with you, you will kill me'."

The grotesque saga began for al-Haj on 15 December, 2001, when he was on his way from the Pakistani capital Islamabad to Kandahar in Afghanistan with Sadah al-Haq, a fellow correspondent from the Arab satellite TV channel, to cover the new regional government. At least 70 other journalists were on their way through the Pakistani border post at Chaman, but an officer stopped al-Haj. "He told me there was a paper from the Pakistani intelligence service for my arrest. My name was misspelled, my passport number was incorrect, it said I was born in 1964 - the right date is 1969. I said I had renewed my visa in Islamabad and asked why, if I was wanted, they had not arrested me there?"

Sami al-Haj speaks slowly and with care, each detail of his suffering and of others' suffering of equal importance to him. He still cannot believe that he is free, able to attend a conference in Norway, to return to his new job as news producer at Al Jazeera, to live once more with his Azeri wife Asma and their eight-year old son Mohamed; when Sami al-Haj disappeared down the black hole of America's secret prisons the boy was only 14 months' old.

Al-Haj's story has a familiar ring to anyone who has investigated the rendition of prisoners from Pakistan to US bases in Afghanistan and Guantanamo. His aircraft flew for an hour and a half and then landed to collect more captives - this may have been in Islamabad, the Pakistani capital - before flying on to the big American base at Bagram.

"We arrived in the early hours of the morning and they took the shackles off our feet and pushed us out of the plane. They hit me and pushed me down on the asphalt. We heard screams and dogs barking. I collapsed with my right leg under me, and I felt the ligaments tearing. When I fell, the soldiers started treading on me. First, they walked on my back, then - when they saw me looking at my leg - they started kicking my leg. One soldier shouted at me: 'Why did you come to fight Americans?' I had a number - I was No 35 and this is how they addressed me, as a number - and the first American shouted at me: 'You filmed Bin Laden.' I said I did not film Bin Laden but that I was a journalist. I again gave my name, my age, my nationality."

After 16 days at Bagram, another aircraft took him to the US base at Kandahar where on arrival the prisoners were again made to lie on the ground. "We were cursed - they said 'fuck your mother' - and again the Americans walked on our backs. Why? Why did they do this? I was taken to a tent and stripped and they pulled hairs out of my beard. They photographed the pupils of my eyes. A doctor found blood on my back and asked me why it was there. I asked him how he thought it was there?"

The same dreary round of interrogations recommenced - he was now "Prisoner No 448" - and yet again, al-Haj says he was told he was being held by mistake. "Then another man - he was in civilian clothes and I think he was from Egyptian intelligence - wanted to know who was the "leader" of the detainees who was with me. The Americans asked: 'Who is the most respected of the prisoners? Who killed [Ah-med Shah] Massoud ([the leader of the anti-Taliban Northern Alliance Afghan militia]?' I said this was not my business and an American sol-dier said: 'Co-operate with us, and you will be released.' They meant I had to work for them. There was another man who spoke perfect Eng-lish. I thought he was British. He was young, good-looking, about 35-years-old, no moustache, blond hair, very polite in a white shirt, no tie. He brought me chocolate - it was Kit Kat-and I was so hungry I could have eaten the wrapping."

On 13 June, al-Haj was put on board a jet aircraft. He was given yet another prison number - No 345 - and once more his head was covered with a black bag. He was forced to take two tablets before he was gagged and his bag replaced by goggles with the eye-pieces painted black. The flight to Guantanamo took 12 to 14 hours.

"They took us on a boat from the Guantanamo runways to the prison, a journey that took an hour." Al-Haj was escorted to a medical clinic and then at once to another interrogation. "They said they'd compared my answers with my original statement and one of them said: 'You are here by mistake. You will be released. You will be the first to be released.' They gave me a picture of my son, which had been taken from my wallet. They asked me if I needed anything. I asked for books. One said he had a copy of One Thousand and One Nights in Ar-abic. He copied it for me. During this interview, they asked me: 'Why did you talk to the British intelligence man so much in Kandahar?' I said I didn't know if he was from British intelligence. They said he was.

"Then after two months, two more British men came to see me. They said they were from UK intelligence. They wanted to know who I knew, who I'd met. I said I couldn't help them." The Americans later referred to one of them as "Martin" and they did not impress al-Haj's senior interrogator at Guantanamo, Stephen Rodriguez, who wanted again to seek al-Haj's help. "He said to me: 'Our job is to prevent "things" happening. I'll give you a chance to think about this. You can have US citizenship, your family will be looked after, you'll have a villa in the US, we'll look after your son's education, you'll have a bank ac-count'. He had brought with him some Arabic magazines and told me I could read them. In those 10 minutes, I felt I had gone back to being a human being again. Then soldiers came to take me back to my cell - and the magazines were taken away."

By the summer of 2003, al-Haj was receiving other strange visitors. "Two Canadian intelligence officers came and they showed me lots of photos of people and wanted to know if I recognised them. I knew none of them."

In more than 200 interrogations, al-Haj was asked about his employers the Al Jazeera television channel in Qatar. In one session, he says another American said to him: "After you get out of here, al-Qa'ida will recruit you and we want to know who you meet. You could become an analyst, we can train you to store information, to sketch people. There is a link between Al Jazeera and al-Qa'ida. How much does al-Qa'ida pay Al Jazeera?"

"I said: 'I will not do this - first of all because I'm a journalist and this is not my job. Also because I fear for my life and my family.'"

Many beatings followed - not from the interrogators but from other US guards. "They would slam my head into the ground, cut off all my hair. They put me into the isolation block - we called it the 'November Block' - for two years. They made my life torture. I wanted to bring it to an end. There were continual punishments without reason. In interrogations, they would tighten the shackles so it hurt. They hadn't allowed me to receive letters for 10 months - even then, they erased words in them, even from my son. Again, Rodriguez demanded I work for the Americans."

In January of last year, Sami al-Haj started a hunger strike - and began the worst months of his imprisonment. "I wanted my rights in the civil courts. The US Supreme Court said I should have my rights. I wanted the right to worship properly. They let me go 30 days without food - then I was tied to a chair with metal shackles and they force-fed me. They would insert a tube through my nose into my stomach. They chose large tubes so that it hurt and sometimes it went into the lung. They used the same tube they had used on other prisoners with muck still on it and then they pumped more food into me than it was possible to absorb. They told us the people administering this were doctors - but they were torturers, not doctors. They forced 24 cans of food into us so we threw up and then gave us laxatives to defecate. My pancreas was affected and I had stomach problems. Then they would forbid us from drinking water."

Al-Haj says he completed 480 days of hunger strike by which time his medical condition had deteriorated and he was bleeding from his anus. That was the moment his interrogators decided to release him.

"There were new interrogators now, but they tried once more with me. 'Will you work with us?' they asked me again. I said 'no' again - but I thanked them for their years of hospitality and for giving me the chance to live among them as a journalist. I said this way I could get the truth to the outside world, that I was not in a hurry to get out because there were a lot more reporters' stories in there." They said: 'You think we did you a favour?' I said: 'You turned me from zero into a hero.' They said: 'We are 100 per cent sure that Bin Laden will be in touch with you...' That night, I was taken to the plane. The interrogators were watching me, hiding behind a tennis net. I waved at them, those four pairs of eyes."

The British authorities have never admitted talking to Sami al-Haj. Nor have the Canadians. Al Jazeera, whose headquarters George Bush wanted to bomb after the invasion of Iraq, kept a job open for Sami al-Haj. But Prisoner No 345 never received an official apology from the Americans. He says he does not expect one.

15 November 2008

CENTURIES OF SAVAGERY

Back in Afghanistan, the mind turns to the small matter of savagery. Not the routine cruelty of war but the deliberate inhumanity with which we behave. The torture and killing of prisoners in this pitiful place - the American variety in Bagram and the Taliban variety in Helmand - is a kind of routine of history. Even execution has to be made more painful. A knife is more terrible than a bullet. The cult of the suicide bomber in the Middle East began its life in Lebanon, moved to "Palestine", arrived in Iraq, leached over the border here to Afghanistan and passed effortlessly through the Khyber Pass into Pakistan. And New York. And Washington. And London...

Are human beings at war - any kind of war - by definition bound to commit atrocities? The International Committee of the Red Cross tried to answer this question in a report four years ago. Were combatants unaware of international humanitarian law? Unlikely, I would think. They just don't care. The Red Cross enquiry interviewed hundreds of fighters in Colombia, Bosnia, Georgia - a bit of real prescience, there, on the part of the ICRC - and the Congo, and suggested that those who commit reprehensible acts see themselves as victims, that this then gives them the right to act savagely against their opponents. Certainly, this might apply to the Palestinian-Israeli conflict, very definitely to the Serbs of Bosnia - I'm not so sure about Georgia - and quite definitely to the Taliban (not least when we've been bombing more wedding parties).

Such cruelty is abetted with a bodyguard of clichés - "police operations", "clean up", "mop up", "surgical strikes" - where you can kill by remote control, "especially when the media are not present to show the realities of a conflict". This is most certainly the case today, for what journalist will now dare to wander the village streets of Helmand or the city of Baquba in Iraq or, for that matter, the border towns of Pakistan? War has never, it seems, been so underreported. And both the good guys and the bad guys like it that way; they prefer to indulge in savagery unseen.

There is nothing new in all this. At the Battle of Omdurman - where the British executed all the Arab wounded - the young Winston Churchill wrote of a sight which is familiar today in a land which was then called Mesopotamia and in another which was already called Afghanistan. He described "grisly apparitions", of "horses spouting blood, struggling on three legs, men staggering on foot, men bleeding from terrible wounds, fish-hook spears stuck right through them, arms and faces cut to pieces, bowels protruding, men gasping, crying, collapsing, expiring...". To the men can now - this very week - be added the suicide-bombed schoolgirls of Baghdad.

In his earlier military campaign on the North West Frontier, Churchill saw how some of the Taliban's ancestors dealt with a wounded British officer: the leader of "half a dozen Pathan swordsmen ... rushed upon the prostrate figure and slashed it three or four times with his sword. I forgot everything else at this moment except a desire to kill this man. I wore my long cavalry sword well sharpened... The savage saw me coming...". Well there's something for the ICRC to think about.

Yet it pays to remember that Afghan wars have always been dreadful. Sir Mortimer Durand - he who created the Durand line which masquerades as the Afghan-Pakistani border, crossed with such impunity today by Americans and Taliban warriors in order to kill each other - witnessed the cruelty of the Afghan war at first hand. "During the action in the Chardeh valley on the 12th of Dec 1879," he wrote, "two squadrons of the 9th Lancers were ordered to charge a large force of Afghans in the hope of saving our guns. The charge failed, and some of our dead were afterwards found dreadfully mutilated by Afghan knives... I saw it all..."

Yet Durand himself objected profoundly to a statement from General Frederick Roberts - he of Kandahar fame - after the murder of the British mission diplomats in Kabul. The killings had been "a treacherous and cowardly crime, which has brought indelible disgrace upon the Afghan people... all persons convicted of playing a part in (the murders) will be dealt with according to their deserts". Durand confronted Roberts over this Victorian version of the message that George Bush would give to the Afghans 122 years later.

"It seemed to me so utterly wrong in tone and in matter," Durand would later write, "that I determined to do my utmost to overthrow it... the stilted language, and the absurd affectation of preaching historical morality to the Afghans, all our troubles with whom began by our own abominable injustice, made the paper to my mind most dangerous for the General's reputation."

Of course, it did Roberts no harm at all. In the age of "shock and awe" - when a Canadian general can call his Taliban opponents "scumbags" - it still doesn't seem to worry Nato officers. They should know better. Montgomery never cursed Rommel; he kept a photograph of the Afrika Korps commander in his caravan to remind him of the man he was fighting. But then again, didn't Montgomery fight in the age of the Holocaust, of industrial killing, of the Hamburg and Dresden firestorms? Indeed, the very Geneva Conventions of 12 August 1949 were supposed to end the mass destruction of human life. And President Bush has torn them up.

I know it's easy to ridicule the Red Cross. There's something very preachy about the post-war conventions. But apart from the precedents of international law, it's all we've got. Maybe a million Pushtulanguage editions should be handed out to the Taliban and their followers as well as to the Nato combatants whom Barack Obama absurdly believes will win the Afghan war. But I doubt it would do much good. Victimhood sits easily on all our shoulders. If Osama bin Laden had a conscience, it would be quickly eased by the destruction of the last Caliphate, the colonial occupation of the Muslim world, the deaths of millions of Arabs. And if we have a conscience, what do we say? Remember 9/11. And so on we go.

22 November 2008

DEJÀ DOUBLE-VU

I sit on the rooftop of the old Central Hotel - pharaonic-decorated elevator, unspeakable apple juice, sublime green tea, and armed Tajik guards at the front door - and look out across the smoky red of the Kabul evening. The Bala Hissar fort glows in the dusk, massive portals, the great keep to which the British army should have moved its men in 1841. Instead, they felt the king should live there and humbly built a cantonment on the undefended plain, thus leading to a "signal catastrophe".

Like automated birds, the kites swoop over the rooftops. Yes, the kite-runners of Kabul, minus Hollywood. At night, the thump of American Sikorsky helicopters and the whisper of high-altitude F-18s invade my room. The United States of America is settling George Bush's scores with the "terrorists" trying to overthrow Hamid Karzai's corrupt government.

Now rewind almost 29 years, and I am on the balcony of the Intercontinental Hotel on the other side of this great, cold, fuggy city. Impeccable staff, frozen Polish beer in the bar, secret policemen in the front lobby, Russian troops parked in the forecourt. The Bala Hissar fort glimmers through the smoke. The kites - green seems a favourite colour - move beyond the trees. At night, the thump of Hind choppers and the whisper of high-altitude MiGs invade my room. The Soviet Union is settling Leonid Brezhnev's scores with the "terrorists" trying to overthrow Barbrak Karmal's corrupt government.

Thirty miles north, all those years ago, a Soviet general told us of the imminent victory over the "terrorists" in the mountains, imperialist "remnants" - the phrase Kabul communist radio always used - who were being supported by America and Saudi Arabia and Pakistan.

Fast forward to 2001 - just seven years ago - and an American general told us of the imminent victory over the "terrorists" in the mountains, the all but conquered Taliban who were being supported by Saudi Arabia and Pakistan. The Russian was pontificating at the big Soviet airbase at Bagram. The American general was pontificating at the big US airbase at Bagram.

This is not dejà-vu. This is dejà double-vu. And it gets worse.

Almost 29 years ago, the Afghan "mujahedin" began a campaign to end the mixed schooling of boys and girls in the remote mountain passes, legislation pushed through by successive communist govern-ments. Schools were burned down. Outside Jalalabad, I found a headmaster and his headmistress wife burned to death. Today, the Af-ghan Taliban are campaigning to end the mixed schooling of boys and girls - indeed the very education of young women - across the great deserts of Kandahar and Helmand. Schools have been burned down. Teachers have been executed.

As the Soviets began to suffer more and more casualties, their of-ficers boasted of the increasing prowess of the Afghan National Army, the ANA. Infiltrated though they were by the "mujahedin", Moscow gave them newer tanks and helped to train new battalions to take on the guerrillas outside the capital.

Fast forward to now. As the Americans and British suffer ever greater casualties, their officers boast of the increasing prowess of the ANA. Infiltrated though they are by the Taliban, America and other Nato states are providing them with newer equipment and training new battalions to take on the guerrillas outside the capital. Back in January of 1980, I could take a bus from Kabul to Kandahar. Seven years later, the broken highway was haunted by "mujahedin" fighters and bandits and the only safe way to travel to Kandahar was by air.

In the immediate aftermath of America's arrival here in 2001, I could take a bus from Kabul to Kandahar. Now, seven years later, the highway - rebuilt on the express instructions of George W but already cracked and swamped with sand - is haunted by Taliban fighters and bandits and the only safe way to travel to Kandahar is by air.

Throughout the 1980s, the Soviets and the ANA held the towns but lost most of the country. Today, America and its allies and the ANA hold most of the towns but have lost the southern half of the country. The Soviets secretly sent another 9,000 troops to join their 115,000-strong occupation force to fight the "mujahedin". Today, the Ameri-cans are publicly sending another 7,000 troops to join their 55,000-strong occupation force to fight the Taliban.

In 1980, I would sneak down to Chicken Street to buy old books in the dust-filled shops, cheap and illegal Pakistani reprints of the memoirs of British Empire officers while my driver watched anxiously lest I be mistaken for a Russian. Last week, I sneaked down to the Shar Book shop, which is filled with the very same illicit volumes, while my driver watched anxiously lest I be mistaken for an American (or, in-deed, a Brit). I find Stephen Tanner's Afghanistan: A Military History

From Alexander The Great To The Fall Of The Taliban and drive back to my hotel through the streets of wood-smoked Kabul to read it in my ill-lit room.

In 1840, Tanner writes, Britain's supply line from the Pakistani city of Karachi up through the Khyber Pass and Jalalabad to Kabul was being threatened by Afghan fighters, "British officers on the crucial supply line through Peshawar... insulted and attacked". I fumble through my bag for a clipping from a recent copy of Le Monde. It marks Nato's main supply route from the Pakistani city of Karachi up through the Khyber Pass and Jalalabad to Kabul, and illustrates the location of each Taliban attack on the convoys bringing fuel and food to America's allies in Afghanistan.

Then I prowl through one of the Pakistani books I have found and discover General Roberts of Kandahar telling the British in 1880 that "we have nothing to fear from Afghanistan, and the best thing to do is to leave it as much as possible to itself... I feel sure I am right when I say that the less the Afghans see of us, the less they will dislike us".

Memo to the Americans, the Brits, the Canadians and the rest of Humpty Dumpty's men. Read Roberts. Read history.

2009: NO END TO THIS MADNESS

Afghanistan War

18 August 2009

WE OWE IT TO THE DEAD TO GO ON KILLING

More than 200 soldiers dead in Afghanistan, and now Gordon Brown advises us that "the best way to honour their memory is to see the course through". I don't know which particular "course" Gordon has in mind - protecting democracy, training the Afghan army, defeating the Taliban, talking to the Taliban, or just fighting them so they don't turn up on British shores - but this is straight out of the George W. Bush tear bucket.

Not so long ago, I seem to remember, Bush was telling us that we would be betraying the American dead in Iraq if we gave up the fight. We owed it to the dead to go on killing more Iraqis. And now we owe it to the dead to go on killing more Afghans. Who, of course, will go on killing us. Is there no end to this madness?

If we are now going to send our soldiers to be killed because the soldiers we sent before have been killed, then we should get out of Afghanistan today. As a matter of fact, I believe that's what we should do. None of our military - or any other Western soldiers - have any business occupying a square metre of the Muslim world. But there you have it.

We've lost more than 200 soldiers but to honour them, we've got to lose some more. The Brits - wise folk, though sometimes a bit slow on the uptake - worked all this out a long time ago. Hence the lines of mourners at Wootton Bassett (no government ministers, of course) every time a flag-draped coffin comes home.

Yet I do wonder whether our concern about this war doesn't just come from the weirdness of the military campaign, but from the funerals themselves.

Until the First World War, our soldiers - unless they were rich or famous - were not even memorialised but simply dumped in mass graves. At Malplaquet and at Waterloo, there were no gravestones. In the First World War, soldiers wrote the names of the fallen on wooden crosses and the bodies were later transferred to the Great War Lutyens cemeteries of the Western Front, where they lie to this day. At Ypres, the local fire brigade still play the Last Post every evening. And our soldiers were buried at Gallipoli, in Palestine and even in Mesopotamia (where other wars, alas, have scythed down their headstones).

So, too, in the Second World War. Our soldiers still lie in rows in Normandy, in Germany, in the Far East. No flag-draped coffins arrived back in Britain. Just a telegram through the door of their families. Did this save us from questioning the wars in which they were dying? Most Brits thought the second great 20th-century conflict worth fighting. Not so - after the Somme - the first.

And let's just remind ourselves of the casualty figures. We've lost just over 200 soldiers - admittedly most of them in the past 14 months - in a war that has lasted for eight years. In the Second World War, which lasted for almost six years, Britain lost 650 men on D-Day, 6 June 1944, alone. The Canadians lost only 335, but the Americans lost 1,465. In just one day. And let's go back to the Great War. On the first day of the Somme - 1 July 1916 - we lost almost 19,500 dead. That's almost a hundred times our Afghan dead in 24 hours.

At the 1917 battles of Arras and Messines, the Brits lost 37,500. But they didn't come home. They stayed on the battlefield. Of course, we cannot keep our soldiers in Afghan graves - indeed, when the Victorians did just that, the Afghans dug them up and mutilated their bodies - but the steady drip-drip of corpses home from foreign fields is something that British prime ministers have never had to deal with before.

Needless to say, few of those who gather at Brize Norton spare a lot of time remembering the Afghan and the Iraqi civilian dead. How many months would it take for their hundreds of thousands of bodies to be driven in solemn cortege through British towns? Their fate is, after all, no less "deeply tragic" - the Ministry of Defence's words for our latest casualties - as the loss of British soldiers.

I guess we've grown used to TV-war, the kind where we live and they - the other, alien people with brown eyes and a strange religion - die. And they must not be allowed to reach the shores of England. Which is why, occasionally and few in number, we die too. Or so Gordon would have us believe.

19 September 2009

OBAMA AND OSAMA

Obama and Osama are at last participating in the same narrative. For the US president's critics - indeed, for many critics of the West's military occupation of Afghanistan - are beginning to speak in the same language as Obama's (and their) greatest enemy. There is a growing suspicion in America that Obama has been socked into the heart of the Afghan darkness by ex-Bushie Robert Gates - once more the Secretary of Defence - and by journalist-adored General David Petraeus whose military "surges" appear to be as successful as the Battle of the Bulge in stemming the insurgent tide in Afghanistan as well as in Iraq.

No wonder Osama bin Laden decided to address "the American people" this week. "You are waging a hopeless and losing war," he said in his 9/11 eighth anniversary audiotape. "The time has come to liberate yourselves from fear and the ideological terrorism of neoconservatives and the Israeli lobby." There was no more talk of Obama as a "house Negro" although it was his "weakness", bin Laden contended, that prevented him from closing down the wars in Iraq and Afghanistan. In any event, Muslim fighters would wear down the US-led coalition in Afghanistan "like we exhausted the Soviet Union for 10 years until it collapsed". Funny, that. It's exactly what bin Laden told me personally in Afghanistan - four years before 9/11 and the start of America's 2001 adventure south of the Amu Darya river.

Almost on cue this week came those in North America who agree with Obama - albeit they would never associate themselves with the Evil One, let alone dare question Israel's cheerleading for the Iraqi war. "I do not believe we can build a democratic state in Afghanistan," announces Dianne Feinstein, the California Democrat who chairs the senate intelligence committee. "I believe it will remain a tribal entity." And Nancy Pelosi, the House Speaker, does not believe "there is a great deal of support for sending more troops to Afghanistan".

Colin Kenny, chair of Canada's senate committee on national security and defence, said this week that "what we hoped to accomplish in Afghanistan has proved to be impossible. We are hurtling towards a Vietnam ending".

Close your eyes and pretend those last words came from the al-Qa'ida cave. Not difficult to believe, is it? Only Obama, it seems, fails to get the message. Afghanistan remains for him the "war of necessity". Send yet more troops, his generals plead. And we are supposed to follow the logic of this nonsense. The Taliban lost in 2001. Then they started winning again. Then we had to preserve Afghan democracy. Then our soldiers had to protect - and die - for a second round of democratic elections. Then they protected - and died - for fraudulent elections. Afghanistan is not Vietnam, Obama assures us. And then the good old German army calls up an air strike - and zaps yet more Afghan civilians.

It is instructive to turn at this moment to the Canadian army, which has in Afghanistan fewer troops than the Brits but who have suffered just as ferociously; their 130th soldier was killed near Kandahar this week. Every three months, the Canadian authorities publish a scorecard on their military "progress" in Afghanistan - a document that is infinitely more honest and detailed than anything put out by the Pentagon or the Ministry of Defence - which proves beyond peradventure (as Enoch Powell would have said) that this is Mission Impossible or, as Toronto's National Post put it in an admirable headline three days' ago, "Operation Sleepwalk". The latest report, revealed this week, proves that Kandahar province is becoming more violent, less stable and less secure - and attacks across the country more frequent - than at any time since the fall of the Taliban in 2001. There was an "exceptionally high" frequency of attacks this spring compared with 2008.

There was a 108 per cent increase in roadside bombs. Afghans are reporting that they are less satisfied with education and employment levels, primarily because of poor or non-existent security. Canada is now concentrating only on the security of Kandahar city, abandoning any real attempt to control the province.

Canada's army will be leaving Afghanistan in 2011, but so far only five of the 50 schools in its school-building project have been completed. Just 28 more are "under construction". But of Kandahar province's existing 364 schools, 180 have been forced to close. Of progress in "democratic governance" in Kandahar, the Canadian report states that the capacity of the Afghan government is "chronically weak and undermined by widespread corruption". Of "reconciliation" - whatever that means these days - "the onset of the summer fighting season and the concentration of politicians and activists for the August elections discouraged expectations of noteworthy initiatives...".

Even the primary aim of polio eradication - Ottawa's most favoured civilian project in Afghanistan - has defeated the Canadian International Development Agency, although this admission is cloaked in truly Blair-like (or Brown-like) mendacity. As the Toronto Star revealed in a serious bit of investigative journalism this week, the aim to "eradicate" polio with the help of UN and World Health Organisation money has been quietly changed to the "prevention of transmission" of polio. Instead of measuring the number of children "immunised" against polio, the target was altered to refer only to the number of children "vaccinated". But of course, children have to be vaccinated several times before they are actually immune.

And what do America's Republican hawks - the subject of bin Laden's latest sermon - now say about the Afghan catastrophe? "More troops will not guarantee success in Afghanistan," failed Republican contender and ex-Vietnam vet John McCain told us this week. "But a failure to send them will be a guarantee of failure." How Osama must have chuckled as this preposterous announcement echoed around al-Qa'ida's dark cave.

3 December 2009

THIS STRATEGY HAS BEEN TRIED BEFORE

"They shoot Russians," the young paratrooper told me. It was cold. We had come across his unit, the Soviet 105th Airborne Division, near Charikar, north of Kabul, and he was holding out a bandaged hand. Blood seeped through, staining the sleeve of his battledress. He was just a teenager with fair hair and blue eyes. Beside us a Soviet transport lorry, its rear section blown to pieces by a mine - yes, an "improvised explosive device", though we didn't call it that yet - lay upended in a ditch. In pain, the young man raised his hand to the mountain-tops where a Soviet helicopter was circling. Could I ever have imagined that Messers Bush and Blair would have landed us in the same sepulchre of armies almost three decades later? Or that a young black American president would do exactly what the Russians did all those years ago?

Within weeks, we would see the Soviet Army securing Kabul and the largest cities of Afghanistan, abandoning the vast areas of mountain and desert to the "terrorists", insisting that they could support a secular, uncorrupt government in the capital and give security to the people. By the spring of 1980, I was watching the Soviet military stage a "surge". Sound familiar? The Russians announced new training for the Afghan army. Sound familiar? Only 60 per cent of the force was following orders at the time. Yes, it does sound familiar.

Victor Sebestyen, who has researched a book about the fall of the Soviet empire, has written at length of those frozen days after the Russian army stormed into Afghanistan just after Christmas of 1979. He quotes General Sergei Akhromeyev, commander of the Soviet armed forces, addressing the Soviet Politburo in 1986. "There is no piece of land in Afghanistan that has not been occupied by one of our soldiers at some time or another. Nevertheless much of the territory stays in the hands of the terrorists. We control the provincial centres, but we cannot maintain political control over the territory we seize."

As Sebestyen points out, Gen Akhromeyev demanded extra troops - or the war in Afghanistan would continue "for a very, very long time". And how's this for a quotation from, say, a British or US commander in Helmand today? "Our soldiers are not to blame. They've fought incredibly bravely in adverse conditions. But to occupy towns and villages temporarily has little value in such a vast land where the insurgents can just disappear into the hills." Yes, of course, this was Gen Akhromeyev in 1986.

I watched the tragedy play out in those bleak early months of 1980. In Kandahar, the people cried "Allahu Akbar" from the rooftops and on the roads outside the city, I met the insurgents - the Taliban of their time - bombing the Soviet convoys.

North of Jalalabad, they even stopped my bus with red roses in the muzzles of their Kalashnikovs, ordering Communist students from the vehicle. I didn't care to dwell on their fate. No different, I guess, than that of pro-government Afghan students caught by the Taliban today. Outside the city, I was told that the "mujahedin" - President Ronald Reagan's favourite "freedom fighters" - had destroyed a school because it was educating girls. Too true. The headmaster and his wife - after they had been burned - were hanging from a tree.

Afghans approached us with strange stories. Political prisoners were being taken from the country and tortured inside the Soviet Union. Secret rendition. In Kandahar, a shopkeeper, an educated man in his fifties who wore both a European sweater and an Afghan turban, approached me in the street. I still have the notes of my interview.

"Every day the government says that food prices are coming down," he said. "Every day we are told that things are getting better thanks to the cooperation of the Soviet Union. But it is not true. Do you realise that the government cannot even control the roads? Fuck them. They only hold on to the cities." The "mujahedin" infested Helmand province and crossed and recrossed the Pakistani border, just as they do today. A Soviet MiG fighter-bomber even crossed the frontier in early 1980 to attack the guerrillas. The Pakistani government - and the United States, of course - condemned this as a flagrant breach of Pakistan's sovereignty. Well, tell that to the young Americans who control the unmanned Predators so often crossing the border today to attack the guerrillas.

In Moscow almost a quarter of a century later, I went to meet the former Russian occupiers of Afghanistan. Some were now addicted to drugs, others suffered from what we call stress disorder.

And on this historic day - when Barack Obama plunges ever deeper into chaos - let us remember the British retreat from Kabul and its destruction in 1842.

2010: MIDDLE EAST PERSPECTIVE

Middle East Correspondent, Robert Fisk. (The Independent)

6 January 2010

CIA'S GREATEST DISASTER SINCE 1983

In the vast American embassy in the hills outside the Jordanian capital Amman a senior US Special Forces officer runs an equally special office. He buys information from Jordanian army and intelligence officers - for cash, of course - but he also helps to train Afghan and Iraqi policemen and soldiers. The information he seeks is not just about al-Qa'ida but about Jordanians themselves, about the army's loyalty to King Abdullah II as well as about the anti-American insurgents who live in Jordan, primarily Iraqi but also Iraqi al-Qa'ida contacts with Afghanistan.

It's easy to buy army officers in the Middle East. The Americans spent much of 2001 and 2002 buying up the warlords of Afghanistan. They paid for Jordanian troops to join their own occupation army in Iraq - which was why the Jordanian embassy in Baghdad was ruthlessly bombed by Washington's enemies.

What the CIA's double agent Humam Khalil Abu-Mulal al-Balawi did - like so many al-Qa'ida followers, he was a doctor - was routine. He worked for both sides, because America's enemies long ago infiltrated Washington's "allies" in the Arab intelligence forces. Even Abu Musab al-Zarqawi, who effectively led the al-Qa'ida side of the insurgency in Iraq and was himself a Jordanian citizen, maintained contacts within Amman's General Intelligence Department, whose own senior officer, Sharif Ali bin Zeid, was killed along with seven Americans this week in the CIA's greatest disaster since the Beirut US embassy bombing of 1983.

There is, however, nothing romantic about espionage in the Middle East. Several of the CIA men killed in Afghanistan were in fact hired mercenaries while the Jordanian "mukhabbarat" spooks, for whom both bin Zeid and al-Balawi worked, use torture routinely on Jordan's supposed enemies; indeed, they tortured men who were equally routinely "renditioned" to Amman by the CIA under the Bush administration.

The mystery, however, is not so much the existence of double agents within the US security apparatus in the Middle East, but just how a Jordanian "mole" could be of use in Afghanistan. Few Arabs speak Pushtun or Dari or Urdu, although a larger percentage of Afghans would speak Arabic. What it does suggest, however, is that there have been much closer links between the anti-American Iraqi insurgents based in Amman and their opposite numbers in Afghanistan.

Hitherto regarded as a purely inspirational transfer of operations, it is now clear that - despite the vast landmass of Iran between the two states - Iraqi and Afghan/al-Qa'ida operatives have been collaborating. In other words, just as the CIA blithely assumed that it could make friends with and trust the local intelligence men in the Muslim world, so the insurgent groups could do the same. The presence of an anti-American Jordanian spy in Afghanistan - one who would sacrifice his life so far from home - proves how close are the links between America's enemies in Amman and in eastern Afghanistan. It would not be going too far to suggest that anti-American Jordanians have connections that reach as far as Islamabad.

If this seems far-fetched, we should remember that just as the CIA first supported Arab fighters against the Soviet army in Afghanistan, it was Saudi money which paid them. In the early Eighties, Saudi Arabia's own intelligence commander held regular meetings with Osama bin Laden in the Saudi embassy in Islamabad and with the Pakistani secret service, which gave logistical help to the "mujahedin" and then to the Taliban - as it still does today. If the Americans believe that the Saudis are not sending money to their enemies in Afghanistan - or to their equally fundamentalist enemies in Iraq and Jordan - then the CIA hasn't much idea of what is going on in the Middle East.

But this, unfortunately, is probably the case. The American desire to be loved as well as feared has long misled their intelligence services into trusting those who are ostensibly their friends, while bestialising those who are their supposed enemies. This is exactly what happened in Lebanon before a Shia Muslim suicide bomber blew up the US embassy in Beirut in 1983, when almost the entire staff of the CIA's operations in the Middle East were meeting inside. Most were killed. The entrance to the CIA's offices in their seafront embassy was closely guarded. But their local operatives in Lebanon included men and women working for both the Israelis and the early version of the Hizbollah. US embassy intelligence staffers dated Lebanese women who had no security clearance.

But the Jordanian-American axis was different. Here, the CIA were operating in an almost totally Sunni Muslim environment, among Jordanians who, while accepting CIA money, had many reasons to oppose Washington's policies, and the Jordanian King's. A large minority of the Jordanian "muhabarrat" are originally Palestinians and believe that America's uncritical, fawning support for Israel has destroyed their "nation" of Palestine and is crushing their people. The CIA's desire to trust its "local hires" is not unlike the British faith in their Indian sepoys on the eve of the Indian Mutiny. "Their" local regiments would never oppose the Raj; "their" Indian officers would remain loyal. But they did not.

Balawi's Jordanian victim, bin Zeid, was given a "martyr's" funeral in the presence of his cousin King Abdullah himself. Let's see who turns up to the burial of his murderer - if there is anything left to bury.

26 March 2010

'DO I LOOK LIKE A TERRORIST?'

For America, the European Union and India, he is the most wanted man in Pakistan, the founder and leader of Lashkar-e-Taiba, the "Army of the Righteous", blamed for the mass killing of 188 civilians, 54 of them women and children, in Mumbai in 2008, for three assaults on Delhi, for the deaths of 211 civilians in a 2005 train bombing also in Mumbai, and last month's suicide attack on Indians in Kabul.

His "army" has been banned as a "terrorist organisation" by the US, the EU, the UN Security Council, Russia, India, Pakistan and Australia. But when Hafiz Muhammad Saeed walks into the bedroom-cum-office of a small suburban house in Lahore, he is all smiles, a white cap on his head, his straggling black Salafist-style beard spreading over his white gown, urging me to eat the biscuits and apricot-topped cream-cake lying on the glass table between us.

He smiles; he occasionally laughs; he wearily takes off his thick-framed brown glasses and lays them on the bed; he talks of the need to "liberate" all of Kashmir, and he produces copious files to show me that the Lahore High Court could not prove he was a violent man, let alone the leader of the "Army of the Righteous". Indeed, he says, he is merely the leader of a charitable organisation, the Jama'at-ud-Da'wah - the "Group of Preaching" - one of the largest welfare NGOs in Pakistan, with 2,000 offices and a reputation as an earthquake and flood relief agency.

For so hated a man, Saeed seems easy-going. I am the first western journalist to meet him. But a tall man with deep-set, dark eyes - presumably a bodyguard - does not bother to search me as I enter the building. Is Saeed over confident? Or is he relying on the two uniformed Pakistani policemen at the entrance, one holding an AK47 assault rifle, the other standing behind a belt-fed machine gun mounted on a pile of sandbags. Are they there to guard against him as a potential enemy of the state - or to protect him? Saeed spends much of the time - when not eating lunch on the floor beside me - sitting on the bed in his office, raising his voice to drown out the air conditioner thumping away in the corner.

"Soon after the Russians evacuated and lost the war in Afghanistan, there were different movements that started in Kashmir - 12 different organisations started at that time, 1990," he says. "Lashkar-e-Taiba was one of those organisations that joined the struggle for the independence of Kashmir. We had so many people and we found the people from Lashkar-e-Taiba were honest and more hard-working than others."

But was Saeed not in Afghanistan? "From the very beginning," he replies, "we were strongly against the Russian occupation of Afghanistan - we thought the people of Afghanistan had been occupied. We supported them and supported the people who were fighting against the occupation and the occupiers. Yes, I went to Afghanistan, I visited to see the situation for myself. But I did not belong to the fighters - I went there because I supported them. We believe that Lashkar are justified in their fight for freedom (in Kashmir). And just like we believe that the Russian occupation (of Afghanistan) was not justified, we believe that the Americans and Nato must leave."

And did he not meet Osama bin Laden in Afghanistan? "Some time in the 1980s, I saw him during the Haj (at Mecca in Saudi Arabia). I saw him only once. I was close to him during the prayers. We greeted each other. It was very simple. It was very brief. There was not much talk."

It all sounds like an admission that Saeed was indeed a Lashkar leader, until he interrupts my questions. "This is one of the biggest falsehoods - that I was said to be the founder," he says angrily. "This is the result of Indian propaganda. The Lahore High Court thoroughly investigated this accusation and they found it was not true. Before 2001, the Pakistan government used to refer very openly - politically and morally - to all those organisations that were fighting for the independence of Kashmir. They included Lashkar-e-Taiba - they had offices here and in Multan and Islamabad. On 12 January 2002, Lashkar-e-Taiba and other organisations, including Jaish-e-Mohammad (the "Army of Mohammad"), were banned. We continued to work under the banner of Jama'at-ud-Da'wah - our organisation is not banned and we are still working under the same name."

It sounds a bit like the old Sinn Fein line: that Sinn Fein is a political movement while the IRA is an armed resistance - and never the twain shall meet. But Saeed is aware of the bruising he has had at the hands of journalists and US members of Congress. Earlier this month, Newsweek described Lashkar - "virulently anti-Jewish ... rabidly anti-Hindu" - as "the next al-Qa'ida", quoting the director of US national intelligence Dennis Blair as saying that Lashkar was "placing Western targets in Europe in its sights".

The US State Department "anti-terror" official Daniel Bergman called Lashkar "a truly malign presence in South Asia." The chairman of the US House of Representatives subcommittee on the Middle East and South Asia, Gary Ackerman, announced that "this bunch of savages needs to be crushed. The LeT is a deadly serious group of fanatics. They are well-financed, ambitious and, most disturbingly, both tolerated by and connected to the Pakistan military."

Saeed plays this for what it's worth. "You have come to see me because I am in the news everywhere, I am in Newsweek and talked about in the US Congress. But the majority of these ideas come from Indian propaganda. They make me out to be the biggest and most evil terrorist. These people you talk about as evil - no court tried them. No evidence was ever put against them. There was no investigation - nobody was ever tried in the courts in Pakistan. I was tried here six times - each time they decided I was not a terrorist. The last court never tried to put evidence against me."

At this point, an aide enters and hands me four bound files on the Jama'at's charitable works, records of the Lahore court hearings against Saeed and a glowing biography of the man himself. It is perfectly true that Saeed's men did rescue Kashmir earthquake victims in 2005, sometimes arriving on scenes of carnage before the Pakistani authorities. Jama'at claims to have rescued 183 victims alive, treated more than half a million survivors in its field hospitals, and clothed more than 12,000 more.

The High Court documents make grimmer reading. They record the evidence of the Lahore Police District Co-ordination Officer - acting, it seems, on evidence from the UN - that he was "satisfied that certain desperate and dangerous persons are moving at large (in Pakistan), instigating and brain-washing the youth to undertake undesirable activities ... and assisting the incitement of hatred and contempt against different segments of the society". Defence lawyers publicly recognised that Saeed was being accused of the Mumbai massacre and links to Al-Qa'ida.

Saeed raises his voice when he talks about these accusations. "We are Pakistanis and our organisations work under the law of Pakistan," he says. "Even though we try to abide by Pakistani law, there have been such serious allegations that I was put under arrest. A lot of people who live round my house were arrested. My movements were restricted. My freedom of speech was restricted. All these limits have been put on me because of the pressure of foreign governments. It isn't important that I happen to be a Pakistani citizen. I did not violate any Pakistani law. I am restricted only because India wants me to be restricted."

But Saeed now feels triumphant. "The Pakistan government has been in court against me and it lost its case against me. There are two cases still in the Lahore High Court. They are allegations about the Mumbai attacks - that I was involved. There have been six cases. One is now in the Supreme Court. The Americans and the Indians, they want us to fight with our government. They are very close to the Pakistani establishment. But we strongly believe we should not fight against the Pakistan authorities."

So who is Saeed? He was born during the bloodshed of Partition; his parents were fleeing north to the new state of Pakistan. Now a professor at the Engineering University of Lahore and formerly chairman of the Department of Islamic Studies, he says he visited Britain in 1995, lecturing on Kashmir and violations of UN resolutions at Islamic centres in London, Birmingham and Rochdale. He is the father of two daughters and a son.

There's a cringe-inducing paragraph at the beginning of his own official CV which needs to be reproduced in full to appreciate the vanity of a man internationally accused of mass murder. "Professor Saeed," it says, is "Teacher. Guide. Philanthropist. Humanitarian. Advocate of tolerance, freedom of thought and worship and high moral values. Can't stand for [sic] religious fanaticism, acts of violence, oppression and the killing of the innocent, armless [sic] people, whosoever." The mistaken use of "armless" for harmless comes as a bit of a shock.

His own explanation to me is only a little less full of self-regard. "I am a simple Muslim and I happen to be head of Jama'at-ud-Dawah and my mission is to educate people about Islam and tell them that Islam is a religion of peace," he preaches. "I try to follow Islam and people should know the true peace of Islam.... We speak about the rights of people. We do not shut our eyes to Kashmir and Palestine and we speak about the rights of Muslims wherever we are. We don't just speak about the religion..."

When I asked if Lashkar had issued a "fatwa" against Pope Benedict XVI for his criticism of Islam in a speech at Regensburg, the angry reply made no distinction between Lashkar and the Jama'at - nor between the Pope's remarks and the Danish newspaper which published cartoons vilifying the Prophet Mohamed. "We were very strong in showing our reaction to that statement (of the Pope). We announced it to be the biggest insult to our Prophet Mohamed. We mobilised people and staged a huge protest... When someone insults the Prophet, we take it very seriously. We believe in the sanctity of every prophet. When Jesus was insulted in India, we condemned it. Is it justified that you insult our Prophet?... Do you think it is for 'freedom of expression' that they published those cartoons? When we [sic] respond - and if there is, unfortunately, violence - then we are 'terrorists' and extremists. What have the European governments done to stop this? It could lead to violence and extremism. Europe is playing with the emotions of Muslims."

Saeed has bought into the widely discredited Pakistani version of the Mumbai slaughter: that the killings were part of an internal Indian insurgency. "Soon after the Mumbai attacks", Saeed said, "there was an organisation called the Deccan Army which claimed responsibility. But within no time, India blamed Lashkar-e-Taiba and India did not even pay attention to the claim from the Deccan Army. This 'proof' was not accepted by the (Pakistani) court. They found there was no evidence for the claims against us... Soon after the Mumbai attacks, we called a press conference. We said we were not involved. We condemned this."

But what of the surviving Mumbai attacker, Ajmal Amir Kasab, who said he worked for Lashkar-e-Taiba? There is a pause. Saeed speaks slowly. "He has been giving different stories ... In court, he gave this statement. He has been saying so many things - we do not know. Do you think that it is fair that you base everything on this man who is in custody?" Perhaps Saeed notices that I am not impressed.

"In order to understand, you have to realise the precise situation between India and Pakistan. There is a deep conflict. India has been trying to support the separatists in Baluchistan. There are so many insurgencies going on in India itself, dividing and separating the country. Kashmir has been fighting for freedom.

"We support Muslim peoples. What will happen in the future? I have some expectations. Afghanistan is a free country, free of every foreign occupier. Pakistan should be free from foreign influence. Kashmir will be independent. We expect this Muslim area will have freedom - and free rights. I'm talking about India, Pakistan, Bangladesh. Do you realise this region contains the largest Muslim population in the world, with 500 million Muslims?"

I ask Saeed the same question I once asked Osama bin Laden. Is he frightened he will be assassinated? He has obviously thought about this. "I truly believe that my life and my death are in the hands of Allah. As long as he wishes me to be alive - and to continue with my mission - I am in his hands."

Bin Laden would have been a bit smarter than this. Bin Laden did not conceal his anger, explained precisely his intention to destroy America, and always carried an AK-47 during interviews. In Lahore, it was the policemen outside who carried guns and Saeed who constantly announced his peaceful intentions.

The Americans believe that in Hafiz Muhammad Saeed, Pakistan has created a Frankenstein's monster. Perhaps. But Saeed is no Bin Laden.

22 May 2010

TEA WITH BIN LADEN...AND OTHER STORIES

When the Iranian Revolutionary Guards closed the roads to journalists after Ayatollah Khomeini's return from exile in 1979, I decided to travel the country by rail. Secret policemen and soldiers always forget trains. They like road-blocks; and the journalist who wishes to elude them must remember Michael Collins' old maxim, that no one ever sees a man on a bicycle. No one ever sees a journalist on a train. So Iranian state railways - and their single-carriage restaurant cars - became my home for weeks.

Paul Julius Freiherr von Reuter - yes, the founder of the news agency - built half the railways in Iran, and after several days there wasn't much I didn't know about the massive Boy's Own Paper trains that freighted me to Qom and Ahwaz, the Tabriz express and the slow train to the shrine of Mashhad. Numbers of bogie wheels, the horse power of the diesel locos, the maximum gradient to climb below the towering cliffs of Zard Kho - "Yellow Mountain" - on the way to Tehran. And the meals.

For breakfast, it was chicken and chips with warm Pepsi and tea. For lunch, it was chicken and chips with warm Pepsi and tea. For dinner, it was chicken and chips with warm Pepsi and tea. There were variations. You could have your chicken undercooked, your chips over-fried. Every morning I entered the restaurant car with its grimy soldiers and cold families, children huddling beneath their mother's cloak, and the cook would shout out: "What you want for breakfast?" And I would bellow: "Chicken and chips!" There was nothing else. And sure enough, the poor old stringy bit of chicken embedded in fatty chips would turn up on the equally chipped Formica table.

The very train seemed to run on the stuff. On a down run, the carriages would merrily click over the rails: chicken-and-chips, chicken-and-chips, chicken-and-chips, like the mad Night Mail in Auden's movie-poem pulling up Beattock ("a steady climb, the gradient's against her but she's on time"). And after a while, I came to enjoy my chicken and chips. Like a prisoner longing for his hour of exercise, food meant freedom from my stinking bunk compartment - soil buckets were kept by the window - and so the smell of fried chips wafting down the corridors was a symbol of life. Back in Tehran, I missed chicken and chips so much that I sought out the meanest cafes to avoid the wonders of kebab bahrg and Persian salads, the first a mixture of lamb, saffron, tomatoes, onions, butter and black pepper, the second a wodge of cucumbers, onions, tomatoes and lettuce hearts. Given the junk food we reporters consume, I sometimes think we deserve to live short lives.

The one Iranian and Lebanese drink I am addicted to is dukh, or what the Lebanese call "laban sharab", literally, "drinking yoghurt". Mixed with lashings of salt - and with the exception of sweet tea - it's the most refreshing drink in the entire Middle East; one mouthful is to bathe in white paradise. Unless... During the 1980-88 Iran-Iraq war, one of Saddam's Scud missiles blew up the Iranian dukh factory. The substitute was not the same. A senior Iranian intelligence officer and several Hezbollah supporters were dining me out one night during the war and were appalled to hear me ask for dukh. "No - don't touch it," the spy shouted at me when it arrived. "It's not the same as it was." No problem, I said, and gulped away. It tasted like a combination of rubber tyres and hot-water bottles. I coughed it up. Always take culinary advice from spies.

It was almost as bad as the night I stopped at the town of Saropi in Afghanistan during the 1979-80 Soviet invasion. There was no electricity. The invisible hotel staff said they had bread and butter. I buttered the bread in the dark. I was sick. In the morning, I awoke to see that the butter was green with age.

Eating is an odd pastime in the Middle East. I've scoffed meat shawarma from a street stand in the Syrian city of Hama and dined with King Hussein of Jordan. I've gone through every form of gippy tummy in Cairo and Assiut and all towns south during the anti-Sadat food riots, and sat at the impeccable table of Rafik Hariri when he was prime minister of Lebanon. Andreas Whittam Smith, founder and then editor of The Independent, was with me in 1993, eyeing a vast vegetable with giant spiky leaves on the prime minister's table. "Take it!" Hariri commanded him. "Well, to tell you the truth" - those readers who know our humble founder will acknowledge that this quotation must be accurate - "I'm rather frightened of it." "Give it to me," Hariri commanded and, with a twirl of knives, reduced the thing to a few pitiful fruit lozenges.

King Hussein sat centre of a candle-lit table - there were candles in the bookcases, as well - that overflowed with an Arab mezze and flowers. The mezze was traditional: hummus (cooked chickpeas, garlic, tahini paste, lemon juice and black pepper), falafel (white beans, garlic, parsley, onions, coriander and, of course, black pepper), buraks (grated feta and mozzarella cheese, eggs, parsley, chives, mint, pastry, melted butter), tabbouleh (bulgar wheat, lemon juice, olive oil, tomatoes, parsley, mint and yet more black pepper) and yoghurt with cucumber. That was just the first course. There was a packet of cigarettes on the table in front of the king. He acknowledged their presence, his inability to give them up. They killed him.

In truth, I can attest that the humblest family in Afghanistan, Iran, Syria or Egypt will insist on feasting any visiting journalist, no matter the colour of his passport, his infidel status or his failure to remove his shoes before entering their home. Family life revolves around meals. Serious conversation in the Middle East begins after the first onion or sip of water. I suspect that the act of eating is so basic to life that hosts believe their guests will tell them the truth. No nonsense about the weather or the state of the roads. It's straight in. "Mr Robert, will there be another war in Lebanon this year?" (answer: not this year, maybe next, because both the Israelis and the Hezbollah want a war) or "Don't the Americans realise they cannot win in Afghanistan?" (answer: not yet, but they will lose, and then they'll leave saying they've won). By now, we're into the baked fish with nuts, the baked aubergine and the Turkish salad and, yes, the chicken and chips.

Arab men seem to like meat in huge amounts. Osama bin Laden - in the only meal I took with him - was more ascetic. "We will now pray and then eat," he announced the last time I met him, on a mountain in Afghanistan. There were many prayers - not by me - but little food. Bin Laden sat next to me on the ground, a tablecloth laid on the bare earth in front of us, mosquitoes swooping from the hot sky. He sipped hot sweet tea, he ate white cheese on top of the big, floppy naan bread so popular in Afghanistan and Pakistan, he bit at an onion head and he drank yoghurt. Then he went back to his tent to warn me that he prayed to God that He would permit him - Bin Laden - and his follow-ers "to turn America into a shadow of itself".

Being a child of post-war austerity, I grew up in the grey Britain of ration cards. No oranges and bananas. I was fed a diet of cabbage, carrots and beetroot and developed an insane hatred of all three. Alas, one of the specialities of the Lebanese city of Sidon is carrot juice. And one of the favourite street drinks in Tehran is beetroot juice. I've tried both. They are as terrible as ever.

There is no ducking the prohibition on alcohol in the Koran; there's no re-interpretation that can possibly allow wine to bless the dinner table - even though some of the greatest poetry of Iran and Iraq involves the drinking of wine (often by drunken poets). But, of course, there is excellent Lebanese red wine (Kifraya, Musar) and quite good Egyptian wine (the best, I must reveal, is made from grapes imported from France) and there is fine Algerian wine (thank you to the former French colonists) and there is Lebanese arak - the "milk of Lebanon", they claim it to be, probably because this gives alcoholism a healthy veneer. Distilled from rice or coconut milk, it's a close relative of ouzo and absinthe, hangs on the breath and is definitely not to be drunk before interviewing Muslim divines.

I once visited a Christian village in south-east Lebanon, almost 20 of whose inhabitants had gone down with the Titanic in 1912. They insisted I take breakfast with glasses of arak - knocked back by women and children as well as men. My wobbly notes record the villagers' miserable deaths, except for a teenage girl who left her husband and baby behind to cross the Atlantic and make a fortune, was rescued from the Atlantic when the Titanic foundered, made her fortune in the lumber industry in Canada, then returned to her Lebanese village - only to find that her friends accused her of stealing the insurance payments for those who had died. Alas, she had no grave. It is a tradition in this Christian village that coffins stand for 10 years in a chapel; the bones are then thrown down a local well. At least, after several araks, that was the story.

Sometimes it is the simplest drink or food that satisfies. I remember one baking summer day in Qom, waiting to speak to Khomeini, when an English student of Shi'ism offered me a bronze bowl of near-freezing water. Never has mere water tasted so good, another peek into paradise. Or the dust-cloaked journey to the Panjshir Valley in Afghanistan when, famished and finding a "chaikana" - a tea-house - I found they were frying eggs and serving them with naan bread and I spent half an hour in silence slurping egg from bread right out of the frying pan. Once, hot and frightened during an Israeli army raid on a village where I was staying in southern Lebanon, a man working in an orchard - and who may have been helping the resistance - held out to me a dawn-cooled mandarin, slicing it open with a hooked knife. It tasted about as sweet as life could be on that dangerous morning. Do condemned men, I remember thinking, enjoy their last meals?

Beirut is a happy place to live, wars permitting, and probably serves the cleanest and spiciest food in the Middle East. Coffee by the sea at the Manara restaurant, a few hundred metres from my apartment on the Corniche, the waves breaking only two foot away - journalists have a habit of always referring to "hot sticky coffee" and "scalding hot sweet tea", as if the Arabs would serve it cold or (unless asked otherwise) unsugared - is a great way of starting the day. The fishermen perch on rocks beside the table, the waves frothing round them. I like to take lunch in the Abdul-Wahab al-Inglisi restaurant, the only cafe I know that was named after a hanged man. Actually it's named after the street which bears the name of one of the Lebanese martyrs hanged by the Turks in 1915 (in Martyrs' Square in central Beirut, which is how it also got its name) but it lives up to the fulfilment of the independence that Abdul-Wahab sought, the most congenial mezzes, the finest fruit and vegetables, the best arak, the cleanest hubble-bubble pipes.

Or there's the dim old Spaghetteria, set back from the sea in west Beirut - the only restaurant to stay open throughout Lebanon's 15-year civil war. It lost a mirror to shellfire around 1975 and a window to the bomb that killed the aforesaid Hariri 30 years later. Its fish are fresh - I love the "sultan ibrahim" (red snappers), although I always check that the eyes are clear. Many years ago, during the war, when electricity was as scarce as peace, I was served a steak that gave me acute food poisoning for two days and lay in bed calling for the death sentence for all waiters. But the fish are now impeccable, the Italian dishes reasonably priced, the waiters (I always imagine) 150 years old and they know how to serve a gin and tonic.

I guess that sums up the city in which I live. You arrive from London or Paris and smell the cardamom in the coffee and you realise you are in the Middle East. You arrive from Tehran or Baghdad and order a gin and tonic (and buy The Independent) and you have arrived in the West. All things to all dinner guests. Tel Aviv, with its unique blend of Arabic and east European food, comes a close second to Beirut. After all, it's got more Moroccan (Jewish) restaurants and Iranian (Jewish) restaurants than most Middle East cities. Israelis, I long ago concluded, eat well. So do Palestinians, although they will correctly tell you than many of the oranges you eat in Tel Aviv are from orchards which are legally owned by the Arabs who lost them in 1948.

My Beirut driver Abed and I often buy each other cheese "manouches" - big folds of hot, thick-floured bread wrapped around wads of boiling yellow cheese - although my landlord Mustafa probably produces the best (number two being a street concession in the hill-town of Sofar). I have never understood why the manouche - there is a "zaatar" variety, if you like to clog your teeth with thyme - has not migrated to Syria or Jordan or "Palestine". I guess some food never crosses borders. Beirut's chocolates do, of course, along with the finest pistachio nuts from Rifai's Roastery - beware, the Syrian variety: they are thin and have a dry Baathist flavour - and the vast pressed orange juices that you buy on the street. There's a cafe in Hamra street which bears the name "Malek al-asir" - the "King of Juice". I like superlatives because I always remember the flower shop in Yalding, Kent, which assured customers that "Bang's Begonias Bloom the Best".

For obvious reasons, reporters in the Middle East spend a lot of time at funeral feasts, dutifully nibbling the food set out to honour the memory of rogues, dictators, vagabonds, murderers, "martyrs", war criminals and saintly prelates. My saddest meal was in a bleak village called Turungzai, outside Peshawar in the North East Frontier province of Pakistan. It was a place of open sewers and screeching children and was the home of Saifullah, one of the first victims of America's 2001 attack on Afghanistan. He had been a student who had taken money to Kabul for "suffering" Afghans - his brother admitted he might also have been a fighter - and he was blown to bits with 35 other men in one of the first US Cruise missile strikes on Kabul. They had just buried Saifullah - his name means "Sword of God" - as a martyr in the grubby little village cemetery and his father Hedayatullah invited me to eat with the family. There was roast chicken and "mitha" sweets and pots of milk and tea. With his fingers, Hedayatullah tugged hunks of chicken from the brazier, scrunched them up in his bare hands and then handed them to me to eat. I glanced at my Pashto translator who gravely nodded at me. I ate them all. Quite good, really. We survived. My translator is now a bigwig in the Afghan government. I remain a Middle East Correspondent, supposedly immune to all sickness.

But there is one culinary experience that never fails to floor me. It occurs after giving lectures at universities very far from Lebanon. I eat well the week before, lunching out at Lebanese restaurants, drinking the same "hot sticky coffee" that we always write about. And after an 18-hour flight, I arrive in Vancouver or - after a 36-hour flight - in Sydney, give a rip-roaring lecture and then, tottering with tiredness, am given an invitation by my hosts in words that are invariably the same: "Robert, we have a special surprise for you tonight - we are taking you to a Lebanese restaurant!" Oh yes, God bless my soul, what a jolly good idea. In fact, there's nothing I like better than to travel thousands of miles from Lebanon and, swaying with fatigue, eat yet more Lebanese food. The cook, always, is a Druze, who wants to tell me what "really" happened in the 1984 mountain war (at which I was present). Sometimes, even chickpeas can be boring.

But hold on. And this is a real reminder. Memo to Abed, my driver: it's your turn to buy the manouche.

27 May 2010

POWER TO CHANGE

I've always claimed that somewhere across the Atlantic - or perhaps somewhere over the Mediterranean - there lies a geopolitical fault line, perhaps a screen or curtain, through which the loveable old West (once called Christendom) sees the Middle East, and then misinterprets all it observes. An Iranian offer of peaceably resolving its nuclear program becomes a threat and a cause for sanctions. Forthcoming elections in Egypt are seen as another step towards democracy rather than further one-party rule by an 81-year old dictator. The start - yet again - of "indirect" peace talks between the Palestinians and Israelis becomes another partial success for US peacemaking rather than a shameful symbol that there is no hope for the Palestinians. Yet more slaughter in Iraq and Afghanistan are symbols of al-Qa'ida and Taliban "desperation", rather than signs that we have lost our war in both countries.

The fault lines between Russia and the Middle East, however, are not so deep, nor do they obscure so much truth. There are a number of reasons for this. The old Soviet Union maintained a more-than-colonial hold on a clutch of Muslim republics - indeed Tsarist Russia had been fighting in Chechnya in the 19th century. Read Tolstoy's Haaji Murat. "No one spoke of hatred of the Russians," Tolstoy wrote of the men whose descendants would be fighting Putin's army well over a century later. "The feeling experienced ... from the youngest to the oldest, was stronger than hatred. It was not hatred, for they did not regard dogs as human beings, but it was such repulsion, disgust and perplexity at the senseless cruelty of these creatures." He might have been writing of the incendiary anger of the people of Grozny, or of the savage fury of the Afghans after the 1979 Soviet invasion.

Yes, the Russians learned a lot in Afghanistan; and our occupation has now lasted - it's not a point our jolly generals and prime ministers will tell you - longer than theirs. Our great plans for the Battle of Kandahar - a battle I suspect will not be fought - are less ambitious than were the Soviet plans for Herat and Kandahar. But the Russians remember what happened to them.

Bin Laden once boasted to me that he destroyed the Soviet army in Afghanistan - a claim which had the merit of some truth. In Moscow five years ago, I listened to Soviet veterans of Afghanistan - some now crippled by drugs - describing the IEDs which claimed the lives of their comrades in Helmand and Kandahar provinces, the skinning alive and dismembering of captured Soviet patrols. The Soviets, it will be remembered, entered Afghanistan for their own interests - Brezhnev feared that the loss of his Communist ally in Kabul might precipitate attacks from Muslims inside the southern Soviet Union - but claimed they were fighting to prop up a people's government led (of course) by a corrupt leader, to bring socialist equality, especially in schools and healthcare, to train the Afghan army. I won't go on ...

But the Soviets understood much of the Muslim world, certainly the Arab bit of it. They had spent decades helping to teach their dictators how to rule like the Kremlin ruled, setting up a hundred mini-KGBs to crush all opposition, flooding them with arms and military aircraft, training their soldiers to fight their own people.

And when Israel won in 1967, and won again in 1973 and then again in 1982 - one memorable moment in the Israeli siege of Beirut, I recall, came when the leader of the Democratic Front for the Liberation of Palestine pleaded with Moscow to air drop weapons for them into the surrounded Lebanese capital - the Russians witnessed the humiliation of the Arabs. Russian diplomats spoke far better Arabic than their American colleagues (the same is true today) and understood the false claims of support that they - the Russians - were expected to make to the Arab "cause".

So when President Dmitry Medvedev arrived in Damascus for a meeting with President Bashar Assad earlier this month, it was typical of the Arabs to listen to him - and typical of us that we did not. Far from being impressed with "peacemaking", Medvedev declared that the Middle East situation was "very, very bad", pleading with the Americans to take serious action. "In essence, the Middle East peace process has deteriorated," he said. "A further heating up of the situation in the Middle East is fraught with an explosion and a catastrophe." And did the Americans listen? Not a bit of it. Instead, La Clinton flounced up to the Hill to tell America's legislators that the new Turkish-Brazilian-Iran nuclear deal was not good enough; UN sanctions would go ahead - with Russian help. Well, we shall see.

After his warning, the President of Russia - which is a member of the infamous Quartet supposedly run by the equally infamous Tony Blair - then did what Blair and a host of British diplomats should have done long ago; he went off to see Khaled Meshaal, the Hamas leader in

Damascus, and ask for the release of the Israeli soldier imprisoned in Gaza - undiscovered by the heroic Israeli army, let it be remembered, when Israel's warriors stormed into that midden of poverty and injustice almost a year and a half ago. The Israelis scarcely criticised Medvedev - which they would if Blair or Hague or Obama were to pay such a visit - but then again, the crazed Israeli foreign minister, Avigdor Lieberman, happens to be a Russian, doesn't he?

So what happens then? Why, Medvedev stokes the flames by formally announcing the sale of air-defence systems to Syria - Pantsir short-range surface-to-air missiles - anti-aircraft artillery batteries and a fleet of Mig-29 fighters. And on the very same day, what does Obama do? He asks Congress to approve £133m for Israel's rocket air defence. This is just a month after President Shimon Peres of Israel claimed - to considerable American scepticism, though of course they cannot show that in the face of Israeli allegations - that Syria had been sending hosts of mighty (and outdated) Scud missiles to the Hizbollah in Lebanon. These old behemoths would be of little use to the Hizbollah, though the latter - who have already claimed to have 20,000 rockets to fire at Israel - slyly chose not to deny the Scud nonsense.

This vast waste of money by the US and Russia and by the Syrians - though not by the Israelis whose economy floats on US financial grants - simply goes unnoticed in the West, where we play our little games of UN sanctions and concern for Israeli "security" (and no concern at all for Palestinian "security"). And where Obama lays out the red carpet - quite literally - for the corrupt and corrupting Hamid Karzai.

Why, oh why, I keep asking myself, doesn't Obama - who spent months debating a "surge" (how I hate that word) in Afghanistan - bring in all his foreign policy "experts" and get a hold on the deepening tragedy of this region? From sea to shining sea, the US possesses armies of deans of departments of Middle East Studies, Islamic Studies, Hebrew Studies, Arabic Studies - and yet their wisdom is never called upon. Why not? Because the foreign policy "experts" - and their disreputable clones on CNN, Fox News, ABC, NBC, CBS, etc - want no part of their wisdom. For Harvard, read the Brookings Institute; for Berkeley, read the Rand Corporation, etc, etc.

And what lies behind this? I turn to my old mate John Mearsheimer, co-author of The Israel Lobby and US Foreign Policy which became a best- seller among ordinary Americans - despite the usual ravings of Alan Dershowitz (he of "Judge Goldstone is an evil man" infamy) - who has now published yet another brave article on the woeful influence of the Israeli lobby on Washington; actually, it is the Likud party lobby, but let's not worry about the difference right now. Mearsheimer says that President Barack Obama has "finally coaxed Israel and the Palestinians back to the negotiating table", hoping that this will lead to the creation of a Palestinian state in Gaza and the West Bank. "Regrettably, that is not going to happen," Mearsheimer states. "Instead, those territories are almost certain to be incorporated into a 'Greater Israel' which will then be an apartheid state bearing a marked resemblance to white-ruled South Africa."

No American president can pressure Israel to change its policies towards Palestinians. Mearsheimer does not mince his words. "The main reason is the Israeli lobby, a powerful coalition of American Jews and Christian evangelicals that has a profound influence on US Middle East policy. Alan Dershowitz" - yes, the same - "was spot on when he said, 'My generation of Jews ... became part of what is perhaps the most effective lobbying and fund-raising effort in the history of democracy.'"

It isn't the first time that an American academic has been so blunt. Since 1967, every US president has opposed the internationally illegal Israeli colonisation of Arab land in the West Bank. None has been successful. Obama isn't going to have any more luck that his predecessors. After becoming President, he demanded an end to these colonies. Netanyahu told him to get lost. Obama - Mearsheimer's accurate words - "caved in". When Obama demanded no more Israeli building in East Jerusalem, Netanyahu said Israel would never stop building there because it was "an integral part of the Jewish state". Obama flunked again.

Netanyahu has yet again repeated there will be no halt in building in that part of Jerusalem which the Palestinians need as their capital. Obama didn't even respond. And don't think for a moment that Clinton will - she wants to be the next American president after Obama.

The flaw of the Europeans, of course, is that they will not themselves take any steps over Israel because - this is the sublime and false message of all EU foreign ministers - it is America that has "leverage" over Israel. Yes, it should be America that has leverage over Israel - given its massive economic subventions to the Jewish state - but it's not; because, as Mearsheimer says, the lobby has too much control over US policy in the Middle East. This is not to suggest that there is some kind of Jewish "conspiracy", merely that this Israeli-Likudist lobby deprives the US of any independent rights as a negotiator and emasculates American policy by endangering American relations with the rest of the region.

Former Israeli prime minister Ehud Olmert - who like many ex-ministers and presidents tells the self-evident truth when he no longer has the ability to enforce that truth - says that if the two-state solution collapses (which it will), "Israel will face a South African-style struggle" and "as soon as that happens, the state of Israel is finished". Mearsheimer's argument is that "the lobby in the US is effectively helping Israel destroy its own future as a Jewish state".

And what do we do? We go on supporting all the outrageous dictators and potentates of the region, encouraging them to trust the US, to make more concessions to Israel, but to keep their people down. We do sometimes ask them to be "more democratic". This was a George W Bush idea - summed up by his wife, who thought King Abdullah of Jordan and his wife were good examples of democrats - this, in an unconstitutional monarchy! I do sometimes wonder at the irony - and the hypocrisy - of European countries which urge democracy on the Arabs.

We all want little Houses of Commons dotted over the Middle East at a time when most EU countries are turning into presidential-style nations. The prestige of the real House of Commons has been steadily deteriorating for years - no British paper, for example, even carries a parliamentary page today - and Blairite rule has a lot to do with this. Perhaps that's why this wretched man doesn't push the democracy thing too much in the Middle East.

Yet, it is all true. Arab rulers are so sure of themselves that they now say boo to the golden goose. When the Obama administration criticised Hosni Mubarak's decision to continue its three-decade-old emergency law - Clinton said the extension ignored "a broad range of Egyptian voices" - the Egyptian foreign minister blithely replied that the statement was "overly politicised", adding that the criticism was aimed at the US media and human rights groups. He was absolutely right about the latter.

So is the American age ending? Alas, not yet. Perhaps some of our illusions about the Middle East are being amended. Perhaps the latest attacks in Iraq, and the more spectacular ones in Afghanistan, including the astonishing attack on Bagram air base - I thought we were supposed to be fighting the Battle of Kandahar, not the Battle of Bagram - will force us to acknowledge more truths. That the Muslim people - not their corrupt leaders - cannot be put down, will not be put down, even when the insurgencies against the West are as ruthless as they are regressive. But are we learning? The US sends flocks of drones over Pakistan, shoots missiles into Waziristan, a Pakistani-born American then tries to blow up a car bomb in Times Square in revenge - and the Americans then in revenge use drones to kill 15 more men in Pakistan, and then ... Readers can write the next bit for themselves.

On top of all this, we still graft our own extraordinary preemptive history onto this massive conflict. I'm often reminded of the way we went to war in Northern Ireland in the early 1970s. We journalists arrived there with little historical knowledge, save for a vague image of the Punch cartoon Irishman, drunk and carrying a cudgel, anxious to kill without reason all the refined Englishmen who came to invade his country - and the faint memory that Catholic Ireland was neutral in the Second World War (true), that de Valera paid a visit of condolence to the German legation on Hitler's death (true), that Irishmen refuelled German U-boats (untrue).

The Muslims find themselves in a similar situation; we believe they want to Islamicise the West (untrue), they want to expand into the West - untrue, they did that in Andalucia - that their expansion is achieved by the sword. Do we really believe that Indonesia, the largest Muslim nation in the world, was invaded by Arabs? There's even the Second World War bit - that the Arabs were pro-Nazi. Well, it's true that the Grand Mufti of Jerusalem met Hitler and made several disgraceful broadcasts against the Jews though he did not - as Israel's propagandists claim - ever visit Auschwitz. But then again, Anwar Sadat was a spy for Rommel in Egypt - and would happily have watched the Wehrmacht continue on its way to Palestine - but he became Israel's greatest Arab friend, invited to Jerusalem when he wanted to make peace.

But our preconceptions go much further back - to the days when we generally used the word "Turk" for Muslims. In Italy, they were using the word "Turks" as a curse before the 16th century. As Swedish diplomat Ingmar Karlsson discovered when researching for a paper he delivered in Istanbul in 2005, the Italians used to have a phrase "puzza come un Turco" which meant "he stinks like a Turk". Today, we still use the phrase "to talk turkey" and my own 1949 Random House American College Dictionary gives one definition of "Turk" as "a cruel, barbarous, or tyrannical person".

And so it goes on, not without a little help from our dear Pope at Regensburg. Yet Arabs became Roman emperors and were visiting the east before us. When Vasco Da Gama "discovered" India and reached Calicut (Calcutta) on 20 May 1498 - I owe this possibly apocryphal story to Warwick Ball in his remarkable Out of Arabia - he was greeted by an Arab from Tunisia with the words "May the devil take you! What brought you here?" But a contemporary chronicle from Hadramaut (in modern-day Yemen) describes how French vessels appeared at sea one day heading for India. "They took about seven (Arab) vessels, killing those on board and making some prisoners. This was their first action, may God curse them!" The Europeans were arriving in the Indian Ocean when we think the Arabs were trying to enter Europe.

Maybe that was the original fault line. Or it was the Crusades? Or the Ottoman Empire - remember how Turkey was "the sick man of Europe"? - or our lies to the Arabs about Palestine? Or the Iranian revolution? Or our unconditional support for Israel? Or our fostering of all those awful dictatorships? But it's time we got rid of fault lines, saw the reality of history and listened - dare I repeat it? - to the likes of Dmitry Medvedev.

DEATH OF BIN LADEN

2011: 'A RESOUNDING TRIUMPH'

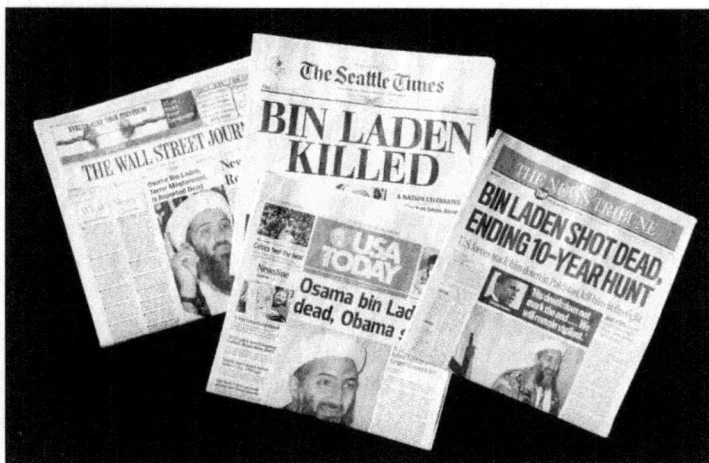

Death of Osama bin Laden

3 May 2011

PAKISTAN KNEW HIS HIDING PLACE ALL ALONG

A middle-aged nonentity, a political failure outstripped by history - by the millions of Arabs demanding freedom and democracy in the Middle East - died in Pakistan yesterday. And then the world went mad.

Fresh from providing us with a copy of his birth certificate, the American President turned up in the middle of the night to provide us with a live-time death certificate for Osama bin Laden, killed in a town named after a major in the army of the old British Empire. A single shot to the head, we were told. But the body's secret flight to Afghanistan, an equally secret burial at sea? The weird and creepy disposal of the body - no shrines, please - was almost as creepy as the man and his vicious organisation.

The Americans were drunk with joy. David Cameron thought it "a massive step forward". India described it as a "victorious milestone". "A resounding triumph," Israeli Prime Minister Netanyahu boasted. But after 3,000 American dead on 9/11, countless more in the Middle East, up to half a million Muslims dead in Iraq and Afghanistan and 10 years trying to find Bin Laden, pray let us have no more "resounding triumphs". Revenge attacks? Perhaps they will come, by the little groupuscules in the West, who have no direct contact with al-Qa'ida. Be sure, someone is already dreaming up a "Brigade of the Martyr Osama bin Laden". Maybe in Afghanistan, among the Taliban.

But the mass revolutions in the Arab world over the past four months mean that al-Qa'ida was already politically dead. Bin Laden told the world - indeed, he told me personally - that he wanted to destroy the pro-Western regimes in the Arab world, the dictatorships of the Mubaraks and the Ben Alis. He wanted to create a new Islamic Caliphate. But these past few months, millions of Arab Muslims rose up and were prepared for their own martyrdom - not for Islam but for freedom and liberty and democracy. Bin Laden didn't get rid of the tyrants. The people did. And they didn't want a caliph.

I met the man three times and have only one question left unasked: what did he think as he watched those revolutions unfold this year - under the flags of nations rather than Islam, Christians and Muslims together, the kind of people his own al-Qa'ida men were happy to butcher?

In his own eyes, his achievement was the creation of al-Qa'ida, the institution which had no card-carrying membership. You just woke up in the morning, wanted to be in al-Qa'ida - and you were. He was the founder. But he was never a hands-on warrior. There was no computer in his cave, no phone calls to set bombs off. While the Arab dictators ruled uncontested with our support, they largely avoided condemning American policy; only Bin Laden said these things. Arabs never wanted to fly planes into tall buildings, but they did admire a man who said what they wanted to say. But now, increasingly, they can say these things. They don't need Bin Laden. He had become a nonentity.

But talking of caves, Bin Laden's demise does bring Pakistan into grim focus. For months, President Ali Zardari has been telling us that

Bin Laden was living in a cave in Afghanistan. Now it turns out he was living in a mansion in Pakistan. Betrayed? Of course he was. By the Pakistan military or the Pakistan Inter-Services Intelligence? Quite possibly both. Pakistan knew where he was.

Not only was Abbottabad the home of the country's military college - the town was founded by Major James Abbott of the British Army in 1853 - but it is headquarters of Pakistan's Northern Army Corps' 2nd Division. Scarcely a year ago, I sought an interview with another "most wanted man" - the leader of the group believed responsible for the Mumbai massacres. I found him in the Pakistani city of Lahore - guarded by uniformed Pakistani policemen holding machine guns.

Of course, there is one more obvious question unanswered: couldn't they have captured Bin Laden? Didn't the CIA or the Navy Seals or the US Special Forces or whatever American outfit killed him have the means to throw a net over the tiger? "Justice," Barack Obama called his death. In the old days, of course, "justice" meant due process, a court, a hearing, a defence, a trial. Like the sons of Saddam, Bin Laden was gunned down. Sure, he never wanted to be taken alive - and there were buckets of blood in the room in which he died.

But a court would have worried more people than Bin Laden. After all, he might have talked about his contacts with the CIA during the Soviet occupation of Afghanistan, or about his cosy meetings in Islamabad with Prince Turki, Saudi Arabia's head of intelligence. Just as Saddam - who was tried for the murder of a mere 153 people rather than thousands of gassed Kurds - was hanged before he had the chance to tell us about the gas components that came from America, his friendship with Donald Rumsfeld, the US military assistance he received when he invaded Iran in 1980.

Oddly, he was not the "most wanted man" for the international crimes against humanity of 11 September 2001. He gained his Wild West status by al-Qa'ida's earlier attacks on the US embassies in Africa and the attack on the US barracks in Dhahran. He was always waiting for Cruise missiles - so was I when I met him. He had waited for death before, in the caves of Tora Bora in 2001 when his bodyguards refused to let him stand and fight and forced him to walk over the mountains to Pakistan. Some of his time he would spend in Karachi - he was obsessed with Karachi; he even, weirdly, gave me photographs of pro-

Bin Laden graffiti on the walls of the former Pakistani capital and praised the city's imams.

His relations with other Muslims were mysterious; when I met him in Afghanistan, he initially feared the Taliban, refusing to let me travel to Jalalabad at night from his training camp - he handed me over to his al-Qa'ida lieutenants to protect me on the journey next day. His followers hated all Shia Muslims as heretics and all dictators as infidels - though he was prepared to cooperate with Iraq's ex-Baathists against the country's American occupiers, and said so in an audiotape which the CIA typically ignored. He never praised Hamas and was scarcely worthy of their "holy warrior" definition yesterday which played - as usual - straight into Israel's hands.

In the years after 2001, I maintained a faint indirect communication with Bin Laden, once meeting one of his trusted al-Qa'ida associates at a secret location in Pakistan. I wrote out a list of 12 questions, the first of which was obvious: what kind of victory could he claim when his actions resulted in the US occupation of two Muslim countries? There was no reply for weeks. Then one weekend, waiting to give a lecture in Saint Louis in the US, I was told that Al Jazeera had produced a new audiotape from Bin Laden. And one by one - without mentioning me - he answered my 12 questions. And yes, he wanted the Americans to come to the Muslim world - so he could destroy them.

When Wall Street journalist Daniel Pearl was kidnapped, I wrote a long article in The Independent, pleading with Bin Laden to try to save his life. Pearl and his wife had looked after me when I was beaten on the Afghan border in 2001; he even gave me the contents of his contacts book. Much later, I was told that Bin Laden had read my report with sadness. But Pearl had already been murdered. Or so he said.

Yet Bin Laden's own obsessions blighted even his family. One wife left him, two more appeared to have been killed in Sunday's American attack. I met one of his sons, Omar, in Afghanistan with his father in 1994. He was a handsome little boy and I asked him if he was happy. He said "yes" in English. But last year, he published a book called Living Bin Laden and - recalling how his father killed his beloved dogs in a chemical warfare experiment - described him as an "evil man". In his book, he too remembered our meeting; and concluded that he should have told me that no, he was not a happy child.

By midday yesterday, I had three phone calls from Arabs, all certain that it was Bin Laden's double who was killed by the Americans - just as I know many Iraqis who still believe that Saddam's sons were not killed in 2003, nor Saddam really hanged. In due course, al-Qa'ida will tell us. Of course, if we are all wrong and it was a double, we're going to be treated to yet another videotape from the real Bin Laden - and President Barack Obama will lose the next election.

4 May 2011

DOES THIS MEAN IT'S TIME TO GO HOME?

So why are we in Afghanistan? Didn't the Americans and the British go there in 2001 to fight Osama bin Laden? Wasn't he killed on Monday? There was painful symbolism in the Nato airstrike yesterday - scarcely 24 hours after Bin Laden's death - that killed yet more Afghan security guards. For the truth is that we long ago lost the plot in the graveyard of empires, turning a hunt for a now largely irrelevant inventor of global jihad into a war against tens of thousands of Taliban insurgents who have little interest in al-Qa'ida, but much enthusiasm to drive Western armies out of their country.

The gentle hopes of Hamid Karzai and Hillary Clinton - that the Taliban will be so cowed by the killing of Bin Laden that they will want to become pleasant democrats and humbly join the Western-supported and utterly corrupt leadership of Afghanistan - shows just how out of touch they are with the blood-soaked reality of the country. Some of the Taliban admired Bin Laden, but they did not love him and he had been no part of their campaign against Nato. Mullah Omar is more dangerous to the West in Afghanistan than Bin Laden. And we haven't killed Omar.

Iran, for once, spoke for millions of Arabs in its response to Bin Laden's death. "An excuse for alien countries to deploy troops in this region under the pretext of fighting terrorism has been eliminated," its foreign ministry spokesman has said. "We hope this development will end war, conflict, unrest and the death of innocent people, and help to establish peace and tranquillity in the region."

Newspapers across the Arab world said the same thing. If this is such a great victory for the United States, it's time to go home; which, of course, the US has no intention of doing just now.

That many Americans think the same thing is not going to change the topsy-turvy world in which US policy is framed. For there is one home truth which the world still has not grasped: that the revolutions in Tunisia and Egypt - and, more pressing, the bloodbaths in Libya and Syria and the dangers to Lebanon - are of infinitely graver importance than blowing away a bearded man who has been elevated in the West's immature imagination into Hitlerian proportions.

Turkish prime minister Erdogan's brilliant address in Istanbul yesterday - calling for the Syrians to stop killing their people and for Gaddafi to leave Libya - was more eloquent, more powerful and more historic than the petty, boastful, Hollywood speeches of Obama and Clinton on Monday. We are now wasting our time speculating who will "take over" al-Qa'ida - Zawahiri or Saif al-Adel - when the movement has no "leadership" as such, Bin Laden being the founder rather than the boss.

But, a day being a long time in the killing fields of the Middle East, just 24 hours after Osama Bin Laden died, other questions were growing thicker yesterday. If, for example, Barack Obama really thinks the world is "a safer place" after Bin Laden's death, how come the US has increased its threat alert and embassies around the world are being told to take extra precautions against attack?

And just what did happen in that tatty compound - no longer, it seems, a million-dollar "mansion" - when Bin Laden's sulphurous life was brought to an end? Human Rights Watch is unlikely to be the only institution to demand a "thorough, transparent investigation" into the killing.

There was an initial story from Pentagon "sources" which had two of Bin Laden's wives killed and a woman held as a "human shield" dying too. Within hours, the wives were alive and in some accounts, the third woman simply disappeared.

And then of course, there's Pakistan, eagerly telling the world that it participated in the attack on Bin Laden, only to have President Zardari retract the entire story yesterday. Two hours later, we had an American official describing the attack on Bin Laden as a "shared achievement".

And there's Bin Laden's secret burial in the Arabian Sea. Was this planned before the attack on Bin Laden, with the clear plan to kill rather than capture him? And if it was carried out "according to Islamic rights" - the dead man's body washed and placed in a white shroud -

it must have taken a long time for the officer on the USS Carl Vinson to devise a 50-minute religious ceremony and arrange for an Arabic-speaking sailor to translate it.

So now for a reality check. The world is not safer for Bin Laden's killing. It is safer because of the winds of freedom blowing through the Middle East. If the West treats the people of this region with justice rather than military firepower, then al-Qa'ida becomes even more irrelevant than it has been since the Arab revolutions.

Of course, there is one positive side for the Arab world. With Bin Laden killed, the Gaddafis and the Salehs and the Assads will find it all the more difficult to claim that a man who is now dead is behind the popular revolutions trying to overthrow them.

13 September 2012

BENGHAZI

So another internet clever-clogs sets the Middle East on fire: Prophet cartoons, then Koranic book-burning, now a video of robed "terrorists" and a fake desert. The Western-Christian perpetrators then go into hiding (an essential requisite for publicity) while the innocent are asphyxiated, beheaded and otherwise done to death - outrageous Muslim revenge thus "proving" the racist claims of the trash peddlers that Islam is a violent religion.

The provocateurs, of course, know that politics and religion don't mix in the Middle East. They are the same. Chris Stevens, his diplomat colleagues in Benghazi, priests in Turkey and Africa, UN personnel in Afghanistan; they have all paid the price for those "Christian priests", "cartoonists", "film-makers" and "authors" - the inverted commas are necessary to mark a thin line between illusionists and the real thing - who knowingly choose to provoke 1.6 billion Muslims.

When a Danish cartoon in a hitherto unknown newspaper drew a picture of the Prophet Mohamed with a bomb in his turban, the Danish embassy in Beirut went up in flames. When a Texas pastor decided to "sentence the Koran to death", the knives came out in Afghanistan - we are leaving aside the little matter of the "accidental" burning of Koranic pages by US personnel in Bagram. And now a deliberately abusive film provokes the murder of one of the State Department's fairest diplomats.

In many ways, it's familiar territory. In 15th-century Spain, Christian cartoonists drew illustrations of the Prophet committing unspeakable acts. And - just so we don't think we have clean claws today - when a Paris cinema showed a film in which Christ made love to a woman, the building was burned down, one person was killed and the killer was a Christian. With the help of our wonderful new technology it only takes a couple of loonies to kick off a miniature war in the Muslim world within seconds. I doubt if poor Christopher Stevens - a man who really understood the Arabs as many of his colleagues do not - had ever heard of the "film" that unleashed the storming of the US consulate in Benghazi and his own death. It's one thing to witlessly claim that the US would go on a "crusade" against al-Qa'ida - thank you, George W Bush - but another to insult, quite deliberately, an entire people. Racism of this kind stirs many a crazed heart.

And has al-Qa'ida - defeated by the Arab revolutionaries who demanded dignity rather than a Bin Laden caliphate across the Middle East - now decided to cash in on populist grievances to advance its Islamist cause? Libya's largely impotent government blames the Americans themselves for Stevens' killing - since the consulate should have been evacuated - and suggests that a Gaddafi clique was behind the attack. This is ridiculous. If the armed militia in Benghazi, calling itself the "Islamic Law Supporters", are more than telephone gunmen, then al-Qa'ida involvement has to be suspected.

Ironically, there is room for a serious discussion among Muslims about, for example, a reinterpretation of the Koran. But Western provocation - and Western, alas, it is - closes down such a narrative. Meanwhile, we beat our chests in favour of a "free press". A New Zealand editor once proudly told me how his own newspaper had republished the cartoon of the Prophet with a bomb-filled turban. But when I asked him if he planned to publish a cartoon of a Rabbi with a bomb on his head next time Israel invaded Lebanon, he hastily agreed with me that this would be anti-Semitic.

25 Janurary 2013

THE NEW FACE OF AL-QA'IDA

"Had he his hurts before?" Siward asks of his slain son in Macbeth. He wants to know if his son's wounds proved he was fighting Macbeth's goons when he died, or whether - if stabbed in the back -

he had been running away. Macbeth would have made a pretty good Middle Eastern dictator, obsessed with power, murdering his rivals, oppressing his people under the fatal influence of a spoiled, ruthless wife. And al-Qa'ida, in its battles with its infidel enemies - the Russians, the Americans, Israel, the West and the Arab potentates who do, or did, our bidding - does not run away. Their battle wounds are part of their personalities.

Osama bin Laden boasted to me of the Russian bullet scars burnt into his body in Afghanistan - three in all - and the Taliban leader Mullah Omar, who wore the Prophet's cloak in Kandahar, has always rejoiced in the eye he lost to his enemies. And now we have Mokhtar Belmokhtar with another eye lost to God's enemies.

This Cyclops wears no patch to hide his wound. Was it shot out by the pro-Western "mujahedin" in Afghanistan after the Soviet withdrawal? Or blown from his face when he was "mishandling" explosives during the war, when Belmokhtar and his cronies were still heroes, our equivalent - once, in Ronald Reagan's eyes - of the Founding Fathers?

Now he hides in - or bestrides, if you believe what you are told - Mali. Al-Qa'ida is back in action, but this Algerian war veteran is an intriguing symbol of the path down which Osama bin Laden's damaged creation now slouches. For Belmokhtar's Afghan war record is clouded by his cruel participation in the vicious 1990s conflict with the military regime in his own country - he was born in the Algerian city of Ghardaia 40 years ago - and by the corruption which has embraced so many North African Islamist militias.

When he travelled to Afghanistan, he was only 19; when he fought the equally ruthless pro-government paramilitaries in Algeria, he had learnt that wars do not necessarily end, that victory is achieved through the humiliation of your enemies, rather than military conquest.

But Belmokhtar was a child of his country's history. Born almost exactly a year after the French colonial power retreated from Algeria, he grew up speaking the language of his country's former oppressors. His French was perfect, and those few Westerners who met him - usually as his captives - were to recall his fluency. Kalashnikov at his feet, Belmokhtar would ostentatiously read the Koran - the mirror image of Bin Laden - as a leader of al-Qa'ida in the Islamic Maghreb and then, having left its ranks long after its apparent defeat in Algeria, as the chef of al-Muwaqqiun bil Dima, uncomfortably but chillingly trans-lated as "Those Who Sign With Blood". Those who were to survive the atrocities at the In Amenas gas field last week - and, I suppose, those who did not - were to discover what this meant.

In a video, Belmokhtar has spoken of the struggle against disbe-lief - in other words, us, the West - the importance of Islamic law and the Islamic project in northern Mali. He is too canny a man not to have realised that Mali's torment springs from the decades-long northern Tuareg-Berber-Arabophone refusal to be governed by a black admin-istration in the south, but he was drawn - like Bin Laden in Afghanistan - into a land where centralised power was weak or non-existent. While human rights groups recorded ferocious Islamist pun-ishments - executions, amputations, the oppression of women; the list is familiar - he spoke of a sharia which fed the poor, created justice between Muslims, and equal rights.

Andrew Lebovich, an Africa analyst in Dakar, has drawn atten-tion to the fact that Belmokhtar's jihadism may be very real, despite his involvement in smuggling and trafficking, and that his public state-ments should be studied and taken seriously. Northern Mali was threatened by "the Crusader Western nations, especially France", Bel-mokhtar announced, and aggressors would be would be fought "in their homes", and "experience the heat of wounds" in their own coun-tries, and their interests attacked. Here, indeed, was a warning about In Amenas. Prophetic, should we say?

Belmokhtar greeted Mullah Omar, the Taliban leader, and Bin Laden's successor, Ayman al-Zawahiri, the "persevering emir". In other words, he was re-asserting his loyalty to original al-Qa'ida prin-ciples. But the problem - which we in the West refuse to comprehend - is that al-Qa'ida itself has changed. The days when this dangerous institution demanded a world-wide Islamic caliphate are long gone. The Arab Awakening - the mass Arab revolts against dictatorship - turned Bin Laden into yesterday's man. His television viewing at Ab-bottabad in the days before his execution by the Americans proved to Bin Laden that not a single protester - from Cairo to Damascus to Yemen - waved an al-Qa'ida flag or carried his photograph.

Indeed, among Bin Laden's last communications with followers in Yemen was a demand for a translation of an article I wrote in The Independent, in which I described al-Qa'ida - following its involve-ment with Sunni suicide killers of Shias in Iraq - as the most sectarian organisation in the world. Bin Laden had long protested against the outfit's role in the sectarian bloodbath in Iraq. And so a re-positioned al-Qa'ida has emerged.

Abdel Bari Atwan of the newspaper Al-Quds al-Arabi - who understands the dark soul of al-Qa'ida better than anyone else - has spoken of how Bin Laden always spoke "longingly" of the Atlas mountains of the Maghreb - the Tora Bora of north Africa - and of America's interests in Africa itself. Many of Bin Laden's legionnaires decamped from Afghanistan to Algeria, Mali, Mauritania, Chad and Niger, even Nigeria. The US now imports as much oil from Nigeria as it does from Saudi Arabia, the country of Bin Laden's own citizenship. Like Gaddafi - whom Bin Laden loathed - al-Qa'ida appreciated the economic importance of Africa. Had Bin Laden himself not spent five years in dangerous exile in Sudan?

In a weird but very clear way, the results of the fearful Algerian civil war were in Belmokhtar's favour. President Bouteflika, France's dearest friend in the new North Africa, called a successful referendum which effectively pardoned Islamist fighters while excusing the government's mass torturers and execution squads. Thus the weaker brethren of the Islamist revolt went home while the hard, unforgiving men emigrated into the deserts and across the Algerian border. Belmokhtar inherited a "cleansed" al-Qa'ida katiba - and a new version of Bin Laden's battle.

Henceforth al-Qa'ida's "purity of arms" - and this was never admitted - would be directed not towards the hopeless aspiration of a world caliphate, but at struggles which could humble Islam's kafir enemies. Bin Laden's battle tactics remained unchanged; only his philosophy would be gently abandoned. Now his fighters - in the hands of Belmokhtar or his latest rival, the supposedly ascetic Abdulhamid Abu Zeid - must humble the Western armies they can persuade to intervene in the Muslim world. Just as every Western soldier that could be induced into Afghanistan and Iraq was a target, so every French soldier arriving in Mali must be a target.

Humble the West's mighty armies and draw them into perfidy with their bloody allies. That is now al-Qa'ida's order of battle. The more France - and America and Britain - can be provoked to ally themselves with the ferocious Algerian government or the killers in the Malian army, the greater al-Qa'ida's victory. Already, French and British horror at the Algerian slaughter of hostages and insurgents alike at In Amenas has been deleted from the record. David Cameron naively - and with a script that might have been written by Belmokhtar - has proclaimed that "our determination is stronger than ever to work with allies right around the world to root out and defeat this terrorist scourge". Quite apart from Cameron's appalling clichés ("root out", "scourge") - which oddly parallel al-Qa'ida's boring rhetoric - this effectively allies the United Kingdom with the killer regime in Algeria. Plenty of Macbeths there.

Now human rights groups are reporting the revenge murder of Tuareg civilians in newly "liberated" towns by the Malian army. "Western diplomats", that all-purpose bunch of mountebanks so beloved of us journos, are now said to "have long warned that the [Malian] army would become involved in revenge killings. Pity they didn't tell us that a month ago. And then we have the French Defence Minister, Jean-Yves le Drian, divulging to us that Belmokhtar's insurgents have "diversified their tactics. They can leave a town at any time, or mingle with the population... It's urban guerrilla warfare, as well as a war, so it's very complicated to manage." And he didn't tell us that a month ago, did he?

The Associated Press - not, I must admit, my favourite agency of world truth - published a remarkable, brilliant report by Rukmini Callimachi this week, an account of how Belmokhtar's fellow jihadist Abdulhamid Abu Zeid arrived in the Malian town of Diabaly, took over civilian homes with the help of veterans from Iraq and Afghanistan, hid to avoid French air strikes, gave gifts to children, offered to pay rent and money for water and, guarded by five armed men, ate boxes of food imported from Algeria. "He ate spaghetti and powdered milk, read the Koran and planned a war,"

And there you have it. Ignore them, and you have lost the "war on terror". Fight them, and you face humiliation. The Algerian Belmokhtar understands this. We do not. Diversified tactics, the French minister tells us. Mingling with the population. Camouflage. Birnam Wood comes to Dunsinane.

2 September 2013

ONCE WASHINGTON MADE THE MIDDLE EAST TREMBLE

Watershed. It's the only word for it. Once Lebanon and Syria and Egypt trembled when Washington spoke. Now they laugh. It's not just a question of what happened to the statesmen of the past. No one believed that Cameron was Churchill or that the silly man in the White House was Roosevelt - although Putin might make a rather good Stalin. It's more a question of credibility; no one in the Middle East takes America seriously anymore. And you only had to watch Obama on Saturday to see why.

For there he was, prattling on in the most racist way about "ancient sectarian differences" in the Middle East. Since when was the president of the United States an expert on these supposed "sectarian differences"? Constantly we are shown maps of the Arab world with Shias and Sunnis and Christians colour-coded onto the nations which we generously bequeathed to the region after the First World War. But when is an American paper going to carry a colour-coded map of Washington or Chicago with black and white areas delineated by streets?

But what was amazing was the sheer audacity of our leaders in thinking that they could yet again bamboozle their electorates with their lies and trumperies and tomfooleries.

This doesn't mean that the Syrian regime did not use gas "on its own people" - a phrase we used to use about Saddam when we wanted a war in Iraq - but it does mean that our present leaders are now paying the price for the dishonesty of Bush and Blair.

Obama, who is becoming more and more preacher-like, wants to be the Punisher-in-Chief of the Western World, the Avenger-in-Chief. There is something oddly Roman about him. And the Romans were good at two things. They believed in law and they believed in crucifixion. The US constitution - American "values" and the cruise missile have a faintly similar focus. The lesser races must be civilized and they must be punished, even if the itsy-bitsy tiny missile launches look more like perniciousness than war. Everyone outside the Roman Empire was called a barbarian. Everyone outside Obama's empire is called a terrorist.

And as usual, the Big Picture has a habit of taking away some of the little details we should know about.

Take Afghanistan, for example. I had an interesting phone call from Kabul three days ago. And it seems that the Americans are preventing President Karzai purchasing new Russian Mi helicopters - because Moscow sells the same helicopters to Syria. Well, how about that. The US, it seems, is now trying to damage Russian trade relations with Afghanistan - why the Afghans would want to do business with the country that enslaved them for eight years is another matter - because of Damascus.

Now another little piece of news. Just over a week ago, two massive car bombs blew up outside two Salafist mosques in the north Lebanese city of Tripoli. They killed 47 people and wounded another 500. Now it has emerged that five people have been charged by the Lebanese security services over these bombings and one of them is said to be a captain in the Syrian government intelligence service.

His charge is "in absentia", as they say, and we all like to think that men and women are innocent until proved guilty. But two sheikhs have also been charged, one of them apparently the head of a pro-Damascus Islamist organization. The other sheikh is also said to be close to Syrian intelligence. Typically, Obama is so keen on bombarding Syria for gassing that he has missed out on this nugget of information which has angered and infuriated millions of Lebanese.

But I guess this is what happens when you take your eye off the ball.

It reminds me of a book that was published by Yale University Press in 2005. It was called The New Lion of Damascus by David Lesch, a professor at Trinity University in Texas. Those were the days when Bashar al-Assad was still being held up as the bright new broom in Syria.

"Bashar," Lesch concluded, "is, indeed, the hope - and the promise of a better future."

Then last year - by which time the West had abandoned its dreams of Bashar - the good professor came up with another book, again published by Yale. This time it was called Syria: The Fall of the House of Assad, and Lesch concluded: "He (Bashar) was short-sighted and became deluded. He failed miserably."

EPILOGUE

COMING FULL CIRCLE

ISIS threat

28 December 2015

THE NEWS FROM AFGHANISTAN MUST BE VERY BAD

The news from Afghanistan is very bad. No one says that, of course. President Ghani has a "national unity government" that "supports a strong partnership with the United States", according to Barack Obama two months ago. Sure, Kunduz was captured by the Taliban - but then the Afghans got it back (though minus one American-bombed hospital, along with most of its patients and doctors). Sure, Sangin was captured by the Taliban - but now the Afghan army is fighting to get it back. But didn't more than a hundred British soldiers die to hold Sangin? Sure, but American troops in Iraq died to hold and keep Mosul - and Mosul is now the home of the Isis leader, Abu Bakr al-Baghdadi. And US troops in Iraq died to capture Fallujah, then lost it, and died all over again to recapture it - and Fallujah is now in the hands of Isis.

We don't do "bad news" from Afghanistan or Iraq. It's like a movie, replayed over and over again each Christmas. Just two weeks ago, General John F Campbell, the US commander of American and Nato forces in the country, admitted that Isis has surfaced in Afghanistan. There could be 3,000 or 4,000 or 5,000 Isis men who are now trying to consolidate links to their "mothership" in Iraq and Syria; note the Hollywood language here. Isis wants to establish its pre-Afghan "Khorasan Province" in Afghanistan's Nangarhar province.

But Obama assures us that America's "commitment to Afghanistan and its people endures" and Afghan forces are "fighting for their country bravely and tenaciously" and "continue to hold most [sic] urban areas". Taliban successes were "predictable", the US president says, but almost 10,000 troops will remain in Afghanistan - even though the war is over - and 14 months ago, David Cameron told our own chaps that their achievements in Afghanistan "will live for ever". Not any more.

As our very own ex-chief of the general staff, General Dannatt, said last week, he was "not surprised" by the fall of Sangin. Not at all. After all, "we always knew that the situation once we left Sangin would be difficult. We left Afghanistan in a situation where the Afghans were in control and the future was in their hands. It is not a great surprise that the Taliban have continued to push in southern Afghanistan, it's their heartland."

So Isis men are now fighting in their thousands in the country we arrived to "liberate" 14 years ago, quite apart from tens of thousands of Taliban "pushing" in to their "heartland" around Sangin (so much for Cameron's stuff about achievements living for ever). And yet Obama tells Americans that in the corrupt Afghan government, the US has "a serious partner", a "stable and committed ally" to prevent "future threats".

It was in 1940, when German soldiers were swarming into France - a rather more dangerous swarm than the one Cameron obsesses about in exactly the same area today - that Churchill decided to tell Britons the truth. "The news from France is very bad..." he began.

And British soldiers, in their thousands, were dying to stem the invasion. Their "achievement" was not victory, but Dunkirk.

Yet we are not permitted to use this same expression - "very bad" - about Afghanistan. No, Cameron had to talk about an "achievement", and now the mother of a terribly wounded soldier speaks of her "desperate sense of waste". For Gen Dannatt, the future's up to those Afghan army chappies now. No big deal; we always knew the Taliban would fight on.

You only have to read Afghan journalists' reports from the country to know that even the old Churchillian "very bad" is a bit on the optimistic side. Take the case of the Shia Muslim Hazara Afghans taken from a bus on the way to Kabul this year. The lads from Isis stopped the bus, abducted 30 Shias and wanted to exchange them for family prisoners - Uzbeks, it seems - in Afghan government hands. The captives were subjected to the usual Isis treatment: at least one beheading, days of beatings, more videos of the Shias wearing suicide belts. Only after nine months were they freed, after an armed assault on their Isis captors by the Taliban. Yes, the bad guys suddenly turned into the good guys, the same bad guys who have captured Sangin, but are now fighting the even-more horrid bad guys. If this wasn't tragic, it would be farce.

And, just for good measure, take the recent local story in Afghanistan about poor Qais Rahmani who, along with his family and four-month-old baby, set off among the refugee army to Europe and in Turkey boarded a boat to Greece which almost immediately sank. Qais's baby died in his arms. Just another Alan Kurdi, you may say, but what struck Afghans was that Qais was a well-known television presenter, his wife and family university-educated. The Rahmanis were not from the poor and huddled masses. They were middle class, the very people who should have wanted to stay and build the new Afghanistan and to work for their government, which is - I quote Obama again - "working to combat corruption, strengthen institutions, and uphold the rule of law".

So just stand back and look at the script. The Taliban ended the lawless regime of the Afghan militias and controlled almost all of Afghanistan by 1996. But it also sheltered al-Qaeda post 9/11. So we invaded Afghanistan to destroy both al-Qaeda and the vile misogynist, murderous and undemocratic Taliban. But the Taliban was not conquered. And now it is winning. And today, we surely want it to fight against the even more vile, misogynist and murderous Isis. Which is why, tucked away at the end of his peroration to the American people, Obama said that everyone should "press the Taliban... to do their part in the pursuit of the peace the Afghans deserve". So the horrid Taliban can become the good, brave Taliban again. Truly, the news from Afghanistan must be very bad.

26 March 2016

SON OF OSAMA

Today, Osama bin Laden is like an albatross for me, a seabird you can't shake off, the guy everyone knows you met three times. But it was at the end of our second meeting - in Afghanistan - that I turned to his young son, sitting proudly by his father, and asked him if he was happy. "Yes," he replied, and I could say nothing more.

His father had been condemning the Saudi royal family - I always suspected bin Laden wanted to be King of Arabia - and this was two years before he warned me, at our third and final meeting, that with God's help, he and his comrades would "turn America into a shadow of itself". I was crossing the Atlantic on 11 September 2001. My plane turned back to Europe where I watched TV pictures of the smoke across New York and thought that, yes, Manhattan at least had been turned into a shadow of itself.

There remain too many secrets around 9/11, but I never doubted bin Laden's link. He wanted to see me again afterwards (the Taliban got cold feet and wouldn't take me to him) and that was the end - until I read his son's book years later. He recalled me meeting his father and my question to him. Was he happy? He should have said "No", he wrote, he was bitterly unhappy. Now that would have been an exclusive.

PHOTO CAPTIONS AND COPYRIGHTS

ALSO AVAILABLE FROM THE INDEPENDENT

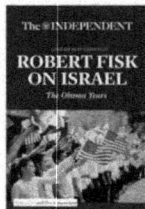

Lightning Source UK Ltd.
Milton Keynes UK
UKHW022238190520
363538UK00009B/503